THE SCOTLAND YARD FILES

THE SCOTLAND YARD FILES

150 YEARS OF THE C.I.D.

Paul Begg and Keith Skinner

HEADLINE

First published in 1992
by HEADLINE BOOK PUBLISHING PLC

First published in paperback in 1992
by HEADLINE BOOK PUBLISHING PLC

10 9 8 7 6 5 4 3 2 1

British Library Cataloguing in Publication Data
Begg, Paul
Scotland Yard Files
I. Title II. Skinner, Keith
363.209421

ISBN 0-7472-0371-7

Printed and bound in Great Britain by
Richard Clay Ltd, Bungay, Suffolk

HEADLINE BOOK PUBLISHING PLC
Headline House
79 Great Titchfield Street
London W1P 7FN

For
George Joshua Begg

Contents

Contents

	Acknowledgements	ix
1	Birth of the Police	1
2	The New Police	17
3	The Detective	37
4	Inspector Williamson, and Divisional Detectives	53
5	The Great Scotland Yard Scandal	71
6	The Criminal Investigation Department	81
7	Bombs Across London – The Fenians	89
8	Changes	111
9	Jack the Ripper	123
10	New Scotland Yard	141
11	All Change	157
12	The War Years	181
13	The Flying Squad	189
14	The Thirties	209
15	Postwar Blues	215
16	Rock and Roll	231
17	Corruption and Gangbusting	247
18	Increasingly Bizarre Crimes	263
19	Where Do We Go From Here?	279
	Bibliography	283
	Index	295

Acknowledgements

The authors would like to thank the following for their help: Robin Gillis and the staff of the Archives Dept, Metropolitan Police (much appreciation); Directorate of Public Affairs, New Scotland Yard; Mary Clucas, Eva Wade and the staff of the Metropolitan Police Library; the Monro Family; Martin Howells; Chris Ellmers, Museum of London; Jana Ferguson; Joan Lock; Martin Fido; Ernie Ostrowski; Sally Holloway and Jane Carr.

For police history and photographs we are particularly indebted to Richard Sharp, Ken Stone and Paul Williams of the Metropolitan Police Museum. The Press Association also provided more recent photograhs.

Finally, the authors are grateful to Michael Ferguson for generously sharing with them his unpublished research into Constance Kent.

Illustrations

The authors and publishers are grateful to the following for permission to reproduce illustrations:

The Metropolitan Police Museum: 3; 4; 6; 7; 17; 22; 26; 28; 32; 36; 37; 38; 43; 44; 45; 46; 48; 50; 51; 57; 60
Crown Copyright material in the Public Record Office is reproduced with the permission of the Controller of Her Majesty's Stationary Office: 5 (MEPO 3/45); 12 (PCOM 4/62)
Private collection: 27; 30
Ann Reynolds: 49
Press Association: 52; 53; 54; 55; 56; 58; 59

'It is the duty of Parliament to afford to
the inhabitants of the Metropolis and its
vicinity, the full and complete protection
of the law and to take prompt and
decisive measures to check the increase
of crime which is now proceeding at a
frightfully rapid pace.'
Sir Robert Peel, Metropolitan Police Improvement Bill, 1829

'Nulli vendemus, nulli negabimus
aut differemus, rectum aut justitiam.'
(To no man will we sell, or deny,
or delay, right or justice.)
Magna Carta, 1215

Chapter One

BIRTH OF THE POLICE

Today's police force has its roots in the principle that social order is the responsibility of the community. In the Dark Ages, for example, if a person committed a crime then, in simple terms, his community had either to produce the wrongdoer to the authorities or else recompense the victim. Such offices as 'tithingman', 'hundredman' and 'shire reeve' (sheriff) were at that time the mainstay of a system which, over the centuries, has evolved into the policing with which we are familiar in the twentieth century.

In 1285, the Statute of Winchester was a landmark in the history of policing. Its purpose was 'to abate the power of felons' and the reason for its success was that it codified all that was best of the previous law enforcement statutes and also laid down measures to strengthen the judiciary. However, the Statute of Winchester was not made applicable to the City of London since it enjoyed autonomy from Westminster and fiercely resisted any attempt to impose upon it.

The City at this time was divided into twenty-four wards, each with six watchmen under the supervision of an alderman who was answerable to the Lord Mayor. Then, a separate force, called the Marching Watch, was also established. It had the freedom to cross the boundaries of each of the

1

wards in order to patrol the City and assist the ward watchmen if necessary, and was the first time anything like a regular police force had been established in Britain. Another notable development during this period was the passing of a special local City act which set down the precept of *ignorantia iuris neminem excusat*: 'ignorance of the law does not excuse breaking it.'

An act passed by Edward III in 1344 and the Statute of Westminster in 1361 enhanced the importance of the Justice of the Peace, first giving him the powers and responsibilities of a chief of police and later combining them with the functions of magistrate. This combined role continued into the nineteenth and twentieth centuries. In 1829, the Police Act appointed the commissioners of the Metropolitan Police as Justices of the Peace, though they had no judicial powers. They remained JPs until the Administration of Justice Act in 1973.

The increase in the power of the justices made it necessary for someone to carry out their instructions, serve warrants and so on. Thus, side by side with the rise in power of the justices came the development of constables. (The origin of the name 'constable' is uncertain but widely believed to derive from the Latin *comes stabuli* meaning 'Master of the Horse'. Every male adult member of the community was theoretically required to take his turn as constable but for various reasons many people paid someone else to take on the duties. This habit was unrecognised by statute but universally tolerated and from it the system of the paid police force developed. In his *History of the Criminal Law of England*, the renowned judge Sir James Fitzjames Stephen described a constable as 'a person who is paid to perform as a matter of duty acts which if he were so minded he might have done voluntarily'.

While these measures seemed to have worked in the City of London and in small rural communities, as England

2

began to develop into a significant commercial and colonial power there gradually emerged a new middle-class of merchants and artisans. Communities grew, jobs became hard to find and a large percentage of the population found itself destitute. These people took to vagabondage, robbery and violence and the result was an outburst of outright lawlessness with which society was ill-equipped to deal.

The decline of discipline continued during and after the years of the Civil War. The Puritans closed places of entertainment such as theatres and ale houses, suppressed sport and made adultery a hanging offence. The people resented these restrictions and Cromwell was forced to use military force to uphold law and order. It was the only time Britain has been under a military dictatorship. As David Ascoli observed in *The Queen's Peace*:

> All this invasion of personal freedom might have been tolerated, except for one cardinal error of judgement which was to have a lasting effect on our social history and on the future of our police system. This was the introduction of political espionage. Years later Peel was to be reminded more than once of the universal hatred of such practices; and even today there remains a profound and proper public suspicion of anything savouring of a secret police.

In the late fifteenth century, the idea of an officially paid police force was instituted when night watchmen were employed in London. They were Britain's first professional policemen and soon developed a reputation for neglecting their duties, for being otherwise unemployable, being old or infirm, or for being criminals themselves. They are perhaps typified by Elbow in Shakespeare's *Measure for Measure* and Dogberry in *Much Ado About Nothing*. A thousand watchmen were appointed in the City of London during the reign of Charles II. They became known as 'Charlies', although Charles II apparently had no hand in their creation.

Without satisfactory crime prevention the law was enforced by threat of harsh punishments and the 'parliamentary reward'. The reward was paid to anyone who brought a criminal to justice and it led to the growth of private detectives known as 'thief-takers', of whom the most famous was Jonathan Wild. Born in 1683, Wild began his working life as a buckle-maker in Wolverhampton. He became a ponce, then ran a brothel, became a racketeer, and was finally appointed assistant to the thoroughly disreputable Under-City-Marshal, Charles Hitchen.

Hitchen was a cabinet-maker who bought the office of Marshal for about £700. Behind this mask of respectability he operated, establishing a virtual monopoly, as a receiver of stolen goods. During a brief suspension from duty between 1713–4 he met Jonathan Wild who had set up in competition against him, though avoiding prosecution by using a loophole in the law. Wild knew that he could only be convicted as a receiver if he actually handled the stolen goods and so he never took possession, but merely acted as a go-between.

Wild was very successful and soon crippled Hitchen's business. As a result, Hitchen tried to salvage something by suggesting a partnership, which Wild accepted, but the partnership broke up after about a year and Wild opened his Lost Property Office. His technique was simple. He paid a thief for stolen goods, then visited the victim and said that for a price – ostensibly to be paid to the thief – he could arrange for the stolen property to be returned. Thus, he established a reputation for having a network of informers who could tell him the whereabouts of stolen property and victims of theft began visiting Wild's office to arrange the return of their belongings.

Wild ensured the success of his business by making sure that the thieves brought their wares only to him. He did this by making one thief inform on another by threatening to use his evidence to have him hanged if he did not do so. Folklore has it that Wild kept a register in which he listed the names of the thieves who brought him stolen property. When he had enough evidence to hang them he entered a cross against their name. A second cross was marked when they had been hanged and it is said that this is the origin of the expression 'double-cross'.

Between 1721–3, Wild broke up four large gangs, the hard core of London's underworld, and for two years high-waymen avoided the capital. The public, therefore, saw Wild as performing a valuable service by returning stolen property and bringing criminals to justice. His 'Office for the Recovery of Lost and Stolen Property' was as famous as Scotland Yard would be in later years and to some extent the Bow Street Runners were modelled on his band of thief-takers. In fact, Wild has been called the 'Father of the CID'.

Eventually, everything went wrong for both Wild and Hitchen. On 15 February 1725, Wild was arrested on flimsy charges, sentenced to death and later hanged at Tyburn. Hitchen, a notorious homosexual, was charged and found guilty of attempted sodomy. He was fined £20, sentenced to stand in the pillory – the hostile crowd almost killed him – and sentenced to six months imprisonment. He died in extreme poverty.

That the likes of Wild and Hitchen, who were by no means alone in their criminal endeavours, survived so long and so openly is a measure of the widespread corruption of the age. The rule of law was virtually non-existent and, by the mid-eighteenth century, England was on the brink of anarchy. The streets were so dangerous that anyone taking a walk was almost begging to be robbed. Yet it was not even safe

5

to remain indoors and so the homes of the wealthy became virtual fortresses.

It is widely agreed that there were two main reasons for this age of lawlessness: gambling and, more especially, strong drink. Until the eighteenth century, England had been a nation of beer drinkers. For various reasons, not least the misjudged excise duty on alcohol, gin became a popular and cheap alternative and London became a gin-swilling city. For example, in 1735, when the population of London was about 650,000, the consumption of gin was 5,500,000 gallons. Gin turned London into a vast cesspit of crime and violence and the drunkenness and lawlessness cannot be overestimated.

In an attempt to combat this surge of crime and mob rule the punishments became increasingly brutal. In 1729 Thomas de Veil was appointed magistrate for Westminster and Middlesex. Though corrupt, if less so than his fellow London magistrates, he is distinguished for having dealt effectively, but harshly, with criminals and it is claimed that, during his seventeen years in office, he was responsible for the execution or transportation of over 1,900 criminals.

He effectively became the first commissioner of the Metropolitan Police, although he employed no policemen and was mainly concerned with crime detection for which he apparently possessed remarkable skills. De Veil is also noted for having moved his home and magistrate's office from Frith Street to 4 Bow Street and it is also coincidental that he began his career as a commission agent with an office in Scotland Yard.

In 1748 de Veil was succeeded as magistrate by Henry Fielding, who not only took over de Veil's job but also moved into his house in Bow Street. Henry Fielding was born in 1707 at Sharpham Park in Somerset and educated at Eton (where he was contemporary with the elder Pitt and the elder Fox) and at Leyden University, where he studied law. He did not enjoy a flourishing legal career and in London supported himself by writing comedies and farces for the stage. He is today best known as the author of the rumbustious comic masterpiece *Tom Jones* and the satire *The History of the Life of the Late Mr Jonathan Wild the Great*, but he was also an exceptional holder of the magistrate's office at Bow Street and left an indelible mark on the history of British policing.

Fielding was an extraordinary man. He possessed high principles tempered by compassion and understood that some people became criminals by choice, while others were forced into crime by the need to survive. He measured his judgements accordingly and, in this respect, Fielding can be considered the first Englishman to consider the causes of crime. For example, in 1751 he published a pamphlet called *An Enquiry into the Causes of the Late Increase of Robbers*. It was full of new ideas which can now be seen as the origin of several legal institutions in existence today, such as Legal Aid and the Public Prosecutor. However, the Establishment was uncompromising towards criminals and the lower classes, and the views expressed by Fielding in this pamphlet were so far ahead of his time that they were not accepted. From 1742, he began to publish twice-weekly the *Covent Garden Journal*, in which he gave descriptions of robbers and accounts of cases that had come before him as a magistrate. This was the forerunner of the *Police Review*, a journal which still exists today.

Fielding was not corrupt and he managed to gather six like-minded incorruptibles. These men became known as 'Mr Fielding's Men' and were placed under the leadership of himself and Saunders Welch, the High Constable of Holborn. The full history of 'Mr Fielding's Men', or the 'Bow Street Runners' as they came to be known, is lost, since most of Fielding's papers were destroyed in the Gordon Riots of 1780 when the mob sacked Bow Street. It is known

7

however that there were originally six Runners and that all but one were ex-constables of Westminster. Each was paid a small weekly salary, no more than a retainer, and also a share of the statutory reward when a criminal he had caught was convicted. This system provided opportunities for corruption but a good Runner, like John Sayer or John Townsend, could legally make up to £30,000 through various annual retainers. Thus, there was no incentive to be corrupt.

Sayer and Townsend were probably the most famous of all the Bow Street Runners. Various thefts and the attempt by Margaret Nicholson in 1786 to assassinate King George III resulted in Bow Street officers being appointed to protect the Court. In 1792, Townsend and Sayer commenced this duty and went with the Court when it moved to Windsor and later under the Regency when it went to Brighton. Townsend, who was paid £200 a year for his services as a Court detective, was a favourite of George III and George IV. Courtiers were fascinated by his tales of crime and his use of criminal jargon.

The Runners were not uniformed (contrary to some claims which are the result of confusion with the later Bow Street Horse Patrol), but identified themselves by showing a small brass tipstaff surmounted by a crown. It is believed that the presentation of this tipstaff by the Runners gives us the expression 'I'll crown you', which originally meant 'I arrest you'. Until 1838, the Runners were the only 'policemen' allowed inside Buckingham Palace.

In 1754 Fielding's co-commander of the Bow Street Runners, Saunders Welch, published a pamphlet called *Observations on the Office of Constable* which was a set of guide-lines for the conduct of petty constables. His primary responsibility was to oversee the Runners and he complemented Fielding's judicial responsibilities for six years before they fell out and Welch opened a Magistrate's

Office in Litchfield Street. He continued to operate until retirement in 1774.

Henry Fielding died in 1754 and was succeeded by his half-brother John Fielding who, although blind from the age of nineteen, was reputed to be able to recognise 3,000 thieves by their voices. He occupied the Bow Street office for twenty-five years and under his guidance it became the clearing-house of crime information. Fielding significantly influenced the development of policing. He was a pioneer and innovator and probably the first magistrate in the country to conceive and advance the idea of preventative policing.

He strengthened and extended the powers of 'Mr Fielding's Men' and, in October 1763, managed to persuade the Government to give him enough money to acquire two 'pursuit horses' to guard the approaches to London. They were so successful that within a year travellers felt completely safe but then the penny-pinching Government withdrew their finance and the Horse Patrol had to be abandoned. 'There is nothing I so sincerely lament as the want of an opportunity of convincing Mr Granville [First Lord of the Treasury] of the amazing importance of the police to the Government,' said Fielding.

Civil disturbances were continuing and also growing in ferocity. In 1763 John Wilkes, the MP for Aylesbury and publisher of *The North Briton*, was accused of libelling the King and expelled from the House of Commons. The proceedings against him were illegal, which Wilkes made known with such wit and humour that both Court and Government emerged humiliated. Wilkes was adopted as a figurehead by groups who had real or imagined grievances and mobs of people staged a series of exceptional riots. Civil order virtually collapsed.

In May 1770, a Select Committee undertook an inquiry into the policing of London (excluding the City). Eleven further committees would follow but all except one were marked by inactivity. In 1772 John Fielding published the first issue of what became a regular broadsheet entitled *The Quarterly Pursuit of Criminals*. This was supplemented by *The Weekly Pursuit*, and occasionally by *The Extraordinary Pursuit*. These contained descriptions of offenders, like 'wanted posters' of gunslingers in the Old West, and were displayed in public places such as churches and inns under the heading 'Weekly Hue and Cry'.

If one event stands out as indicating the need for an organised police force it was the Gordon Riots during the first week of June 1780. Lord George Gordon was the figurehead for an explosion of mob violence, which literally left the heart of London ablaze. The existing police force proved ineffectual at controlling the rioters and was swept aside while the politicians argued among themselves. Eventually the King ordered the military to take action and this resulted in 'Bloody Wednesday', when at least 250 rioters attacking the Bank of England were shot and killed. However, although the military quickly restored order the politicians responded ineffectually as usual by merely holding a debate. This was public disorder on a grand scale, which alone should have demonstrated the need for a trained and organised police force.

At the time of the Gordon Riots John Fielding was seriously ill. He died soon afterwards and was succeeded as magistrate at Bow Street by Sampson Wright, whose tenure was marked by two significant events. The first was that, in 1782, the Government authorised the creation of the sixty-eight strong Bow Street Foot Patrol to patrol the metropolis at night. Apart from John Fielding's short-lived Horse Patrol, the Foot Patrol was Britain's first preventative police force and was further distinguished by being armed! It was a successful supplement to the handful of Runners and, together, they remained in existence until both were absorbed by the Metropolitan Police in 1839.

The second significant development during Sampson Wright's tenure at Bow Street was in 1786 when the weekly crime bulletin was converted into a newspaper called *Public Hue and Cry*. It was later called *Hue and Cry and Police Gazette* and, in 1828, simply the *Police Gazette*. In 1883 the editorial office was transferred to Scotland Yard and, since 1914, the *Police Gazette* has been published daily.

In 1785 Sir Archibald Macdonald, the Solicitor-General, prompted by the Gordon Riots, introduced a 'Bill for the Further Prevention of Crime and the more speedy Detection and Punishment of Offenders against the Peace in the Cities of London, Westminster, the Borough of Southwark and certain parts adjacent to them'. This became known as 'Pitt's Bill' and is one of the most remarkable documents in British police history because fifty-four years later it was embodied in Peel's Act, which established the Metropolitan Police.

The bill would probably have been passed in 1785 if it had not incorporated the City of London. Instead, it provoked an outraged response from the Lord Mayor and sheriffs and Pitt was forced to bow before the storm and to withdraw it. Ireland, however, wholeheartedly seized the plans and the abortive bill was enacted substantially in its original form by the Dublin Parliament in 1786. Thus were laid the foundations of the Royal Irish Constabulary.

In March 1792, the Middlesex Justices Act was introduced with the object of ending corruption among the Metropolitan magistrates. One of its leading proponents was the chairman of the Middlesex Sessions, William Mainwaring, who was described by David Ascoli in his book *The Queen's Peace* as 'one of the most corrupt and distasteful characters to have disgraced the Bench'. The act established eight police offices: Bow Street, Great Marlborough Street, Queen Square, Hatton Garden, Worship Street, Whitechapel, Shadwell and Southwark. In 1798 the Marine Police Office

11

at Wapping was added. Each had three stipendiary magistrates, six police officers, and a treasurer (the forerunner of the Receiver of the Metropolitan Police). The new magistrates were an odd assortment, but one man among them justifiably has a place in the history of British policing: Patrick Colquhoun.

A Scotsman, Colquhoun lived for a while in Virginia but returned to Glasgow in 1766, where for three consecutive years he was Lord Provost. He founded the Glasgow Chamber of Commerce and made his name and fortune in the cloth trade. In 1789 he went to London and, in 1792, for no particular reason except that he was a man of established integrity (itself something of a rarity at the time), he was appointed a magistrate. Four years later he published a *Treatise on the Police of the Metropolis*. It went through seven editions in ten years, which suggests that more people were concerned about burgeoning crime than the inactivity of Parliament would suggest.

The theme of the treatise was the causes and effects of crime and public disorder and Colquhoun reinforced his unassailable arguments with numerous statistics. It made chilling reading and convincingly supported his agitation for the creation of a police force. However, Colquhoun made the usual and serious mistake of incorporating the City of London in his proposals and, once again, the City scuppered the proposal, with one exception. His plan for the creation of a River Police was picked up in 1797 by Captain John Harriott, who incorporated it into his own plans for a similar force which was presented to the Lord Mayor of London. The City gave Harriott short shrift but he met Colquhoun and together they were able to persuade the Government to authorise and finance the creation of the River Police. Thus, on 26 June 1798, the Marine Police Office was established but without City jurisdiction, which left City wharfs prey to criminals. Harriott was appointed

Resident Magistrate and Colquhoun, Superintendent Magistrate.

By this time, Richard Ford had succeeded as magistrate at Bow Street and in 1805 he managed to persuade the Government to revive the Horse Patrol. Known as 'Robin Redbreasts' because of their distinctive uniform, the Horse Patrol was armed. Within a year the approaches to London were once again safe from highwaymen but the situation lasted only until 1812 when the gruesome Ratcliffe Highway murders caused widespread panic. Twenty-four-year-old former sailor Timothy Marr, his family and a shop-boy were savagely butchered at 29 Ratcliffe Highway in London's East End with a ripping chisel and maul. The shop-boy's head was savagely beaten to a pulp with blood and brains even splashed on the ceiling. Nearby lay Celia Marr, her head also brutally beaten. Hidden behind the shop counter was her husband Timothy but the greatest horror waited in the basement. Still in its cot lay their three-and-a-half-month-old baby whose head, also battered, was almost severed from its body.

The brutal murders, especially that of the child, created a wave of public horror which had hardly begun to subside when, near to where the Marrs were killed, a man named John Williamson and his wife and servant were found with their skulls fractured and throats cut. A bloodstained iron crowbar and maul lay beside the bodies. These crimes, which were the foundation for De Quincey's *Murder Considered as One of the Fine Arts*, were inadequately investigated because there were few men capable or available to investigate them properly. The Government offered a large reward for the discovery of the perpetrators and eventually a man named John Williams was tried, convicted and executed for the murders. Doubts about his guilt have remained ever since.

The murders demonstrated the ineffectiveness of the

policing system and, among the judiciary and public, complacency about the need for reforming the police temporarily vanished – except in the Government, whose response was to set up a Select Committee on Police. The Tories remained blinkered to the social collapse around them. They could hardly have expected that anything fruitful would result from the Committee – nothing had in the past – but committees made it look as if action was being taken and so, hopefully things would quieten down for a while. Crime would flare up again, of course, and there would be another committee. This sequence was repeated time and again and was a proven formula which might have been useful for the Government, but did not make the streets any safer.

The Industrial Revolution caused extensive changes to British society, not the least of which was the emergence of an organised working class determined to defend themselves against the genuine and terrible injustices heaped upon them by the Establishment. There were violent demonstrations and riots. Revolution was in the air. Then, the British victory against the French at Waterloo and the subsequent disbandment of the army threw thousands of men on to the unstable labour market. It crumpled under their weight and, as a result, there was massive unemployment. Feelings of injustice overboiled so that, during the winter of 1815–6, London was virtually under siege by rioting gangs and mobs. Property was destroyed and buildings set alight. It was the start of what could have been revolution.

Home Secretary Henry Addington, Lord Sidmouth, quickly responded by creating sixteen police districts and almost doubling the number of men at Bow Street. Unsurprisingly he also set up a Parliamentary committee, some of the conclusions of which were incredible: 'the police of a free country is to be found in rational and humane laws, in the effective and enlightened magistracy ... above all in the moral habits and opinions of the people'. It is astonishing that this conclusion was reached at a time when 'begging by soldiers and sailors without a permit from their commanding officer' was among the 'rational and humane laws' which carried the death penalty; when until recently corruption within the magistracy was commonplace; and when 'the moral habits and opinions of the people' had only a couple of years earlier sent them through the streets of London in an orgy of destruction.

However, in January 1822 Henry Addington resigned and, in his place, the Prime Minister appointed Robert Peel. Peel succeeded where others had failed and, as is well-known, he 'created' the Metropolitan Police and policemen were called 'Peelers' and 'Bobbies' after him. Much of the organisation of the Metropolitan Police was Peel's own plan but he was also able to recognise other people's good ideas and had the tenacity and political acumen to make them a reality.

Born in Lancashire in 1788, the son of a very wealthy and self-made cotton manufacturer, he entered Parliament shortly after reaching his majority and at the age of only twenty-four was appointed Secretary for Ireland. Here he cut his teeth in the arena of social and policing reforms. In March 1822, three years after accepting the position of Home Secretary, he set up yet another Select Committee to examine the police organisation. The committee reported three months later and its final conclusion was the following:

It is difficult to reconcile an effective system of police with the perfect freedom of action and exemption from interference which are the great privileges and blessings of society in this country; and Your Committee think that the forfeiture or curtailment of such advantages would be too great a sacrifice for improvements in police, or facilities in detection of crime, however desirable in themselves if abstractly considered.

This judgement was a severe blow to Peel's plans, but he busied himself by reforming the judiciary and reducing the number of capital offences. Eventually, he became Prime Minister and on 15 April 1829 introduced his bill for improving the police.

It was a perfectly phrased and carefully argued masterpiece of diplomacy, excluding the City of London and avoiding any suggestion of radical change. The conclusion remains relevant today:

It is the duty of Parliament to afford to the inhabitants of the Metropolis and its vicinity, the full and complete protection of the law and to take prompt and decisive measures to check the increase of crime which is now proceeding at a frightfully rapid pace.

There was little opposition to Peel's 'Metropolitan Police Improvement Bill' and on 19 June 1829 it became law.

Chapter Two

THE NEW POLICE

The headquarters of the Metropolitan Police, called the Metropolitan Police Office, was at 4 Whitehall Place. At the rear of the building there was a station house for the local A Division which faced a small street called Great Scotland Yard. Soon this was the name by which the Police Office in Whitehall Place was known.

The origin of the name 'Scotland Yard' is supposed to come from the area having once been the location of a residence reserved for the Kings of Scotland on their visits to London to pay homage to the English kings. The authority for this story is John Stow's *Survey of London*, published in 1598. Stow's source was almost certainly a pamphlet published fifty years earlier by Nicholas Bodrugan. This stated that King Edgar had given lands to Kenneth II of Scotland in the late 900s. The lands reverted to King Henry II following the rebellion of William, King of the Scots.

Unfortunately Bodrugan's source seems to have been documents allegedly found in Scotland by the chronicler Hardynge (1378–1465?). Hardynge was anxious to prove that from ancient times the Scottish kings had been subservient to the English and those documents are now known to be forgeries.

The real origin of the name is less glamorous. Determined and detailed research (by N. W. H. Fairfax, *The Mystery*

of Scotland Yard, an article published in a police magazine) has shown the land to have once been owned by a
man named Walter Scot and known as 'Scottes grounde'.
Walter's son, Adam, gave it to the prior of the chapel of
St Mary Rounceval and, in 1437, the parcel of ground, now
called 'Scot's land', was placed in the custody of a John
Prud. The land thereafter passed through various hands. It
would appear that the name alone sparked off Hardynge's
imaginings.

When the Commissioners' Office moved to a new building
in 1890 the commissioner, James Monro, christened it New
Scotland Yard and the name survived a third move in
1967 to the present twenty-storey tower block at 10, The
Broadway.

Peel's New Police were underpaid, received no pension,
and were rarely compensated for injuries sustained whilst
on duty. They also had somewhat less than six weeks
cursory training and no one, not even the two joint commissioners, really had any idea what they were supposed
to do or how they were supposed to do it. The latter were
forty-six-year-old ex-soldier Colonel Charles Rowan and
thirty-two-year-old lawyer Richard Mayne.

Every policeman was clearly distinguished from ordinary
citizens by a distinctive and exceedingly uncomfortable
uniform which they were obliged by Police Regulations
to wear at all times, even when off duty. The uniform
of even thirty years later was so intolerable that it left
a lasting impression in the mind of Tim Cavanagh, who
wrote an account of his experiences in the early days of the
police force:

> I had to put on a swallow-tail coat, and a rabbit-skin
> high-top-hat, covered with leather, weighing eighteen
> ounces; a pair of Wellington boots, the leather of which
> must have been at least a sixteenth of an inch thick,

and a belt about four inches broad, with a great brass buckle some six inches deep.

The 'General Instructions on the New Police' emphasised that the purpose of the new force was to prevent crime: to patrol streets, check property and keep a wary eye open for suspicious individuals. They were obliged to investigate any crime brought to their attention but the detection of crime was not part of the original idea and there were no detectives. This was just as well. Few of the early policemen had the experience or the necessary mental equipment for detective work.

The British people believed the New Police would be used by the Government as a political tool, not to preserve public order but for spying and to enforce the status quo. Despite efforts therefore to dispel the spectre of a secret police, the press and public remained hostile. *The Times*, in particular, launched a vitriolic campaign and public opposition was displayed in verbal and physical attacks on policemen and a blizzard of complaints to the new commissioners. The depth of this animosity towards the police is reflected by the reaction to the first policeman killed in the furtherance of his duties. On 29 June 1830, PC Joseph Grantham attempted to break up a fight between two drunken Irishmen. They turned on him and in the struggle he was kicked on the temple, dying minutes later. The general reaction was that PC Grantham got what he asked for and his death was so rapidly forgotten that he is not even mentioned in most police histories. The distinction of being the first policeman killed in the line of duty is instead given to PC John Long.

On 16 August 1830, thirty-two-year-old PC John Long was patrolling his beat in Gray's Inn Road when he saw three men behaving suspiciously. He followed them. It is not certainly known what happened next but in Mecklenburg

Square PC Long probably questioned the men, one of whom stabbed him in the heart. Three men were noticed running from the scene and a few passers-by gave chase. One of them managed to grab a man who was arrested despite protesting that he was a pursuer and not the pursued. He gave his name as John Smith.

The murder inquiry was taken over by Inspector John Busalin of G Division. According to author Belton Cobb, Busalin's method of crime detection 'was to arrest everyone who could possibly be a suspect, it being better to be safe than sorry'. Busalin's trawl included a youth named Lawrence Summers who was found sitting on a doorstep in Gray's Inn Road two hours after the crime had been committed. Summers said that he was not in Gray's Inn Road when the murder happened and had only gone there to wait for a friend named Charles Baldwin. Baldwin went to the police station to confirm Summers's story and was promptly arrested by Inspector Busalin.

Smith, Summers and Baldwin were shackled with leg-irons and handcuffs and brought before the magistrates who immediately released Summers and Baldwin, but John Smith remained in custody. A witness to the murder said that the murderer had worn a brown coat. John Smith was wearing a brown coat and he also behaved very suspiciously by refusing to give information about himself. It turned out that this was because his real name was William Sapwell and ten years earlier he had been arrested for housebreaking. He had escaped punishment by informing on two accomplices who had recently finished their ten-year prison sentences. Inspector Busalin went after the accomplices, found one, arrested him but was soon forced to let him go.

William Sapwell, alias John Smith, was eventually tried. He strenuously proclaimed his innocence but the brown coat he was wearing appears to have constituted overwhelming evidence of his guilt. He was convicted and on 23 September 1830 hanged. It is worth observing that Sapwell went to the gallows on the evidence of two witnesses, one of whom declared herself to be named Stevens, the widow 'of a surgeon of great respectability', and currently living 'under the protection of a nobleman'. In fact her name was Griffiths and she was a prostitute who at the time of the murder was making a deal with a potential customer. Her evidence given at the inquest and at the trial differed substantially. The other witness was a boy who also identified Sapwell as the man in brown. He, too, contradicted himself, and his credibility as a witness seems overall to have been only marginally better than that of Griffiths.

The Long, or Sapwell, case is not so much an illustration of the deficiencies of the New Police as an illustration of the deficiencies of the judiciary. Inspector Busalin applied a degree of logic, followed up new lines of inquiry, produced a few suspects, and generally seems to have taken the view that the judicial process would assess the evidence (such as it was) and determine innocence or guilt. On the other hand, Inspector Busalin did not display what could be recognised as detective skills and, even if Sapwell was guilty, his accomplices were never found and no effort seems to have been made to find them.

However, with hindsight, the birth of the detective can be seen in actions which were somewhat distantly removed from crime detection. In spite of all the efforts made to reassure the public that the police were not spies, policemen were occasionally employed in plain clothes for special duties. This is revealed by a succession of *Police Orders* dating from as early as the 1830s. One in particular about the Lord Mayor's Show, dated 8 November 1831, lists the number of men needed along the route and states that ten of 'the most active men are to be present in plain clothes'. Another, for 8 November 1833, states: '. . . each Division is to have a number of men in readiness during the procession of the Lord Mayor. Each Division will have two of their most active and intelligent men in plain clothes to apprehend thieves and pick pockets.' The use of plain-clothes policemen to catch pickpockets may have been necessary but it marks the first step away from the original preventative role of the police and the first rung on the ladder towards the feared 'secret' police. Using plain-clothes policemen to watch the crowds for pickpockets was only a small step away from using them to listen to conversations in public houses or even to infiltrate meetings of various kinds.

In May 1833, the police broke up a demonstration in Cold Bath Fields by the National Political Union of the Working Classes. Later that year, evidence was produced showing that for over twelve months a policeman named William Popay had been attending meetings of the NPU in plain clothes to gather 'inside' information. The revelation caused uproar. A Select Committee of the House of Commons investigated the case and it remained alive in the minds of people for many years. Popay was dismissed from the police service and some effort seems to have been made to suggest that he had acted on his own initiative. In fact, even the Select Committee was told that he acted on the instructions of a Superintendent McLean and that his reports had been sent to the commissioners and passed on to the Home Office. The police and Government were therefore both aware of and had sanctioned his actions.

It is claimed that for two years after the Popay case the Metropolitan Police did not put any men into plain clothes. This may or may not be true but the first reference to the employment of plain-clothes policemen after the Popay case is contained in *Police Orders* for 26 April 1837. It refers to men detached to preserve order at a Drawing Room held by their Majesties at St James's Palace and states that officers to be present would consist of: '6 Superintendents,

16 Inspectors, 41 Sergeants, 310 Police Constables and 44 in addition in plain clothes.' Reference to the use of plain-clothes men is also made in *Police Orders* of 1837 concerning their presence during the nomination of members of Parliament for Westminster and during the election. Again, on 1 October 1838, *Police Orders* refer to the employment of policemen in plain clothes, but this time in connection with crime detection:

> From the great difficulty in detecting the perpetrators of Garden robberies by men on beats and which robberies are principally committed by persons employed on the premises who carry the property away as opportunity offers concealed about them the Superintendents of the outer Divisions may occasionally when they consider it advisable employ a man in plain clothes to detect if possible the persons committing these offences.

It seems that gradually the deficiencies of the uniformed police were recognised and that tentative steps were taken towards specialisation. This is clear from *Police Orders* of 2 February 1840: following a serious jewel robbery in Welbeck Street, instructions were issued for 'an active intelligent man in each division' to trace the missing property.

Yet, since these tasks could still be classified as crime prevention, they were not strictly detective work. True detective work at this time was still carried out by the Bow Street Runners, the most famous of whom was Henry Goddard who, in January 1835, investigated a burglary in Southampton. According to the butler, Joseph Randall, one of the burglars fired a gun. Goddard searched for and found the bullet. He examined Randall's gun and found the burglar's and Randall's bullets were marked by a pinhead pimple which showed they had been cast from the same mould. Because of this evidence Randall admitted that he had committed the crime himself. The story shows the detective talents of the Runners and that they used forensic methods of detection but it is also interesting to note that the local police, who accepted Randall's story, had called for the expert assistance of the Runners. In later years, local forces would call in Scotland Yard but for now even the Yard needed the Runners.

On 27 December 1836, a sweeper clearing away the snow from the pavements in Edgware Road, near Paddington Green, found a large sack by the roadside which contained the body of a woman, minus the head and legs. Also in the sack was an old towel bearing the initials 'J. C. B.', a child's blue frock patched with nankeen, a piece of material later found to be part of a carpenter's apron, and a quantity of wood shavings covered with blood. The Runners were called in to help with the detective work. They did not make much progress until the middle of January when a bargeman hooked a woman's head from the Regent's Canal with his pole. Next, the legs were found tied in a sack left in a field off Coldharbour Lane, Brixton.

These discoveries were of little help in identifying the woman or her killer, but eventually a man reported his sister missing. Hannah Brown was last seen at her lodgings on Christmas Eve with a man believed to be her fiancé, named Greenacre. The brother was able to identify the remains as those of his sister and the hunt for Greenacre began. The Runners found him living in Lambeth with a woman named Sarah Gale and a child. A Runner searched Greenacre's lodgings, and found a child's frock patched with nankeen.

This case is significant because the police had questioned Greenacre and, unlike the Sapwell case, noted inconsistencies in his story. James Greenacre claimed that he and Hannah Brown were to be married on Christmas Day.

On Christmas Eve, they went out drinking and Hannah admitted that she was penniless and did not have savings amounting to several hundred pounds as Greenacre believed. There was an argument and Greenacre claimed that, furious at the deception, he had pushed Hannah Brown. She had fallen and struck her head on a log of wood by the fire, and died. Terrified that he would be charged with her murder, Greenacre's Christmas Day festivities included dismembering her body and taking the pieces to the places where they were found.

At his trial at the Old Bailey, the prosecution proved that Hannah Brown's stomach contained no trace of alcohol, which suggested that the drunken confession and row was a lie; that she was struck on the front of the head, not the back as Greenacre claimed; and, damning for Greenacre, that her throat had been cut before, not after, death. Greenacre admitted his original story was untrue and said he had struck her with a silk-weaving roller. He continued to maintain that it was an accident – his family was dogged by accidents, a brother, Samuel Greenacre, having accidentally killed his wife and shot off the hand of her sister – but he was convicted and executed. Sarah Gale was transported for life.

As good as the Runners were, they were not part of the New Police or subject to any recognised organisational conventions. Requesting a Runner's assistance therefore seemed to undermine the capabilities of the police who obviously needed detectives of its own. Commissioner Rowan was apparently opposed to the idea, but the author Belton Cobb claims (on unstated authority) that throughout this period Commissioner Mayne had been keeping a record of any policemen who displayed above average detective abilities. Among those who were placed on his list were Charles Burgess Goff, who was to be distinguished as one of the first detectives, and Charles Frederick Field who would become the most famous detective of his day.

Circumstances brought these two men together in May 1838 when a very beautiful prostitute known as 'the Countess' was found murdered. Her real name was Eliza Grimwood. She was twenty-eight years old and lived at 12 Waterloo Terrace near Waterloo Bridge. Her body was discovered by her 'lover', a bricklayer named William Hubbard who notified the other occupants of the house, then went to fetch a doctor. Someone, it is not known whom, then raised the alarm. First to respond from his beat in Waterloo Road was PC Charles Goff.

Charles Field took charge of the case. The son of a Chelsea publican, Field had joined the Metropolitan Police on its creation in 1829 and had recently been appointed Inspector of L Division. Field was told that in the opinion of the examining surgeon, Dr Cooke, Eliza Grimwood had committed suicide by cutting her throat. Field looked at the body. The head had almost been decapitated, there was a deep cut across the back of the neck and the hands bore cuts which looked as if they had been made while the victim tried to defend herself. For these reasons, it seemed unlikely to be a case of suicide. The surgeon then returned to re-examine the body. He now observed that Eliza had also been stabbed in the chest and stomach and conceded that the death looked suspicious.

Field seems to have immediately suspected William Hubbard, but he knew from the maidservant that on the night of her death Eliza had brought home a well-dressed, gentlemanly-looking man. Field went in search of this man, leaving PC Goff at the house to watch Hubbard. The investigation was remarkable for the large number of witnesses who were gathered, yet it got nowhere. Goff watched Hubbard carefully and he shared Field's suspicions, but although Hubbard was arrested he was released by the magistrate because of insufficient evidence against him. The murder of Eliza Grimwood was never solved but

Field and Goff impressed Commissioner Mayne and the case further highlighted the crying need for the New Police to have a trained detective department of its own.

The days of the Bow Street Runners had long been numbered and in 1839 they were disbanded. Supposed to be absorbed by the Metropolitan Police, it is not known how many, if any, of them moved over to the police except, that is, for Nicholas Pearce, the only Runner actually known to have joined the Metropolitan Police several years earlier. Born in St Anthony, Cornwall, on 10 November 1800, Pearce was a tall man with brown hair and blue eyes and, like so many of the detectives who were to follow him, he began his career with the Metropolitan Police attached to H Division in Whitechapel. By 1840, Pearce was an inspector attached to A Division – Scotland Yard – with special responsibilities for watching the activities of London's habitual criminals and investigating certain cases of murder or other serious crimes in the Metropolis.

The first notable case he had investigated was the murder of fifty-five-year-old clock- and watch-maker Robert Westwood at his home at 35 Princes Street, Soho, at about midnight on 3 June 1839. The ground floor of the house was Mr Westwood's shop. He had taken to sleeping in the shop since a recent robbery but the rooms above were occupied by seventy-three-year-old Mrs Westwood, a seventy-year-old Frenchman named Gerard who lodged with the Westwoods, and on the top floor a new maid named Maria Petty. There had been two other lodgers, William and Caroline Stephenson, but they had left a few days earlier following a marital row. Mrs Westwood was in bed when she heard 'scuffling' from the passage below. Later, a door slammed. She thought her husband had been chasing the cat and then put it out for the night. She was not immediately alarmed but, after about fifteen minutes, the recent robbery preying on her mind, Mrs Westwood became concerned and went upstairs to fetch Maria Petty, the maid. They went downstairs to see what was happening and found smoke was billowing up from below. Maria Petty made a brave dash to the front door and sent a passer-by for the fire engine. Fortunately the fire had not got a hold and was extinguished by neighbours before the engine arrived but Mr Westwood was found dead in his bed. He had been struck on the head, apparently with a window-sash, and his throat had been savagely cut.

Superintendent Baker, Inspector Beresford and Inspector Jervis of C Division at once took charge of the case and, with exceptional skill and thoroughness, they collected the preliminary evidence. There were no signs of forced entry but cash and watches worth about £2,000 had been taken, some of the watches from secret hiding places. Apart from these indications that the crime had been committed by or with the assistance of someone familiar with Mr Westwood's business, evidence was meagre. Suspicion fell on Mrs Westwood, the maid Maria Petty, a young man named George Robinson (because he looked like one of the two men whom a neighbour said he had seen leaving the shop at about 12.30 a.m.), the former lodgers Mr and Mrs Stephenson, Westwood's foreman Charles Louis Serouche, and even one of the coroner's jury alleged to have once threatened Westwood's life.

The case attracted a great deal of press attention and Inspector Pearce and Sergeant Charles Otway were appointed to 'assist' Inspector Beresford. However, Pearce and Otway did not greatly distinguish themselves on this occasion. Pearce circulated descriptions of the stolen watches to all likely buyers in London. He learned that a large number of watches were offered for sale in Gravesend on the evening after the murder and that a boat stolen from nearby Ramsgate Harbour was seen heading for France. Pearce and Otway went to Boulogne but their efforts were to no avail.

In spite of a string of suspects, Mr Westwood's murderer(s) were never caught but Pearce established a reputation as a dogged pursuer. No matter where a criminal went, it was believed that Pearce would follow.

For the following year, Pearce and Otway often acted as a kind of two-man detective team operating out of Scotland Yard, sometimes known as HQ or Reserve Division (because the men stationed there could be deployed in other divisions as and when necessary), but in 1840 Otway blotted his copybook in the Templeman murder.

On 17 March 1840 an old man named John Templeman went out to collect rents from his tenants. He returned and gave some money to his charwoman, Mrs Thornton, to do some shopping. The next day Mrs Thornton sent her daughter to Templeman's house to deliver the things which she had bought, but her daughter was unable to obtain a reply. Mrs Thornton then went herself and on looking through a ground-floor bedroom window she saw the old man on the floor 'brutally murdered'. His hands were tied with cord and his eyes bandaged with a stocking. His forehead had been smashed with a blunt instrument, there were severe wounds to the back of his head, and his nose and jaw bones had been broken. For several hours Mrs Thornton did nothing except wait for her son-in-law to come home. He was a Frenchman named Capriani and worked as night-watchman at the Sadler's Wells Theatre. He arrived home in the middle of the morning and reported what he had been told to Templeman's grandson, a solicitor, who immediately notified the police.

N Division's Superintendant James Johnston took charge of the case and he put Inspector Miller to work on it. Miller immediately arrested Capriani, apparently for no better reason than that Capriani was late in bringing news of the murder. Yet Capriani had an impeccable alibi and was released by order of the magistrates. A few days later,

Inspector Miller made another arrest. He learned from Mr Templeman's neighbours that their lodger, an out-of-work pot-boy named Richard Gould, had been out on the night of the crime until 3 a.m. The next day he bought himself a new pair of shoes. Further inquiries revealed that shortly before the crime Gould had bought a pick-lock and a dark lantern, had talked of stealing money from an 'old man' and had tried to persuade someone to join him in a robbery. Miller charged Gould with the murder of Mr Templeman and the case was tried at the Central Criminal Court. However, Inspector Miller's evidence only showed that Gould had contemplated a robbery, not that he had committed one or murdered Mr Templeman.

The police believed Gould to be guilty but knew that he could not be charged and tried again for Templeman's murder but that he could, however, be charged with burglary. Sergeant Otway was sent to arrest Gould, who was on board a ship about to sail for Australia. For some reason, Otway did not immediately arrest him but instead told Gould the police believed he could give them important information about the murder. Otway added that Gould might then be eligible to claim the £200 reward offered in return for 'information'. Gould accordingly related how he had committed the robbery with two accomplices and how one of them had killed the old man. He even signed a statement and Otway, believing he had a confession signed and sealed, arrested Gould.

At Gould's trial it was held that a confession 'bought' by the promise of a reward was inadmissible as evidence. Fortunately the police had managed to acquire additional evidence against Gould and this was sufficient to secure a conviction for burglary. However, Otway's conduct was clearly out-of-order and he ceased thereafter to be Pearce's right-hand man. Nevertheless, he rose to the rank of Superintendent C Division, retiring in May 1853 after nineteen years service, his discharge papers stating that he was 'worn out and unfit for further service'.

Soon after the Templeman case there occurred one of the most sensational murders of the day, and it is generally believed, along with a handful of other incidents, to have resulted in the formal creation of a detective branch at Scotland Yard. In May 1840 Lord William Russell, the seventy-two-year-old uncle of Lord John Russell (the former Home Secretary and future Prime Minister), was murdered at his home off Park Lane. The murder attracted considerable attention, not the least of which was that of Queen Victoria, and at first Commissioner Mayne took charge. Initial inquiries were conducted by Superintendent Baker (who had been involved in the Westwood investigation) and the housemaid told him she had discovered Russell's study in disarray and his desk broken open. She had therefore alerted the valet, François Courvoisier, who decided that the house had been robbed and went to tell Lord Russell, whom he found dead.

The police searched the house and in Courvoisier's bedroom they found a screwdriver and a chisel which matched marks discovered in the pantry, from where it was learned that some silver spoons had been taken. At this point, Nicholas Pearce took charge of the investigation. In spite of the evidence, Courvoisier was not the only suspect and particular attention was paid to a former servant named Carr who had visited Lord Russell the evening before the murder but, when eventually found and questioned, he was able satisfactorily to account for himself.

Within two days The Times, ever hostile towards the police, declared that a 'foul and horrible crime' had again defeated Scotland Yard. The article went on to say that whilst the Metropolitan Police had success at preventing crime, as a drop in crime statistics indicated, they were useless at discovering the perpetrators once a crime had been committed. *The Times* concluded by calling for the reinstatement of the Runners.

However, as the days passed Courvoisier appeared increasingly edgy, especially when the police entered the butler's pantry. Thus alerted, Pearce made a closer examination of the room and found behind the skirting board a medal, rings and coins. The butler denied knowledge of these things and additionally no trace could be found of other property believed to have been stolen, such as the silver spoons, but Courvoisier's behaviour was regarded as sufficient to justify his arrest.

At the trial, Inspector Pearce was subjected to a rigorous cross-questioning during which a barely veiled challenge of his honesty was made. It appeared that a substantial reward had been offered for evidence resulting in the conviction of Lord Russell's murderer and that, when asked, Pearce admitted he anticipated receiving a share of the reward money if Courvoisier was convicted. It was then pointed out that all the evidence against Courvoisier had been found subsequent to the reward being offered.

It is quite possible that Courvoisier might have been found 'not guilty' and for Pearce to have been stained thereafter by the implied allegation of having 'fitted-up' Courvoisier. However, thankfully for Pearce, the missing silver turned up. It had been left by Courvoisier with the manageress of a hotel at which he had previously worked. A verdict of guilty was therefore brought in by the jury despite a spirited defence of Courvoisier by his counsel, Charles Phillips – to whom, as Phillips admitted in a letter to *The Times* nine years later, Courvoisier had in fact earlier admitted his guilt. Thus, Courvoisier was hanged outside Newgate Gaol on 6 July 1840.

The execution was witnessed by Charles Dickens and William Makepeace Thackeray and was described by the latter: 'It seems to me that I have been abetting an act of frightful wickedness and violence, performed by a set of men against one of their fellows . . .' Dickens, writing in a letter to the *Daily News* of the behaviour of the crowd, said that he saw:

> No sorrow, no salutary terror, no abhorrence, no seriousness; nothing but ribaldry, debauchery, levity, drunkenness, and flaunting vice in fifty other shapes, I should have deemed it impossible that I could have ever felt any large assemblage of my fellow-creatures to be so odious . . .

Considering that frightful punishments had been regularly meted out even to petty wrongdoers only a few decades earlier, these comments illustrate that attitudes in British society were changing. The Courvoisier case once again raised the question of the absence of and possible need for detectives at Scotland Yard and subsequent events, such as several attempts to kill the Queen, and also the notorious Daniel Good case, made the issue a pressing one.

At about 6 p.m. on 10 June 1840, the first attempt on Queen Victoria's life was made. She and Prince Albert left Buckingham Palace and, just as their carriage turned up Constitution Hill, seventeen-year-old Edward Oxford fired a pistol. Prince Albert actually heard the whistle of the ball and pulled Queen Victoria back into the seat. Oxford was then seen to draw a second gun, take careful aim and fire. When Oxford's rooms were searched, among the things found was a document setting out the rules of a society called 'Young England'. Among other things it stated that the members were to meet masked and armed. This gave rise to the suggestion that there was a conspiracy to assassinate the young queen, but it is probable that 'Young England' was Oxford's own creation and Oxford its only member. The jury fully accepted that he was of unsound mind – this appears to have been hereditary since both his father and grandfather had been committed to mental institutions – but they did not accept the prosecution's contention that he had attempted to kill the Queen since no evidence had been presented to show that either of Oxford's guns had actually been loaded. Finally, they agreed to a verdict of guilty but insane and Oxford was committed to an asylum.

In 1842 there were two more attempts made on the Queen's life. The first was by John Francis while the Queen was once more travelling in her carriage down Constitution Hill. Francis fired from only seven feet away and was tried and given a sentence of death which was commuted to transportation for life. A few weeks later, a hunch-backed youth named John William Bean was seen to level a gun at Queen Victoria. It did not go off and Bean fled. In the search which followed, numerous young hunch-backed men were arrested. Bean, when caught, received a sentence of eighteen months.

There were further attempts in 1849, 1850 and 1882. In the first, an Irishman from County Limerick, named William Hamilton, fired a blank charge at Queen Victoria's carriage. He was found guilty of presenting a pistol towards Her Majesty and sentenced to transportation for seven years. In 1850 a former Army officer, Robert Pate, actually managed to strike Queen Victoria on the head with a stick outside Cambridge House, Piccadilly. He pleaded insanity but this was rejected and he was sentenced to be transported for seven years. Finally, in 1882 at Windsor railway station, Roderick McLean fired a gun at Queen Victoria's carriage. He was judged to be insane and was committed to a mental institution.

As well as these attempts on Queen Victoria's life, the Daniel Good case was probably the single most influential incident leading to the formal creation of the 'Detective', as the force became known. On 6 April 1842, a coachman named Daniel Good had bought a pair of knee-breeches from a pawnbroker's shop in Wandsworth High Street. Good was known to the shopkeeper and was allowed to take them on credit but, as he was leaving, the shop-boy informed the shopkeeper that Good had also taken, stolen, a pair of trousers.

By this time Good had gone so a local constable, William Gardner, was dispatched to question him. Good vehemently denied the theft but PC Gardner insisted on searching the stable where Good worked. Pushing away some trusses of straw he discovered something, he was not sure what – a dead goose or pig? – which made him cry out. Good seized the constable's moment of inattention to flee, making sure to bolt the stable door behind him.

PC Gardner now discovered that he had stumbled upon the naked torso of a woman but it was fifteen minutes before he was able to free himself from the stable and summon assistance. Investigation turned up a blood-stained axe, a handsaw, a knife and a number of charred bones were found in the grate of the harness-room. It was also discovered that the torso was that of Jane Good (also known as Jones and Sparks).

In the ensuing days, no fewer than nine divisions of the Metropolitan Police were involved in the case but there was no coordination and each followed its own line of inquiry. D Division learned that Good had a son who lived off Manchester Square but they delayed making inquiries there until the afternoon, only to learn that Good had spent the night and early morning in the house. A Mrs Good ('Old Molly' Good), Good's wife, who lived in what was then Flower and Dean Street, Spitalfields, was also interviewed. Good is widely believed to have been in the house at the time.

The search for Good, closely followed by the Press, turned

out to be an almost farcical series of accidents and Good always seemed to be ahead of the police. The commissioners angrily dismissed some of the men involved and turned the case over to Inspector Pearce, assisted by a sergeant named Stephen Thornton (who had also been involved in the Westwood investigation). They began a methodical search of Good's cold trail, beginning in Spitalfields where after a few inquiries they arrested Molly Good and a second-hand clothes dealer called Gamble. The trail led to Deptford, then Bromley, then . . . nowhere. Two weeks later, Daniel Good was arrested by pure chance in Tonbridge where he had found a job as a bricklayer's labourer. It so happened that another labourer, Thomas Rose, was a former Metropolitan Police constable who knew Good by sight and was aware of the hunt for him. He told the local police.

Good was tried, found guilty of murder and hanged before a large crowd at Newgate on 23 May 1842. The case was closed but the appalling muddle in the Force over bringing Good to justice finally persuaded the commissioners that the Yard needed a detective department.

Chapter Three

THE DETECTIVE

Soon after the end of the Good case, Commissioners Rowan and Mayne sent the Home Secretary a memorandum entitled 'Relative to the detective powers of the police' in which they proposed the creation of a detective branch. No copies of the memorandum have been found but the commissioners must have advanced a convincing argument because, on 8th June 1842, the Home Secretary accepted the proposal in principle, cautioning the commissioners to 'ensure the proper employment of the detective officers when not immediately occupied in the pursuit of offenders'.

On 15 August 1842, the formation of the Detective Branch, otherwise known as 'the Detective', was formally announced in *Police Orders*. This marked the birth of what nearly forty years later was to become the Criminal Investigation Department, or the CID. Pearce was appointed Senior Inspector, with Haynes his deputy. The first detectives were:

Inspector Nicholas Pearce
Inspector John Haynes
Sergeant Stephen Thornton
Sergeant William Gerrett
Sergeant Frederick Shaw
Sergeant Braddick

Sergeant Charles Burgess Goff
Sergeant Jonathan Whicher

It has sometimes been suggested that, like Pearce, Haynes was a former Bow Street Runner but in fact he had been a chemist. This gave him an analytical turn of mind but he also had a well-known knack of catching horse-thieves. These talents were combined in 1840 when a ship was wrecked off Margate. Thieves stripped the vessel of 2,000 lb of cargo and made off towards London with it loaded on a horse-drawn cart. Haynes calculated the probable distance the thieves could cover in a day, then worked out which inns they would most likely have stayed at. A quick check proved his calculations to be correct and Haynes was able to arrest the thieves and recover most of the stolen property which they had sold during their journey.

Pearce did not stay with the Detective for long. In 1844 he was promoted Superintendent of F Division and replaced by Inspector Joseph Shackell. Shackell had joined the Metropolitan Police when it was formed in 1829. Within eight months he had been promoted to inspector but in 1834 left to be gaoler at the Bow Street police office. Then, after rejoining the Force in 1839 he was appointed to the rank of detective in 1843 to replace Charles Burgess Goff, who had been promoted out of the department. Shackell became truly famous and, in March 1839, for instance, assisted in the daring arrest of the armed and immensely popular Chartist, the Reverend Joseph Stephens. Stephen's arrest slowed the growth and ultimately aided the decline of the revolutionary Chartist movement.

The new detectives worked in difficult times. Society was changing. People were becoming more concerned about moral issues and, on 24 January 1843, a crime was committed which affected the murder laws for well over a century. On that day, a wood-turner from Glasgow named Daniel

McNaghten shot and fatally wounded Edward Drummond, Private Secretary to Prime Minister Sir Robert Peel. McNaghten, who initially believed that he had shot Peel, explained to the police that the Tories had been persecuting him for years. During McNaghten's trial at the Old Bailey it was decided that the crime had been committed while McNaghten was temporarily insane. He was accordingly found not guilty and committed to an asylum. As a result Her Majesty's judges drew up the McNaghten Rules in which were set out the rules for a plea and acquittal on grounds of diminished responsibility.

The case of the murder of Sarah Hart by John Tawell illustrates not only the changing times but also how new technology was beginning to be used in the capture of criminals. On 1 January 1845, Sarah Hart was found unconscious and dying on the floor in her house at Salt Hill, near Slough. A neighbour said she had heard stifled screams, went to investigate and saw an agitated man dressed like a Quaker leave the house. The local police soon learned that a man looking like a Quaker had boarded a train for London and so a description of the man was immediately sent to the Metropolitan Police via the newly installed railway telegraph, the first time it had been used for such a purpose. A policeman was sent to Paddington Station and there he arrested the 'Quaker', a man named John Tawell.

Tawell was indeed a Quaker but he was also a criminal on ticket-of-leave (being obliged to report monthly to the police) following the completion of a twenty-one years' sentence for bank fraud. A married man, Tawell had earlier had an affair with Sarah Hart. Recently, though, she had begun to send him letters pressing for money and claiming that he was the father of her children. Tawell, in dread of his wife learning about the affair, saw no escape except to murder his former mistress. He was found guilty of murder and executed.

Another crime which reflects these changing times was the Manning case.

Marie De Roux was born in Switzerland and, by most accounts, was an attractive woman. Two men, Frederick Manning and Patrick O'Connor, sought her hand in marriage but it was Frederick Manning who won it. Following their marriage, Frederick and Marie, on the advice of O'Connor, took the tenancy of a pub in Shoreditch. The business failed. Marie believed that this was O'Connor's fault and that he owed them compensation. One evening, O'Connor was persuaded to visit the Mannings's home. Marie took him down to the basement, put a gun to his head and pulled the trigger. O'Connor inconsiderately clung to life and Frederick Manning was forced to resolve the problem. As he later succinctly put it, he 'battered his head with a chisel'. They buried the body in a small grave prepared by Marie in her kitchen and thoroughly cleaned the house.

The Mannings then cheated on each other. Frederick tried to sell all their property to a furniture dealer while, unknown to him, Marie took all her valuables and went to Edinburgh. En route she coolly visited O'Connor's lodgings and stole cash and valuables including railway stock from a cashbox and a small safe. O'Connor's friends reported his continued absence to the police. It was learned that he had last been seen at the Mannings's house and the body was indeed found when the house was searched. It was buried in quicklime and badly decomposed but O'Connor's false teeth were identified by his dentist.

The search for the Mannings was led by Sergeants Thornton and Langley of the Detective Department. Marie was arrested when she tried to sell the railway stock in Edinburgh but Frederick had vanished. He was thought to have boarded a ship bound for the United States and so Thornton and Langley commandeered a naval steamship and eventually caught up with what was believed to be Manning's vessel. Unfortunately, the suspect was not Manning. The next lead took Sergeant Langley and a PC Lockyer to Jersey. This was where Frederick Manning was indeed hiding and he was arrested.

The Mannings were hanged together in 1847 before an enormous crowd outside Horsemonger Lane gaol in Southwark. Charles Dickens was a witness, as he had been at the execution of Courvoisier, and he later wrote to *The Times* about it. His distaste for public hanging contributed to the growing pressure which brought about the exclusion of members of the public from hangings.

The executioner was William Calcraft, who also executed Courvoisier, James Greenacre and John Tawell, as well as other notable criminals of the day such as the body-snatchers John Bishop and Thomas Head. Calcraft is especially noted for having hanged at Chelmsford in 1831 a nine-year-old boy found guilty of setting fire to a house. Calcraft, however, was also known as a particularly inefficient hangman, death by slow strangulation being his trademark. *The Times* reported that at the execution of John Tawell at Aylesbury:

> The length of drop allowed him was so little that he struggled most violently. His whole frame was convulsed: he writhed horribly, and his limbs rose and fell again repeatedly, while he wrung his hands . . . It was nearly ten minutes after the rope had been fixed before the convulsions which indicated his extreme suffering ceased.

At any rate, Marie Manning's execution is often said to have been a bad day for manufacturers of black satin. She wore a dress made from this popular material to her execution and demand for it is said to have dramatically declined as a result. This story, though, may be a myth since Albert Borowitz in his account of the case, *The Bermondsey Horror*, found no evidence for it. However, there seems to be truth in the claim that Marie Manning left a more permanent mark in being the model for Mademoiselle Hortense, the French maid to Lady Deadlock in Dickens's *Bleak House*. The novel also featured Inspector Bucket of the Detective who was modelled on the real-life detective, Inspector Field.

In January 1850 Commissioner Rowan retired and was replaced by one of the superintendents, Captain William Hay. Hay caused friction by refusing to accept the otherwise generally agreed seniority of Mayne and, when Hay died in 1855, it was decided that in future the Metropolitan Police would have only one commissioner. In the year of Rowan's retirement, the Detective at Scotland Yard received some welcome good publicity. Charles Dickens wrote warmly about a visit by most of the department to the editorial offices of the weekly periodical *Household Words*. First, though, his article began with an attack on the Bow Street Runners:

> To say the truth, we think there was a vast amount of humbug about those worthies. Apart from many of them being men of very indifferent character, and far too much in the habit of consorting with thieves and the like, they never lost a public occasion of jobbing and trading in mystery and making the most of themselves. Continually puffed besides by incompetent magistrates anxious to conceal their own deficiencies, and hand-in-glove with the penny-a-liners of that time, they became a sort of superstition.
>
> Although as a Preventative Police they were utterly ineffective, and as a Detective Police were very loose and uncertain in their operations, they remain with some people a superstition to the present day.

In contrast, Dickens praised the Detective Force of the Metropolitan Police and left us a valuable, if perhaps exaggerated, impression of his guests. Barely veiled by the false names supplied by Dickens, they were described thus:

Inspector Wield (Charles Frederick Field):
... a middle-aged man of a portly presence, with a large, moist, knowing eye, a husky voice, and a habit of emphasising his conversation by the air of a corpulent fore-finger, which is constantly in juxta-position with his eyes or nose.

Inspector Stalker (Superintendent Robert Walker of A Division; he was not in fact a detective, but a member of the Yard's Executive Branch):
... is a shrewd, hard-headed Scotchman – in appearance not at all unlike a very acute, thoroughly-trained schoolmaster, from the Normal Establishment at Glasgow.
Inspector Wield one might have known, perhaps, for what he is – Inspector Stalker, never.

Sergeant Dornton (Stephen Thornton):
... about fifty years of age, with a ruddy face and a high sun-burnt forehead, has the air of one who has been a Sergeant in the army ... He is famous for steadily pursuing the inductive process, and, from small beginnings, working on from clue to clue until he bags his man.

Sergeant Witchem (Jonathan Whicher):
... shorter and thicker-set [than 'Dornton'], and marked with the small pox, has something of a reserved and thoughtful air, as if he were engaged in deep mathematical calculations.

43

Sergeant Mith (Henry Smith):
. . . a smooth-faced man with a fresh bright complexion, and a strange air of simplicity . . .

Sergeant Fendall (Edward Kendall):
. . . a light-haired, well-spoken, polite person, is a prodigious hand at pursuing private inquiries of a delicate nature.

Sergeant Straw (Frederick Shaw):
. . . a little wiry Sergeant of meek demeanour and strong sense, would knock at a door and ask a series of questions in any mild character you chose to prescribe for him, from a charity-boy upwards, and seem as innocent as an infant.

Dickens did not meet two of the detectives, Inspector John Haynes and Sergeant Edward Langley, and did not have the opportunity to smoke cigars, drink brandy-and-water and discuss the art of detection with a man who was ultimately to become the most renowned member of the department: Adolphus Frederick Williamson. The latter joined the Force in 1850, the year the detectives gathered in Dickens's office. In 1852 he was promoted from constable to sergeant and transferred from P Division to the Detective Branch, later achieving the ranks of inspector, chief inspector, superintendent and chief constable. Tim Cavanagh, a contemporary of Williamson, left a fascinating portrait of the man who was to become the overseer of the Detective and of its transition to the Criminal Investigation Department:

We always called Williamson 'Dolly', because of his Christian name Adolphus. Now, 'Dolly' was possessed of a considerable amount of dry humour and chaff . . . Scarcely a 'barney' was got up that he was not in; but he had a happy knack of keeping out of trouble, when some of the others easily got 'spotted'.

Adolphus 'Dolly' Williamson was perhaps fortunate to be involved so early in his career in the apprehension of the perpetrators of what was known, at the time, as the 'Great Bullion Robbery' and today could be called the 'First Great Train Robbery'. On the evening of 15 May 1855, three large boxes containing gold bullion were placed on the Folkestone train. At Folkestone they were to be transferred to a boat and taken to the Continent. The boxes were bound with iron bars, sealed and weighted by the carriers, and put in an iron safe secured by double locks in the guard's van. There were three sets of keys to the safes. One kept by the railway's traffic superintendent in London, one by the head of the Folkestone railway office, and a third by the skipper of the Folkestone–Boulogne ferry. When the French railway authorities checked the safes at Boulogne they found them lighter than they should have been. The boxes were opened. Upwards of £20,000 of gold bullion had been removed and replaced by lead shot. Nobody could fathom when or how the substitution had taken place.

The mystery was solved about a year later when the thieves fell out. The robbery was conceived by a man named William Pierce, who printed tickets for the railway company. He enlisted the help of a professional thief named Ted Agar and a guard called James Burgess who was often in charge of the bullion train and was able to describe in detail the arrangements concerning the gold. They decided the robbery could only be committed during the train journey but that two sets of keys were needed to get at the gold. A clerk named William George Tester who worked in the traffic department at London Bridge was able to obtain a wax impression of one set of keys when the safes were sent for repair. The other set of keys was kept in a cupboard in Folkestone. Tester could not get at these but Pierce and Agar kept the cupboard under surveillance and noted that it was often left unlocked. At the first opportunity, they made a wax impression of the needed key. The thieves then made copies of the keys from the wax impressions and, with everything ready, they waited for Tester to send them word of the next bullion shipment. The word came. The robbery was committed.

Pierce and Agar melted most of the gold into small, easily disposable ingots. Some of them were sold to a man named James Saward who was a barrister of the Inner Temple and also a forger known as 'Jim the Penman'. About twelve months later, Agar was convicted of a different offence. He gave Pierce about £15,000 to invest for a woman and her child but Pierce made a few payments, then got greedy and kept the money for himself. Agar was so angry when he heard about Pierce's duplicity that he turned Queen's evidence. All concerned in the robbery were rounded up by Inspector Thornton, with Sergeants Tanner, Williamson, and Henry Smith.

In many ways Williamson's mentor was Jonathan Whicher, one of the original members of the Detective. By now, Whicher was a junior inspector under Stephen Thornton and he worked alongside a team of six others who were:

Sergeant Frederick Adolphus Williamson
Sergeant Richard Tanner
Sergeant William Palmer
Sergeant George Clarke
Sergeant Alexander Thomson
Sergeant Robinson

The Bow Street Runners could be sent on investigations

outside London and this practice was continued by the Metropolitan Police who, in July 1837, sent a sergeant and eleven constables to Huddersfield to keep order during an election in which Chartist Richard Ostler was active. Also, in 1838, a total of 647 Metropolitan Police constables were sent to various parts of Britain to help prevent public disorders. The following year Inspector Haynes and Sergeant Thornton were sent to gather information about the Chartists in the North of England but these were general Metropolitan Police operations, not specifically investigations by the Detective.

The first recorded instance of the Detective's assistance being requested was in 1860 and in subsequent years it became the custom for the provincial forces to ask for the help of Scotland Yard when circumstances required it. The public was generally alerted to difficult and perhaps sensational cases by the newspaper headline: 'SCOTLAND YARD HAS BEEN CALLED IN'. Thus, in 1860, Whicher and Williamson were asked to investigate the murder of a child at the imposing Road Hill House in the village of Road, near Frome in Somerset. The house was occupied by Mr Kent and his wife, seven children (four of them being from Mr Kent's previous marriage), a nurse, a cook, and a housemaid.

On the morning of 30 June 1860 the nurse gave the alarm that Francis, aged almost four years, was missing from his cot. The child's body was found wrapped in a blanket taken from the nursery. His throat had been cut and the body had been dumped down the privy in the garden probably five hours before. It was a classic 'country house' murder. All the doors and windows had been securely locked and there was no sign of a forced entry. Therefore the murder had been committed, or the murderer had been admitted to the house, by someone who lived there.

Suspicion first fell on the nurse, Elizabeth Gough. She

twice appeared before the magistrates before being discharged because of lack (in fact complete absence of) evidence. Mr Kent was suspected next, then suspicion settled
on Constance Kent, the eldest child. She was said to have
murdered her little half-brother through petty jealousy.
Whicher concluded that Constance Kent was indeed the
guilty party and procured a warrant for her arrest. The
main cause of suspicion against her was the disappearance
of one of her nightdresses. The housemaid said that she had
received from Constance a nightdress for washing which
appeared to be normally soiled but that as she was packing
the clothes basket for the laundress, Constance came and
asked her for a glass of water which she took about a
minute to fetch. There was no evidence that Constance had
used that time to retrieve the nightdress from the basket
but, when unpacked by the laundress, the nightdress was
missing.

Constance was tried. The judgement when passed was not
that she was innocent but that the evidence was insufficient
for a verdict of guilty. Constance was released on bail of
£200 to come up for judgement if called. However, the
particularly brutal murder of the child and the rumours
concerning Constance and the adults in Road Hill House
caused a sensation and the Press was hostile towards the
police, criticising them for failing to arrest the perpetrator
of the crime. Then the Press accused the police, principally
Jonathan Whicher, of falsely accusing Constance and of very
nearly causing a gross miscarriage of justice. Whicher was
badly affected by the criticism and it is generally regarded
as having broken his health since he was forced to retire
three years later.

In 1865, Constance Kent confessed. She claimed that she
had taken one of her father's razors and hidden it a few days
before the murder. On the night of the murder she said that
she had gone downstairs, opened the drawing-room window,

then returned upstairs for the child, whom she carried out into the privy in the garden. There she had cut the child's throat. As for the nightdress, she said that on returning to her room she found it spotted with blood. She managed to wash it out in a pan in her room, but a few days later noticed that the blood-stains were still visible against the light. As had been surmised, Constance said she took the nightdress from the washing basket and hid it in various places before finally burning it in her bedroom fire. She was sentenced to death, though this was commuted to life imprisonment, and she was eventually released in July 1885 after serving a twenty-year term. The following year, using the name Ruth Emilie Kaye, she went to Tasmania with her brother William, later moving with him and his wife to Australia and devoting the rest of her life to nursing. She died on 10 April 1944, shortly after celebrating her 100th birthday.

Was Constance Kent Guilty? Constance's confession contains some remarkable inconsistencies and a determined emphasis that she had committed the murder alone. There are suggestions that the whole truth was not admitted and that Constance's public admissions of guilt were carefully calculated to protect someone else. Television producer Michael Ferguson has been conducting detailed research into the case for a proposed drama and we are grateful to him for drawing our attention to and allowing us to use a note by Jonathan Whicher in the surviving records. As far as we are aware, Michael Ferguson is the first person to have recognised the significance of Whicher's observation. In a report to his superior Whicher wrote:

> I beg to add that, as far as I am able to form an opinion, the murder was committed either by Miss Constance alone while in a fit of insanity, or by her and her brother William from motives of spite and jealousy entertained towards the younger children and their parents, and I

am strongly impressed with the latter opinion judging from the sympathy existing between the two . . .

Constance's guilt does not seem to be in question. She would have confessed to clear her conscience but William stands alone as her closest confidant, the one person she would be most likely to want to protect. Whicher had probably divined the truth and at the same time been unable to prove his case. As a result his career came to an end.

Another famous detective of these early days was Richard Tanner who was involved in solving the Stepney murder. Mary Emsley owned property and was reputed to be wealthy, having an income estimated by some to be £5,000 a year – which in 1860 was wealthy by the standards of the great majority. She made this money from the rents on several properties she owned. Walter Thomas Emm, a cobbler who collected some of these rents for her, became disturbed after four days had passed without Mrs Emsley answering the door of her house at 9 Grove Road, off the Mile End Road, to take the rents he had gathered. Emm reported his concerns to Mrs Emsley's solicitor and on 17 August 1860 the house was broken into and Mrs Emsley's body was discovered, with severe head injuries.

The police soon established that there was no evidence of forced entry and reached the inevitable conclusion that Mrs Emsley was killed by someone she knew. Suspicion fell on James Mullins, a plasterer employed by Mary Emsley. Mullins was an ex-policeman who had served with both the Irish Police and the Metropolitan Police but had been automatically dismissed from the Force after a conviction for larceny and a six-year prison sentence. No evidence could be brought against Mullins except the testimony of a sailor named Mitchell who said that on the morning after the murder he had seen Mullins in an agitated state.

Mullins was questioned by Inspector Thornton and accounted for himself satisfactorily but when a reward of £300 was offered for information leading to the apprehension of Mrs Emsley's killer James Mullins turned up one evening at the Stepney home of Sergeant Richard Tanner of the Detective. Mullins explained that he had been doing some detective work of his own and had seen Walter Emm behaving very suspiciously, hiding packages in a shed adjoining his house. To quote Sergeant Tanner:

> I suspected this to be a plant of Mullins and I consulted Inspector Thornton and he considered so also, and the next morning, the 9th September, we took Mullins to point out where the parcel was and he did so. In consequence we took them both, but Emm clearly showed that he did not put the parcel there.

Unfortunately for Mullins, his story completely lacked credibility. He pointed out where he had been standing on the other side of the road when he allegedly observed Emm. How, then, had he managed to see what Emm was doing inside his shed? Mullins was unable to answer and, when his home was searched, sufficient evidence was unearthed to convict him of the murder of Mrs Emsley. On 19 November 1860 he was hanged by Mr Calcraft.

The point about the Mullins case is that the murderer would probably never have been caught had he not been tempted by the £300 reward. However, if his story had been better thought out and the planted evidence against Emm substantial, then the latter, an innocent man, could have gone to the gallows. The case illustrates the dangers of the reward system, a subject which was to be the cause of much criticism in later years, especially in connection with the Jack the Ripper murders.

Chapter Four

INSPECTOR WILLIAMSON, AND DIVISIONAL DETECTIVES

In 1863, the burden of running the Department fell on 'Dolly' Williamson and Sergeant Richard Tanner. Tanner was promoted to inspector in 1864, but his career was cut short through ill-health. Eventually he was forced to retire early and he moved to Winchester where he kept the White Swan Inn until his death from apoplexy on 19 October 1873.

Though not as experienced as Wicher, Tanner's teeth had been cut on some memorable cases. He had shown flair in the Mullins investigation, for example, and in 1864 investigated the first murder to be committed on the railway. On 9 July 1864, two young bank clerks boarded at Hackney a train bound for Highbury. Entering a first-class compartment, they were horrified to find blood soaked into the seat cushions. There was blood elsewhere in the compartment and on a silver-topped cane and a hat. About twenty minutes later the driver of a train heading in the opposite direction saw something on the track. He was able to stop before hitting the obstruction and, on investigation, found it to be an unconscious man, beaten badly about the head and barely alive.

Some letters in the victim's possession led to his identification as seventy-year-old Thomas Briggs and the silver-topped cane found in the carriage by the two bank clerks was later identified as belonging to Briggs, although the hat did not. Briggs always wore a tall silk top-hat made specially for him by a hatters in the City of London. Thus, his hat was missing and also, it was believed, his watch and chain. Briggs never regained consciousness and died the following day.

Inspector Tanner took over the investigation. A watch and chain was believed to have been taken from Mr Briggs and so Tanner circulated its description among jewellers and pawnbrokers. A Cheapside jeweller named Death came forward to say that he had taken the watch-chain in exchange for another from a young foreigner, possibly a German. A cab-driver named Matthews also came to the police and told them that an acquaintance had given Matthews's daughter one of Mr Death's jewellery boxes. It was unfortunate for the murderer of Mr Briggs that he had chosen to take the watch-chain to a jeweller with such a memorable name because its unusualness caused Matthews to pay more attention to the murder reports than he might otherwise have done. He consequently noted that the hat found in the railway carriage exactly matched the one he had acquired for this acquaintance who was a foreigner, a German named Franz Müller.

Unfortunately, four days earlier, Franz Müller had sailed aboard the *Victoria* for the United States. Tanner set off in pursuit aboard the faster *SS City of Manchester*, taking with him Sergeant George Clark, Matthews the cab-man and Death the jeweller. They arrived in New York three weeks ahead of the *Victoria*. A disgruntled Tanner later described the unexpected trip, for which he had been given only an hour and a half's notice and which caused him to be out of pocket:

I was twenty days and nights in the Harbour of New York, during which time I do not think I ever went to sleep, waiting for that ship and then there was the anxiety of coming home with Müller, besides the trouble of getting him and going to law in New York. It was very wearing and I had a reward of £20 when I thought I should have had £100.

Müller was duly arrested. His extradition papers were signed by the President of the United States and he was returned to London to stand trial where he was found guilty and hanged by Calcraft. *The Times* reported the scene: 'Before the slight slow vibrations of the body had ended, robbery and violence, loud laughing and oaths, fighting, obscene conduct and still more filthy language reigned round the gallows far and near.' The behaviour of the crowd that day did much to persuade the more responsible members of the public to back the abolition of public hanging.

In 1866 the Detective Branch was increased by the addition of one inspector and one sergeant. The new inspector was James J. Thomson and he enjoyed a particularly varied career as one of the Yard's most accomplished detectives. His father had been a merchant in the East in the firm of Jacob Van Lennep, Thomson and Co., which had houses at Constantinople, Smyrna and London. Thomson was born in Smyrna and only came to England following the great fire in 1844. His mother was Italian and for some time the family had lived in Paris. Thomson was able to speak several languages fluently, including French, Italian and English.

In 1866 he undertook the investigation of 'The Great Stamp Office Robbery' since Scotland Yard was called in following the theft of a quantity of stamps from the Government Stamp Office in Manchester in May of that year. Later, in 1868, Thomson delivered a paper to a departmental commission on the Detective Police and it provides a fascinating first-hand account of this major inquiry which involved a specialist team of detectives:

The office was situated at the north-east corner of the block of buildings formed by Cross Street, Robinson Street, New Market Street, and Moult Street; it was in the basement; there were cellars beneath and a warehouse at the side, and general offices on the second and third floors. The public entrance was in Moult Street, but there was a side entrance in Cross Street, chiefly used by the gentlemen having offices upstairs and by Mr Howard [Richard Howard, the Distributor of Stamps in Manchester]. I examined the premises from the basement to the roof, and noticed every-thing, and took the name and address of every person known or in any way connected with the entire block of buildings. After this close examination, Mr Maybury [the detective superintendent of the Manchester police] and I came to the conclusion that the thieves had obtained a thorough knowledge of the movements of the people connected with the stamp office; that they had entered on Saturday afternoon by the private entrance in Cross Street, that they had proceeded to the first floor, and by means of a skeleton key had entered the office of a firm above the warehouse below, and that they had done so at an hour when there was no one upon the premises, namely between 2 and 3 or 4 on the Saturday afternoon; that having obtained access they had fastened themselves in, had proceeded to the warehouse below, and to the cellars below that; had removed the bricks forming a partition between the two houses; had passed through to the cellars beneath the stamp office, and had broken open one or two doors, through which they had to pass to arrive at the stamp office . . .

The robbery had evidently been undertaken by professionals and Thomson went on to explain to the commission how the thieves had expertly opened the safe and taken items, including stamps and money, worth £10,000 or more. Thomson returned to London and in an interview with Commissioner Mayne asked permission to form a special team to investigate the case. This seems to have been a very unusual request at the time, but Mayne sanctioned it.

> I picked out Inspector Potter of the G division, who had shown himself to be a very good detective while a sergeant in the D division, and had been promoted; I picked out Sergeant Dunnaway of the H division, a man who did not seem to have had much education, but who was known as a good detective, and as a man who had an extensive knowledge of thieves, and so on, and was capable of obtaining information where others, perhaps, failed. I had also Police Constable 199 G. Ranger, likewise known as a good plain-clothes man at that time, and one or two others. I think that I had Sergeant Newey of the P Division.

The first thing to do was to follow up the leads given by the Manchester police. Investigations showed that the men suspected by them were innocent and that the word on the street was that the robbery had been committed by two men known in London as 'The Countrymen'. Further inquiries established that 'The Countrymen' were brothers Tom and 'Big Bill' Douglas and a man named Gleeson.

Nothing further could be learned and the investigation came to a standstill. Then, towards the end of July, a man who gave the name Charles Batt was arrested at Somerset House on suspicion of possessing a stamp stolen in the Manchester robbery.

I suggested to Potter and Ranger that they should be at the police court the next day, and that they should mix amongst the crowd and see whether this man had any friends or anybody who took an interest in the case . . . Ranger noticed that a man with a wooden leg passed a little tobacco in a piece of paper to Batt . . .

The man with the wooden leg was identified as Richard Shaw, a burglar who had damaged his leg so badly during an attempted prison escape that it had been amputated. He was known thereafter by the nickname 'Peg-leg Dick'. Potter and Ranger picked up the man and questioned him. Dick thought himself hard done by. He had been one of the top men in his profession before his accident, but since then had found himself ill-used by his former equals. He hated them and was willing to inform on them providing that nobody ever knew that he had done so. Thomson continued:

. . . Potter turned him over entirely to me, and a more trying man I never came across in my experience, he was not truthful; he was seldom sober; he was never otherwise than filthy; and he persecuted me day and night by coming to my house, and even when I was not at home he would lie dead drunk on the doorstep, saying that he should be sure to meet me sometime by doing so.

Peg-leg led the police a merry chase but eventually 'The Countrymen' were arrested and convicted. Thomson's story is a singular first-hand account of a major investigation conducted in the early days of the Detective Branch. It also demonstrates that the methodology of the investigation was not radically different from today. Thomson selected a team of specialists. He set up an operational headquarters away from Scotland Yard. He went after minor associates of the criminals. This is essentially what the police did one hundred years later when they pursued the Krays and the Richardsons.

Of considerably greater significance on the historical stage, however, were the activities in the 1860s of the Republican faction in Ireland. They called themselves the Irish Republican Brotherhood or Fenians and, over the succeeding decades, their terrorist activities in England had a profound and long-term effect on the development of the Metropolitan Police. The Fenians, both in Ireland and in their military activities elsewhere, including the organisation of a rising against the English, were under the control of Captain T. J. Kelly, who had fought in the American Civil War with the 10th Ohio Regiment. In January 1867, Kelly sailed from New York to Ireland with his companions, among whom was Captain Richard O'Sullivan Burke, the armaments' organiser. Burke was born in Macroom, county Cork, but had emigrated to America in 1857 and taken part in the Civil War, serving with the 15th New York Engineers.

Later in 1867 the 200-ton brig *Jacknell Packet* sailed from New York with a cargo of about 5,000 modern breech-loading and repeating rifles, 1.5 million rounds of ammunition and three unmounted cannons. There were also thirty-eight officers of the Irish Republican Army. The vessel put in at Sligo Bay and was met by Richard O'Sullivan Burke, now Kelly's second-in-command, who explained that nobody was willing to accept the weapons. The ship sailed on but the same thing happened at other Irish ports. The weapons consequently returned to America. However, twenty-eight Fenians did land in Ireland, but were all in police custody within twenty-four hours.

In September of the same year, two men were arrested in

Manchester as vagrants. They gave the names Wright and Williams, but one was Captain Kelly and the other a Captain Deasy. They were remanded in custody and taken to prison but en route the prison van was ambushed by about thirty Fenians, some of them armed. One, Peter Rice,* scrambled to the roof of the van, prized open a ventilator and shot Sergeant Brett who was inside. On Rice's instructions, a terrified woman prisoner took the keys of the prison van from Brett's pocket and Kelly and Deasy were freed. They were never recaptured. Subsequently, the Manchester police arrested a great many Irishmen and, as Robert Kee has observed:

> The identification procedure employed by the police was so questionable, and much of the eye-witness' evidence so doubtful, that the surprising thing was not that one of the five men eventually put on trial for their lives should have been entirely innocent, but that the other four were in fact all involved in one way or another in the rescue attempt.

The four were Edward Condon, William Allen, Philip Larkin, and Michael O'Brien; the innocent man was an Irish marine named Maguire who was on leave at the time and who was not only *not* involved with the Fenians but had never been near the scene of the escape. In English law, anyone taking part in an illegal act which results in someone being killed is deemed guilty of constructive murder.†

---

* It is often said that Sergeant Brett was shot by a man named William Allen, but the murderer was Rice and he escaped to America with Kelly and Deasy.
† See the case of Craig and Bentley in the early 1950s for a more recent example of this.

Therefore, although none of those arrested had actually killed Sergeant Brett, all were found guilty and sentenced to death – including poor Maguire, although he was finally released and granted a free pardon. Edward Condon, who on leaving the dock after conviction had uttered the famous words: 'I have nothing to regret, nothing to retract or take back. I can only say: God Save Ireland!,' was also released. He was an American citizen and was released subsequent to appeals from the American legation in London. Allen, Larkin and O'Brien were executed in public on 24 November 1867. The hangman was somewhat less than professional and Larkin and O'Brien died in agony on the gallows.

The following month Richard O'Sullivan Burke, Kelly's second-in-command, was arrested in London, remanded in custody and sent to Clerkenwell prison. On 11 December Scotland Yard received a letter from Daniel Ryan, Superintendent of the Dublin Metropolitan Police, which read:

I have to report that I have information from a reliable source to the effect that the rescue of Richard Burke from prison in London is contemplated. The plan is to blow up the exercise wall by means of gunpowder – the hour between 3 and 4 p.m. and the signal for all right, a white ball thrown up outside when he is at exercise.

On 12 December a policeman in Corporation Row, which was bounded by the prison wall, saw some men bring up a barrel and insert and light a fuse, but it was damp. The men calmly took the barrel away – all under the thoroughly disinterested eye of the policeman. The next day, the conspirators tried again. At 3.45 p.m. on 13 December some men wheeled a barrel into the street alongside a section of the prison wall. One man crossed to the barrel, put a fuse in the end, applied a match, and ran off. Several people saw this happen. There was a tremendous explosion and about sixty yards of the prison wall were blown in. Many of the houses opposite the prison, occupied mainly by poor people, were destroyed and windows over a wide area were broken. Far more seriously, 6 people were killed, another 6 later died from injuries sustained in the explosion and 120 people, mainly women and children, were hurt.

The area was immediately cordoned off, the army was brought in to give assistance and a man and two women were arrested on suspicion. A week later, two men were arrested in Glasgow for using firearms. They were recognised as Fenians and sent to London where they were identified as having been concerned in the Clerkenwell explosion. One of the men, Michael Barrett, was identified as the man who fired the barrel. Two other conspirators, James Murphy and Patrick Casey, escaped to Paris and the French Government refused extradition. Of all the people arrested only Michael Barret was convicted and, on 26 May 1868, he was executed in front of Newgate Prison. Today he has the distinction of being the last person executed in public in England.

The police attempted to excuse their incompetence by arguing that they had believed the conspirators' intention had been to blow *up* the wall, not to blow it down. They had therefore restricted their searches to below the prison wall, apparently suspecting that an attempt would be made to put a bomb in the drains or for a tunnel to be dug under the wall! As a result, one Irish policeman observed of the British police: 'They know as little how to discharge duty in connection with Fenianism as I do about translating Hebrew.' Commissioner Mayne dutifully shouldered the responsibility for the fiasco and tendered his resignation but the Home Secretary, Walpole, refused to accept it. 'We told Mayne,' he is reported to have said, 'that he made a damned fool of himself, but that we weren't going to throw him over after his long public service.'

Earlier the Irish viceroy, Lord Mayo, had suggested that Scotland Yard create a special Fenian department with Williamson at the head. The Government now decided not to do so and instead formed a special secret branch attached to the Home Office. They brought over from Ireland an army Intelligence colonel named Fielding to head it and a barrister named Robert Anderson to be his assistant. The Metropolitan Police also enrolled 50,000 special constables, created the rank of Detective Chief Inspector (to which Williamson was appointed) and increased the department to three inspectors, eleven sergeants, and one clerk sergeant. It was also decided that detectives should possess their own form of authority and they were issued with brass tipstaves similar to those held earlier by the Bow Street Runners. The Police Orders which announced the issue added:

> When called upon to act, and if there is any doubt as to their being constables, the police are to draw their truncheons (i.e. tipstaves) which will be readily distinguished as a distinctive badge by persons doubting or resisting the lawful authority of the constable.

By 1868, however, the Detective Department was still so small that it could boast a personnel of only sixteen within a force numbering nearly 8,000. A government committee in that year also decided that each Metropolitan Police Division should have a detective department under the immediate supervision of the Divisional Superintendent. The recommendation was shelved until the following year but by this time Sir Richard Mayne had died and the Metropolitan Police had its first new commissioner in forty years.

The new man at the top was Lieutenant-Colonel Edmund

Henderson. Born on 19 April 1821 in Muddiford, near Christchurch, Hampshire, he was noted as a fluent speaker with a good sense of humour and never lost for an anecdote. He was also a skilled water-colour artist. His qualifications for the job consisted of having been Comptroller-General of Convicts in Western Australia from 1850–63 and a few years spent in England as Surveyor-General of Prisons. It has never been entirely clear why the proven ability to handle hardened prisoners was seen as a recommendation for handling policemen. His term of office was marked by gaining sanction for an increase in the detective force and for the establishment of Divisional detectives but he is chiefly remembered today for the series of disasters which befell the police during his commissionership, some of which we will touch on later.

Under Rowan and Mayne, the handful of Metropolitan Police detectives had been headquartered at Scotland Yard and their assistance was given to the Divisional police as and when requested. The Divisions are not supposed to have had detectives of their own, but there is some evidence that they did, although this evidence is admittedly patchy since so many files from this period no longer exist. On 10 December 1845, for example, *Police Orders* contained the following rebuke:

> I have reiterated to Superintendents that there should be no particular men in the Division called plain clothes men and that no man should disguise himself without particular orders from the Superintendent and that this should not be done even by them without some very strong case of necessity being made out.

The Commissioner issued a similar complaint in a memo dated 23 January 1854, which is also interesting because it shows that twenty-five years after the creation of the New

Police, the authorities were still concerned to allay public suspicions that the police were employed as spies.

I find a considerable number of sergeants and constables employed in plain clothes, 15 sergeants and 53 constables permanently and 2 sergeants and 102 constables temporarily are in effect permanently employed. I understand also that the same men are not always employed. The numbers employed in the different Divisions whether permanently or temporarily vary greatly and in some of the Divisions when the duties are as satisfactorily performed as in any other Division the numbers employed in plain clothes are very small.

Superintendents are reminded that there is no regulation in the service authorising the employment of police in plain clothes, and by doing so two very important objects are lost sight of, namely the prevention of crime by the presence, so that it shall be known, of a Constable, and the satisfaction to the public on seeing that a Constable is at the place. Also such constables are not under the control of public observation, not being known from their dress to belong to the police, and such a practice gives occasion to a charge of police being employed as spies and in other improper ways.

Each Superintendent will report the objects of his employing the number of Sergeants and Constables who are now employed, and the duties specially assigned to each and in future on every occasion in which any of the police are employed in plain clothes a report is to be made of the cause of such employment either at the time or as soon as possible afterwards, this is not however to be understood to apply to the employment of police to make inquiry in any case of crime which has occurred in which the Superintendent considers the inquiry may be made more effectively by men in plain clothes nor in cases of inquiry directed by Commissioners.

In 1869, Henderson pushed through the recommendations for the formal creation of Divisional detectives. He organised detective constables under a sergeant and hoped they would be selected 'from the most promising men in the service.' The pay was fixed at 28s a week for constables and 35s for sergeants, with an allowance for plain clothes of £5 per annum.

Yet an interesting analysis of the new system comes from a memo written by Sir Howard Vincent, future head of the Detective Branch. He did not have a high regard for Henderson's choice of men or of the organisation of the Divisional Detective Force:

> Great as was the improvement of this system over that which previously prevailed, it was nevertheless attended by many defects. A Division was looked upon in the light of a separate police district, and there was neither interchange of information, nor communications with the detectives of other divisions, or with the detective department at Scotland Yard.

Vincent went to say the main problem was that money and conditions in the Detective were poor in comparison to the uniform police:

> The divisional detectives consisted for the most part of illiterate men, many of whom had been put into plain clothes to screen personal defects which marred their smart appearance in uniform. They were but nominally controlled by a sergeant, little superior to themselves. Every Inspector gave them orders, and in reality they were employed as much as messengers, as in detective duties, which they discharged pretty much as they liked. They never were withdrawn from duty so

long as they committed no flagrant breach of discipline and with some exceptions lived a life unprofitable to themselves, discreditable to the service, useless to the public.

Yet it is easy to be critical. Henderson's creation of the Divisional Detective was a major achievement, especially given the continuing public distrust of plain-clothes policemen. It was Henderson, too, who relaxed the rule that all uniformed policemen had to wear their uniform even when off duty. Another change instituted in Henderson's first year as commissioner was the division of the Metropolitan Police into four districts, each in the charge of a district superintendent. Thus, under Henderson's commissionership, the Detective Branch entered the new decade of the 1870s with Williamson being promoted to the new rank of detective superintendent. Under him were three chief inspectors, three inspectors, six sergeants (first class) and thirteen sergeants (second class).

Henderson also oversaw the creation of a small team similar to that formed by Thomson to investigate the Great Stamp Robbery. In 1875 the Home Secretary sent a note to the Commissioner saying that he felt sure that there was a gang of thieves particularly concerned with jewel robberies. 'I desire special care may be taken to prevent them for the future and that all known thieves be well watched.' Therefore, On 24 May, Williamson suggested that Inspector Shore and Sergeants Moon and Meiklejohn be relieved from their general duties in the department and devote the whole of their time to trying to track down the thieves. He also asked that £20 should be supplied to enable them to buy information as opportunity offered. Unfortunately, although we know that Shore reported on three men, we do not know the outcome and whether this mini 'Flying Squad' was successful.

Despite these considerable advances it has to be said that at this time the Detective was also suffering a series of setbacks. There were examples of fine detective work, of course, but a catalogue of blunders made the headlines and did nothing to help it win the respect and trust of the public. They also seriously affected morale within the Force.

One such classic blunder followed the discovery of the body of Harriet Buswell at a house in what was then Great Coram Street, Bloomsbury, in December 1872. One of the first on the scene was Superintendent Thomson, now superintendent of the local Division. Thomson noted such clues as there were, estimated the time of death from the oil remaining in a lamp and even had a plaster cast made of teeth marks in an apple (they turned out to be Miss Buswell's), but the investigation got nowhere and the press became increasingly critical of the handling of the case.

Meanwhile, a brig bound for America had put in to Ramsgate for repairs. A clergyman named Hassel, his wife, a ship-broker named Wohlebbe and a member of the crew took the opportunity to visit London for Christmas. They returned to Ramsgate in early January and it was here that an inspector of the Ramsgate police noticed that Wohlebbe looked like the published description of a man last seen in the company of Harriet Buswell and arrested him.

Superintendent Thomson sent an inspector to Ramsgate together with a fruiterer, at whose shop Miss Buswell and a male companion had bought some apples, and also a waiter who had served the couple. An identification parade was held. Neither witness picked out Wohlebbe, standing with Dr Hassel and some twenty crewmen from the ship, but both identified the clergyman, Dr Hassel, as Harriet Buswell's companion. Superintendent Thomson himself then went to Ramsgate with several other witnesses, two of whom also picked out Dr Hassel. The poor clergyman was duly arrested. Taken to London, he was charged at Bow Street with the murder. At the hearing before the magistrate, the defence was able to show that at the time of the murder Dr Hassel was ill in bed in his hotel room some distance away from Coram Street and the case against him was dismissed. On 31 January 1873, The *Daily Telegraph* caustically observed:

> The public will learn with satisfaction that a step has actually been taken towards the detection of the Coram Street murder. The step though small, is certain. It has now been conclusively shown, by an indisputable chain of evidence, that, whoever murdered the woman Buswell, it was not Dr Hassel. We have only to pursue the same course of action with reference to every grown-up man who slept in London on Christmas Eve and, by process of elimination, we must at last arrive at the guilty man. The only objection to this process is the limited duration of mortal life.

Inquiries continued – suspects included a member of a troop of Japanese jugglers and a Fellow of the Society of Antiquaries – but the whole thing had become a farce and the murderer of Harriet Buswell was never found. The case shows how much the early police trusted eye-witness identification but also how unreliable such evidence can be. However, it is extraordinary that, throughout all these trials and tribulations, 'Dolly' Williamson, the effective head of the Detective Department, emerged intact. He even survived the catastrophe of what became known as the 'Great Scotland Yard Scandal.'

Chapter Five

THE GREAT SCOTLAND YARD
SCANDAL

It is known by several names: the 'De Goncourt Case', the 'Turf Fraud Scandal' and the 'Montgomery Scandal', but it is best known as the 'Great Scotland Yard Scandal'. This particular case became one of the blackest parts of the history of the Detective and was also the cause of radical change in the department. John Littlechild, then a sergeant and involved in the investigation, wrote in 1895 that: 'Apart from dynamite conspiracies, and explosions, and the Whitechapel murders, perhaps no matter has been regarded of such great importance at Scotland Yard as the discovery of the Great Turf Frauds of 1876.'

Harry Benson was born in Paris where his father was a prosperous merchant with offices in the Faubourg St Honoré. Tall, black-haired, with brown eyes and a sallow complexion, he received a good education and was able to speak German and French. A former sub-editor for the Brussels-based journal *Gaulois*, in 1872 he came to London to make a series of impassioned speeches on behalf of a French town that had suffered terribly in the Franco-German war. Benson touched the compassion in all who heard him and was soon presented with a substantial cheque for the relief of the French town. However, since he was a con-man, he pocketed the money.

After being caught, Benson was tried at the Central

Criminal Court in July 1872 and received a twelve-month gaol sentence. In prison he tried to commit suicide by piling his clothes on the floor, setting them alight and sitting on them with the result that he was temporarily lamed and permanently scarred by large burn marks on both thighs and buttocks. On release from prison, Benson took the name George Henry Yonge and said he intended to 'go straight'. He set out to find employment but his partial lameness made it possible for him to consider only those jobs involving light duties. One day he replied to an advertisement in the *Daily Telegraph* for 'literary assistance' and so met William Kurr.

Kurr was the son of a baker and had started work at thirteen as a clerk on the South-Eastern Railway but, after about a year, he ran away and started betting on horses. Although he did not have Benson's education or brains he was a very able swindler and he also possessed a daring which Benson lacked. They therefore complemented one another perfectly.

In 1877 Kurr was planning a 'sting', the idea of which was to make it known in France that a 'Mr Montgomery' in England had acquired such success betting on horses that he could no longer get decent odds from the bookmakers. He was accordingly looking for people in France to whom he could send money and who would place the bets in their own name, collect the winnings and return them to him. The plan was that the specified bookmaker would be one of the gang and the bank issuing the winnings would likewise be a front. Kurr and Benson anticipated that on seeing 'Mr Montgomery's' success the 'mark' would be unable to resist wagering his own money. The plan also involved renting an office for the fake bookmaker and having some cheques printed for the fictitious Royal Bank of London.

Among the people who responded was the extremely wealthy and naive Madame la Comtesse de Goncourt. She duly received a cheque from 'Mr Montgomery' drawn on the Royal Bank of London and was requested to return it as a bet to a particular bookmaker. A few days later a large cheque arrived for her from the London bookmaker and, in accordance with the agreement, the cheque was forwarded to 'Mr Montgomery'. Mme de Goncourt was hooked. Seeing Mr Montgomery's success she added a small cheque of her own to that of his when she next placed a wager for him with the London bookmaker. After a couple of days she received her 'winnings' in the form of a cheque on the Royal Bank of London. This is where the plan could have failed but Kurr and Benson knew their mark. Instead of cashing the cheque, Madame de Goncourt sent it back with a cheque of her own for £10,000 for further 'investment'.

Clever criminals are often brought to book by greed. Such was the case with the perpetrators of the First Great Train Robbery and such was the case with Kurr and Benson. They would probably have got away with the £10,000 but instead they sent a letter to the countess telling her that by English law the £10,000 she had already deposited would be forfeited unless she sent a further £30,000. Although uncertain, Madame de Goncourt was prepared to send the money but her local bank did not have enough funds to transfer this sum for her. She accordingly went to Paris to arrange the transaction and there met her lawyer. She explained her business and he became suspicious. The investigations which he instituted led to the arrest of Kurr and Benson (the latter being armed with a loaded gun when arrested by Detective Sergeants Manton, Littlechild and Roots). They received sentences of fifteen years. Other members of the gang – Edwin Murray and Frederick Kurr, the brother of William, and a few lesser figures – also went to prison.

What bothered the police was the difficulty they had encountered in catching up with the criminals. Every time they seemed on the verge of making an arrest, the gang vanished, almost as if they knew every move the police were about to make. After the gang had been sentenced and, in the hope of obtaining remission, Kurr and Benson told the authorities that for several years they had been bribing several senior officers of the Detective at Scotland Yard. They named Chief Inspectors Nathanial Druscovitch, William Palmer and George Clarke, and Inspector John Meiklejohn. For several years, they said, these men had given them information about any police interest in their activities. They had got away with several previous swindles because of this and had hoped to do the same with the de Goncourt fraud. Kurr and Benson added that they had in fact decamped from London as a result of such a warning, and gone to Glasgow, where they were again warned and escaped. When three of the gang fled to Rotterdam and were arrested by the Dutch police, Kurr and Benson had used their police contacts in an attempt to free their comrades. A crooked lawyer named Edward Froggatt and Inspector Meiklejohn concocted a telegram purporting to be from Superintendent Williamson telling the Dutch police to let the prisoners go. This did not work and the three were extradited, but it had been a good try.

Although these claims seemed hard to believe, particularly since they were made by two accomplished con-men, the story was investigated and supporting evidence emerged. Eventually the named police officers were arrested, along with Froggatt and stood trial at the Old Bailey in October 1877 on charges of conspiring to defeat the ends of justice. The complexities of the case resulted in a trial lasting nineteen days, the longest in the history of the Old Bailey at that date. Three of the inspectors and Froggatt were found guilty and sentenced to the maximum term permitted at that time: two years hard labour. The fourth officer, Clarke, was acquitted but resigned from the Force a couple of weeks later.

Yet how could three senior members of the Detective, a small department, have been 'turned' by Kurr and Benson and remained undetected for so long? It had happened like this: Meiklejohn was a gambler and through common betting interests was known to Edwin Murray, a member of the Kurr and Benson gang. Murray introduced Meiklejohn to Benson and the two men began to see each other fairly regularly in a pub near Scotland Yard called the Silver Cross. Tempted by large sums of money, usually £100, but sometimes as much as £500, Meiklejohn began warning Benson of any police interest in his activities. Next, Druscovitch became embroiled because, in 1873, he had guaranteed a bill of £60 for his brother. Druscovitch became responsible for the debt when his brother was unable to pay but he could not raise the money and was desperate when Meiklejohn suggested that his friend Mr Kurr might be able to help. Kurr, of course, was only too happy to offer whatever assistance he could and, with relief, Druscovitch accepted a loan.

It was never satisfactorily established how George Clarke became involved. There was a lot of talk about a letter in Meiklejohn's possession which Clarke was anxious to get back but Williamson later said the letter had been official police business, that its contents were known to him and that Clarke had no reason to worry about it in any way. Kurr and Benson both claimed that Clarke had given them warnings and taken money from them but it was shown that some of the meetings said to have been with Clarke could not have taken place.

It is now difficult to establish the truth behind this business. Each of the policemen stated in their own defence that they had in every other respect done their job honestly and honourably. They maintained that they had been drawn into the conspiracy to help Benson and Kurr largely because both men had figured among their informers and had provided information which had led to several arrests. Whatever the truth might be, their downfall served to highlight the continuing problem of the detective branch, namely that the job brought the detectives into close contact with criminals and with temptations sometimes difficult to resist. The distinction between the allowable turning of a blind eye and the unallowable giving active assistance to a criminal sometimes becomes blurred. The opportunity for being compromised is often great, as it appears to have been in the case of Druscovitch and probably Clarke. Of the later careers of these policemen, writer Belton Cobb says in his book, *The Trial of the Detectives*: 'On being released from prison Meiklejohn set up as a private inquiry agent, and later tried his hand at journalism. Druscovitch's health broke down in prison, and he died soon after his release. Palmer became a publican.'

And what of the conspirators? James Monro, a future commissioner of the Metropolitan Police, briefly headed the Detective Department and later had a brush with William Kurr and Edwin Murray. Kurr was released on ticket-of-leave and given the privilege of reporting to the police by letter rather than in person. Monro regarded this concession as a great mistake and at the first opportunity had it revoked. Monro then kept Kurr and Murray under observation and learned that the latter was employing a large number of clerks to write hundreds of envelopes addressed to people all over England. These envelopes were eventually crated and dispatched to a 'Mr Williams' of Geneva. 'Williams' turned out to be William Kurr and the Geneva police informed Monro that Kurr had recently printed thousands of circulars offering a high-class watch at a ludicrously low price. Monro concluded that Kurr and Murray intended to defraud innocent people 'by getting them to buy rotten watches – or probably to remit money for the purchase of watches which 'Williams' would forget to send'.

Given advance warning by the Geneva police that Kurr and Murray had posted their circulars, Monro alerted the Press to the apparent intended fraud. The Press carried a warning story and most of the expensive circulars 'went into the wastepaper basket or the fire'. Murray in particular was furious at the money lost in the printing of the circulars and the postage costs. He sued *The Times* and the *Daily Telegraph* for defamation of character, getting a farthing damages from the former. In a shop in Fleet Street he also displayed a notice telling of the 'injustice' done to him at the hands of the police. He even hired several sandwich-men and dressed them in police uniform to parade the streets imparting the same message. Not surprisingly, this was soon stopped by the real police.

At the time of the Geneva Watch Fraud, Benson was still in prison serving his sentence. Monro had him continually watched on his release but Benson managed to give his shadow the slip. Investigations proved that he had gone to Belgium where he sold mining shares. Scotland Yard informed the Belgian authorities, who it turned out wanted Benson for an earlier crime. He was arrested and sentenced to eighteen months in prison but did not serve this sentence in full and was released on his promise never to cross Belgium's frontiers again. Benson next turned up in Switzerland. Here, according to Monro's 'memoirs', William Kurr, who had taken the name of Clinchwood, met a retired surgeon-general of the Indian Army and persuaded him to hand over his savings of £7,000 for investment. Kurr left Switzerland with the money and was aboard a steamer bound for America when he was arrested. Benson was with him. They escaped punishment by offering to return the money if the doctor dropped all charges. On Monro's advice the doctor did as requested.

Benson was next heard of in Mexico impersonating Mr Abbey, a certain 'Madame Patti's' impresario, selling tickets on her behalf to the amount of $25,000. The fraud was uncovered and he was arrested and taken to New York for trial where he was sentenced to prison and incarcerated in the notorious Tombs prison. Here he committed suicide by throwing himself over the railing from the top storey.

The consequence to the Force of the De Goncourt scandal was immediate. Suddenly, the Detective Department was left with no senior officers except Williamson, who seems to have avoided even the mildest rebuke for having failed to notice what was happening under his very nose. The Commissioner directed that all cases of serious crime in future would be supervised by someone outside the Detective Department who would advise and direct junior and Divisional officers and call for reports as necessary from any officer engaged on any case. Also, a Commission of Inquiry was set up 'to inquire into the State, Discipline and Organisation of the Detective Force of the Metropolitan Police'. The Commission reported in 1878 and made a number of important recommendations. They pressed strongly that an assistant commissioner should be placed at the head of the Detective Branch, ranking next to the Commissioner and having charge of the whole force in his absence. They also recommended that the existing Divisional detective system should be abolished and replaced by a central detective force, with some of its officers stationed in Divisions, though they stressed that the local superintendent should always be told what the detectives were doing. They suggested that registers of crimes and criminals should be kept both locally and at headquarters, that a few officers with knowledge of languages, distinct from the main body, should be attached to headquarters and also that men in the Detective Forces should take precedence over the uniformed branch of the service.

A young barrister, Howard Vincent, who had studied the police system in Paris, submitted to the Government a well-argued paper setting out suggestions for a system of detective police and submitted it to the Commission, which was greatly impressed. The Home Secretary invited Vincent to lead the new Detective Department. The department itself also received a new name. No longer would it be known by the Dickensian 'the Detective'. It emerged as the Criminal Investigation Department.

The CID was born.

Chapter Six

THE CRIMINAL INVESTIGATION DEPARTMENT

Charles Edward Howard Vincent was born in 1849. He began his career with a stint in the army and then studied law at the Inner Temple where he was called to the Bar in 1876. Early in March 1878, Vincent was appointed head of the CID at Scotland Yard. He did not have the rank of Assistant Commissioner, as would his successors, but was styled Director of Criminal Investigations. Within a month of taking office he submitted proposals for the reorganisation of the department. All the detectives, both at Scotland Yard and in the Divisions throughout London, were to be amalgamated into a single reporting structure headed by Chief Superintendent Williamson. Scotland Yard would have 3 chief inspectors, 20 inspectors, and an office staff of 4 sergeants and 1 constable as a central force. The London Divisions would have 15 inspectors, 160 sergeants and 80 constables.

The CID's headquarters at Scotland Yard – known until comparatively recently as 'CO' or Central Office – were largely responsible for extradition, naturalisation, investigations on behalf of government departments and all cases deemed to be of a serious nature either in the Divisions or, when requested, in the provinces. The Detective Force was also deemed separate from the uniformed force. Divisional detectives were directly responsible to the Divisional

Superintendent who, in turn, was obliged to report direct to Scotland Yard.

Initially, there was considerable opposition to the CID from the uniformed police. One reason was that the detectives were paid more and enjoyed better pension arrangements. Another was generated by fears that the detectives were to be used as spies on the rest of the Force, as was the case with the section of the French police known as 'Controle Générale' in Paris. A third reason was a plan to recruit direct into the CID, meaning that detective recruits would not first have to do their bit in uniform. This unfortunately gave an elitist air to the Detective Department and almost made the CID a law unto itself. The repercussions of this are still present within the Force today.

The CID was also unsupported by the public, whose deep-seated hostility towards plain-clothes policemen had been reinforced by the recent scandal and 'Trial of the Detectives'. Two cases over the next few years, however, did a little to restore severely shaken confidence in the Force as a whole. The first involved a thoroughly nasty little man who for some reason not altogether accounted for by the daringness of his crimes, acquired a 'Raffles'-like romantic image with the public. Charles Peace was probably Britain's most notorious criminal until firmly knocked into the shadows by Jack the Ripper.

Born in 1832, Peace was small, agile and very strong. He was a successful and elusive housebreaker who, in 1876, became enamoured of Katherine Dyson, his neighbour's wife. To escape Peace's attentions and threats, Mr and Mrs Dyson moved house. Peace found out their new address and paid them a visit. He lured Mr Dyson into the rear yard and there shot him twice, killing him. Somehow Peace was able to generate a rumour that he had killed himself shortly after the murder so that the police search for him was gradually wound down and eventually stopped.

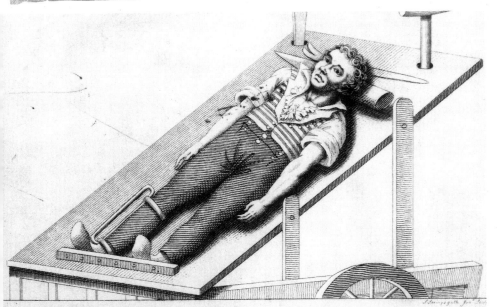

FIFTY POUNDS

REWARD.

Horrid Murder!!

WHEREAS,

The Dwelling House of Mr. TIMOTHY MARR, 29, Ratcliff Highway, Man's Mercer, was entered this morning between the hours of Twelve and Two o'Clock, by some persons unknown, when the said Mr. MARR, Mrs. CELIA MARR, his wife, TIMOTHY their INFANT CHILD in the cradle, and JAMES BIGGS, a servant lad, were all of them most inhumanly and barbarously Murdered!!

A Ship Carpenter's Pæn Maul, broken at the point, and a Bricklayer's long Iron Ripping Chissel about Twenty Inches in length, have been found upon the Premises, with the former of which it is supposed the Murder was committed. Any person having lost such articles, or any Dealer in Old Iron, who has lately Sold or missed such, are earnestly requested to give immediate Information.

The Churchwardens, Overseers, and Trustees, of the Parish of St. George Middlesex, do hereby offer a Reward of FIFTY POUNDS, for the Discovery and Apprehension of the Person or Persons who committed such Murder, to be paid on Conviction.

By Order of the Churchwardens, Overseers, and Trustees,

JOHN CLEMENT,

VESTRY CLERK.

Ratcliff-highway,
SUNDAY, 8th DECEMBER, 1811.

SKIRVEN, Printer, Ratcliff Highway, London.

A Correct likeness of JOHN WILLIAMS, the supposed murderer of the Marr's & Williamson's Families,

1. Reward poster for the Ratcliffe Highway murders

2. John Williams. Charged with the Ratcliffe Highway murders of 1811, Williams hanged himself before any verdict was reached; this was taken as a sign of guilt. His body was paraded through the streets of London before being buried at the crossroads of Cannon Street and Cable Street, a stake driven through his heart

3. Sir John Fielding (1721–80), blind half-brother of Henry Fielding and pioneer in the field of preventative policing

4. A Peeler. Both 'Peeler' and 'Bobby' as nicknames for policemen were derived from the name of Sir Robert Peel, founder of the first police force in 1829

ONE HUNDRED POUNDS
REWARD

WILFUL
MURDER.

DANIEL GOOD

Stands charged with the Wilful Murder of a Female at Putney (whose
Name is at present unknown). He is an Irishman, about 46 Years of Age,
5 Feet 6 Inches high, very dark sallow complexion, long thin features, and
dark piercing Eyes; he is bald at the top of his Head, and combs his Hair
from each side over the bald part. He walks upright, and when he
absconded was dressed in a **Dark Great Coat, Drab Breeches and Gaiters,**
and Black Hat, but is supposed since to have changed his Dress.

The above Reward of ONE HUNDRED POUNDS will be paid by Her
Majesty's Government to any Person who shall give such information and
evidence, as will lead to the apprehension and conviction of the said
DANIEL GOOD.

Information to be given to the Commissioners of Police, Scotland Yard, London, or at
any of the Stations of the Metropolitan Police.

11th April, 1842.

W. Clowes and Sons, 14, Charing Cross.

Reward poster for murderer Daniel Good, eventually hanged 23 May 1842. The
hunt for Good showed up the deficiencies of the police and was instrumental in the
creation of the 'Detective'

6. Colonel Rowan who, with Richard Mayne, became the first Joint Commissioner of the Metropolitan Police

7. Richard Mayne, Joint Commissioner with Colonel Rowan. Mayne is believed to have been the driving force behind the setting up of the 'Detective'

15 August 1842

Memo:

Two Inspectors and six Serjeants are to be employed as a Detective Body, as sanctioned by the letter of the Secretary of State of June 20th. The following Men are appointed to this duty from the dates against their names.—

A.   Inspector Pearce
P.   „   Haynes
A.   Serjeant Gerrett
E.   „   Thornton   } From the 8th Inst.
„   P. Constable Whicher
L.   P. Constable Goff
R.   Serjeant Shaw
F.   „   Braddick (From the 12th Inst

(R.M.)

8. Memorandum from Sir Richard Mayne appointing the first eight detectives, August 1842

9. Husband and wife, the Mannings murdered out of jealousy and for gain and were hanged in November 1847

10. The discovery of the remains of Patrick O'Connor, murdered by the Mannings

11. Charles Frederick Field, one of the early detectives and probably the most famous of his day

12. A rare and previously unpublished photograph of Constance Kent, child murderer

13. The principals involved in the Great Scotland Yard Scandal of 1877 which resulted in the reorganisation of the Detective and its emergence as the Criminal Investigation Department (C.I.D.)

14. Superintendent Williamson is cross-examined at the 'Trial of the Detectives', during the Great Scotland Yard Scandal

15. The convict William Kurr is questioned at Bow Street Police Court

16. Harry Benson and (*below*)
William Kurr

Photo J. Russell

17. Sir Howard Vincent, appointed first head, in 1878, of the newly created C.I.D. at Scotland Yard

18. Railway murderer Percy LeFroy Mapleton, hanged on 29 November 1881. This drawing was the first time an illustration of a wanted man was used by the police

BALCOMBE TUNNEL.

19. Lefroy murdered Isaac Gold in a train carriage then pushed the body out onto the track

WHERE THE BODY OF MR. GOLD WAS FOUND.

20. Inspector Melville

21. Surveying the damage done to Scotland Yard and the adjacent Rising Sun public house after the explosion of a Fenian bomb in May 1884

22. John Sweeney, a member of the Irish Branch and early member of the Special Branch

23. Rare photograph of P.C. Bowden Endacott whose arrest of Miss Cass on charges of soliciting in June 1887 caused a sensation

24. The police were heavily criticised following the riots known as Bloody Sunday. Here police attempt to head off a contingent of unemployed men in St Martin's Lane

25. *Centre*: Jack the Ripper suspect Michael Ostrog

26. Sir Charles Warren, probably one of the most controversial commissioners; he held office at the time of the Ripper murders

27. James Monro, seen here in retirement, headed the C.I.D. before replacing Sir Charles Warren as Metropolitan Police Commissioner

28. Chief Inspector Donald Swanson, officer in overall charge of the Jack the Ripper case

29. Dr Robert Anderson, Assistant Commissioner at the time of the Ripper murders

30. Montague John Druitt, another Ripper suspect

31. Inspector Abberline, who achieved notoriety as the hunter of Jack the Ripper

32. Colonel Sir Edward Bradford succeeded James Monro as Commissioner and brought calm to troubled years

—— IN MEMORIAM. ——

Alas for the splendour of ages departed;
Alas for the pride of the times that are past,
The glory of Bow Street exists but in story.
The best of its Runners has vanished at last!
As long as brave Shonfeld still flourished at
Croydon,
We saw what the "Force" in his lifetime was worth;
But Death, that fell hunter, has caught poor old
Shonfeld—
The last of the Runners is now run to earth.
Let not the spruce Bobby the mem'ry disparage
Of Shonfeld so brave, in his waistcoat so red.
For the sprucest of Bobbies must follow old Shonfeld,
When the days of his street-pacing grandeur are
fled.

33. A tribute to Peter Shonfeld, the last Bow Street Runner, who died in January 1894

34. Inspector Nutkins investigated several infamous cases including the Orrock murder, Mrs Pearcy, and the Fowler and Milsom case

35. Adolf Beck, victim of misidentification. Beck was tried twice as a confidence trickster (in 1896 and 1904) and served a prison sentence

All this had happened in the north of England but, in 1877, a series of daring robberies took place in London. The police believed these to be the work of a large gang but most had been committed by the industrious Peace working alone. On 17 November 1878 PC Edward Robinson, on duty at Blackheath Common, came upon a burglar in a house in St John's Park and attempted to arrest him. The burglar drew a revolver and fired five shots. PC Robinson was severely wounded but nevertheless fought back and was able to blow his whistle to summon assistance. Peace, who claimed to be named John Ward, was identified by a neighbour as a Mr Thomson, ostensibly a most respectable man who had a gracious and expensively decorated home and was even a local churchwarden. It was therefore as 'Thomson' that he was convicted of attempting to murder PC Robinson and sentenced to life imprisonment but he was eventually identified as Charles Peace and convicted of the murder of Mr Dyson. He was hanged at Armley Gaol in Leeds on 25 February 1879. The capture of Peace was through good fortune rather than skilled detective work but PC Robinson's courage and determination restored a gloss to the public image of the police.

PC Robinson became famous for having arrested Charlie Peace but he soon faded from public memory and some mystery has persisted regarding his eventual fate. *The Kentish Mercury* (16 April 1926, 21 May 1926) and *The People* (23 May 1926) contained an interview with PC Robinson and reported his death shortly afterwards. The articles said that he left the Force and for some time worked in a lumber camp in Canada. He spent the last fifteen or more years of his life in Greenwich Workhouse. His last years were spent in poor physical and mental health. The *Mercury* reported that he was so often asked about Charlie Peace 'that recently he had been labouring under the delusion that his name was actually "Charlie Peace"'.

The *Mercury* (26 April 1973) reported that PC Robinson's celebrity as a result of arresting Peace led to him getting drunk several times and his eventual dismissal from the Force. We have not been able to confirm this.

Another successful investigation which raised police spirits slightly during this gloomy decade was the arrest of Thomas Henry Orrock, a man who often waxed lyrical about the adventures and acts of derring-do of criminals. Yet the youthful Orrock was depressed because apart from wearing a wide-brimmed hat which he fancied made him look 'criminal', he had no adventures or acts of derring-do of his own to talk about. However, one day Orrock saw an advertisement for a revolver in the pages of the advertising magazine, *Exchange & Mart*. He bought the weapon and had it in his pocket when he nervously set out on 1 December 1882 to burgle a chapel. As he was about to enter the building he encountered PC George Cole and dropped the chisels with which he had planned to gain access to the building. Attempting to flee, he was firmly held and soon found himself on the way to the police station. Next, Orrock produced his revolver and fired four shots. PC Cole lay dying, Orrock disappeared into the night, and two horrified women who had witnessed the whole incident ran to the police station to get help. They could give no description of PC Cole's murderer, except that he wore a wide-brimmed hat.

Sergeant Cobb was regarded by his fellows on M Division as a nuisance. He was a worrier and worried unnecessarily but he knew about Orrock and his hat. Orrock was brought in and placed in an identity parade. Neither of the women recognised him. Orrock and Sergeant Cobb's suspicions were dismissed by everyone, except Sergeant Cobb. He worried about Orrock and was still worrying a year later when he heard a chance remark by a young man named Henry Mortimer, who was describing a visit to Tottenham Marshes to practise with a revolver. He had gone with a few friends named Evans, Miles and – Orrock. Mortimer took PC Cobb to the very spot where the shooting practice had taken place and, from a tree used as a target, Cobb prised several bullets. These proved to match the ones which had killed PC Cole. Cobb traced Evans and Miles who confirmed that the gun was Orrock's and alleged that Orrock had boasted to them of planning to break into the chapel.

The case was now picked up by Inspector Glass, who shared with Robert Peel a willingness to 'burgle' other people's ideas. He realised that the letters 'r-o-c-k' which he had found engraved on the blades of some chisels found outside the chapel might have some significance after all. Eventually Scotland Yard was brought in and the accumulated evidence was sufficient to justify charges against Orrock. The only problem was that he could not be found, and he beat the best efforts of Scotland Yard to find him. This worried Sergeant Cobb.

Cobb did not believe that Orrock had died, gone abroad or been able to hide himself for such a long time. He reasoned that Orrock therefore had to be somewhere where nobody would look for him: prison. Thomas Henry Orrock was found in Coldbath Fields prison where he had been a 'guest' for two years following conviction under a false name for a bungled burglary. He was charged with the murder of PC Cole, found guilty and executed in 1884. Cobb had done some excellent detective work.

1880, the year when a cardboard warrant card replaced the old tipstave as the means whereby detectives identified themselves, marked the start of what was probably one of the most difficult decades in the history of Scotland Yard and the Titley case was one of the lowest points from the police point of view. The CID knew that Thomas Titley was an abortionist but they could not get evidence against him and, much to the horror of 'Dolly' Williamson, Howard

Vincent, the head of the CID, decided to try a little French police trickery. The wife of a pensioned police constable was persuaded to call on Titley and request something for her daughter who had got herself into 'trouble'. Some slight difficulties were overcome and in return for £4 16s Titley provided bottles of 'medicine'. He was promptly arrested for illegally supplying drugs for the purpose of effecting an illegal abortion.

There was a trial and although Titley was convicted the judge added some caustic comments about the police acting as spies and telling lies to induce Titley to commit the crime. A Bill of Indictment was duly preferred against the police officers involved. Although the Bill was soon withdrawn, Vincent was convinced that his methods were justified and was prepared to fight the case. Other people took a different view of his actions. The use of an *agent provocateur* reopened all the old fears about plain-clothes policemen and French police methods. There was a furore in the press and questions were asked in the House of Commons.

More seriously, a bomb exploded at Salford barracks on 14 January 1881. The Home Secretary believed this to be the start of a Fenian bombing campaign and he informed Vincent that he was 'much disturbed at the absolute want of information in which we seem to be with regard to Fenian organisation in London'. He told him 'to devote himself exclusively for the next month to Irish and Anglo–Irish business'. The result was the creation of the 'Fenian Office' at Scotland Yard to investigate Fenian activities and liaise with various Government experts, including the Home Office's Fenian authority Robert Anderson. However, aside from Fenian activity, other political groups were also causing some degree of concern for the CID and all of these combined to be instrumental in the creation of what the British had always feared the police might become – a political police. The *Die Freiheit* Affair was regarded as a major step along that road.

In 1881, the London-based German-language newspaper *Die Freiheit* published an article by its editor Johann Most praising the recent assassination of the Tsar and advocating the murder of all heads of state 'from St Petersburg to Washington'. Most was arrested on 30 March 1881 by Inspector Donald Swanson, who would later head the Jack the Ripper investigations. He was charged with seditious libel – the British much cherished freedom of speech being limited by the proviso that it did not incite murder. Most was convicted and sentenced to eighteen months hard labour.

Apart from providing writer Henry James with the theme for *The Princess Casamassima*, the *Freiheit* affair created a problem for the police because they had not known about the article until their attention was drawn to it. They were also unaware that Johann Most had (allegedly) made the same observations at a socialist meeting in March.

Although they could not be blamed for not knowing about a 'crime' until it was brought to their attention, they were responsible for keeping the peace and technically this could be interpreted as a licence to maintain a watch on groups and individuals who incited breaches of public order. Home Secretary Harcourt instructed the police to 'look after' such meetings in future. This meant keeping regular surveillance irrespective of whether any crime was suspected.

While some meetings held by the Chartists had been kept under observation, the Chartists openly advocated sedition and for this reason the surveillance was justified. Yet political and semi-political groups such as the socialists and other labour movements were not advocates of sedition (or were not so overt) and so Harcourt's instruction was therefore an instruction to the police to spy.

Meanwhile, considerable press and public attention was generated by the murder of coin-dealer Isaac Frederick

Gold. Percy LeFroy, whose real name was Mapleton, was a twenty-two-year-old unsuccessful journalist. However, his name got into the newspapers when he stabbed and shot Gold aboard a train bound from London Bridge to Brighton. On leaving the train at Preston Park, on the outskirts of Brighton, a ticket-collector noticed bloodstains on Lefroy's clothing and questioned him. LeFroy claimed that he had been struck on the head and knocked unconscious by one of his fellow passengers. When searched, he was found to have in his possession some German coins of the kind Mr Gold dealt in. He was arrested and allowed to return to his lodgings in the company of a constable but gave the constable the slip and escaped. However, LeFroy was soon traced and taken into custody by CID Inspectors Donald Swanson and Frederick Jarvis and Constable Hopkins. He was tried, sentenced to death and hanged on 29 November 1881.

The case is distinguished because for the first time in history the police issued a portrait of a wanted man to the press. The *Daily Telegraph* reported that it was not a good likeness and refuted claims that it directly led to LeFroy's arrest but it was nevertheless a notable 'first' in the use of what may loosely be described as technology in the history of crime detection.

Chapter Seven

BOMBS ACROSS LONDON – THE FENIANS

Although the domestic diversions of Peace, LeFroy and Orrock captured newspaper headlines, more dramatic events were about to influence the structure of the CID and indirectly have a profound effect on the public perception of policing. On 6 May 1882, Lord Frederick Cavendish and Thomas Burke were murdered in Dublin's Phoenix Park and, as a direct result, on 17 March 1883 the CID formed its first specialist section, the 'Irish Bureau'.

Today's Special Branch regards itself as having been created on 17 March 1883 and is widely accepted as being a direct descendant of the Irish Bureau. However, a thorough search of *Police Orders* has failed to find reference to the designation 'Special Irish Branch' and Special Branch records confirm that the word 'special' was merely a nickname. The Irish Branch, or Section B as it was sometimes called, was not in fact the origin of the Special Branch, whose beginnings, as we will see, are altogether more mysterious.

The Irish Bureau was headed by 'Dolly' Williamson, who was instructed 'to be relieved of the greater proportion of his regular duty and to devote his time entirely to Fenianism'. Under him was a staff of twelve 'selected from the officers most conversant with Irish affairs'. Williamson was to keep in daily touch with Vincent, the head of the

CID, and Anderson, the Home Office's Fenian expert, and to report important facts directly to the Home Secretary. *Police Orders* of Monday, 19 March 1883 contained the following notice:

> C.I. DEPARTMENT – CENTRAL – The following are authorised to be employed in plain clothes at the Central Office with departmental allowance, from 20th. To report themselves to Chief Supt. Williamson, at 10am on the date named:-
> C. Inspector Pope
> M. PC 332 Foy
> D. PC 49 O'Sullivan
> R. Inspector Ahern
> E. PC 50 Walsh
> V. PS 3 Jenkins
> L. PC 224 McIntyre
> Y. PC 492 Thorp
> The following are also temporarily attached to the Central Office, and are to report themselves to Chief Superintendent at the same time:-
> H. PC CID Enright
> W. PS CID Melville
> K. PC CID Enright
> TA PS CID Regan

Williamson's new squad was thought little of by Edward Jenkinson, Under Secretary for Police at Dublin Castle in Ireland and soon to be enlisted by the Government to operate on the mainland. He claimed to have not found 'a man in Scotland Yard worth anything'. Even Williamson, who was an exceptional policeman, in Jenkinson's opinion nevertheless lacked even 'a trace of brilliancy or dash'. Jenkinson did not regard Robert Anderson very highly either. However, perhaps he was right in this because Anderson's effectiveness has been questioned, it being argued that his only contribution to anti-Fenianism was to act as postman for Henri Le Caron who had successfully infiltrated the Fenian movement in the United States. Eventually, Anderson was relieved of his Fenian investigations except for his dealings with Henri Le Caron, who refused to deal with anyone else.

Anderson was replaced by Major Nicholas Gosselin, a resident magistrate in Ireland who, on Jenkinson's recommendation, was brought over to Britain to gather intelligence about Fenians and secret societies outside London. Among others considered for the job was a future Metropolitan Police commissioner, Sir Charles Warren, and it is interesting to note how in the 1880s the top jobs in the Force were held by men who were experienced in intelligence work. Gosselin met with initial success in gathering a team of 'agents', including a group of boys for tailing suspects, but within a short time he had to acknowledge that his efforts were producing minimal results.

Next, the Government brought over Jenkinson for the job and he arrived in London in March 1884. He had the tacitly stated but not officially recognised position of authority over all of the United Kingdom's counter-Fenian groups, including Williamson's team at Scotland Yard. He did not receive great support, particularly from the Yard, whose officers he considered inefficient and indiscreet. Jenkinson complained that any clues which came the way of the Yard were used as publicity fodder and consequently made useless. 'There is not a man there with a head on his shoulders,' he wrote, and he believed that Howard Vincent had to go.

Vincent did go, and was replaced by a former chief of police in Bengal named James Monro. Jenkinson thought Monro 'a very good man in his way' but lacking in 'energy and originality' and quite happy to leave things in the hands of the 'very slow and old fashioned' Williamson. Monro left fewer documents than Jenkinson and his opinions and personality have consequently remained mysterious but the discovery of his unpublished memoirs has thrown some light into the shadows of this period and, as might be expected, he saw things rather differently:

When I joined the Met Police, I found that there was a kind of Central Bureau of Intelligence ... At the Home Office Mr E. G. Jenkinson was the Head of this department. His business was to collect all information from many countries, specially America, regarding the dynamiters, and to give to the various police forces concerned any information which concerned people under their jurisdiction, so that any necessary police action might be taken by them. Mr Jenkinson's functions were entirely those of an intelligence department; he was not a member of any police force; he had no police authority anywhere; all that he had to do was to keep the police generally acquainted with any information which, from his various agents, he acquired, suggesting any course of action which he might think desirable. But the responsibility for police action, taken or not taken, lay of course with the police forces concerned, and not with Mr Jenkinson ...

I very soon discovered however that Mr Jenkinson instead of confining his function to the distribution of intelligence to the London police, went far beyond it. He not only collected intelligence regarding London, but he acted upon it, without any reference to the London police, by means of a number of Irish police whom he had, without any authority whatever, stationed in London ... While Assistant Commissioner, I had to fight against the machinations of Mr Jenkinson. I

92

had to do this under four different secretaries of state, and all of them supported me against Mr J. The last Secretary of State dismissed Mr Jenkinson . . .

The Irish Bureau and the various Government Fenian investigators had a difficult job on their hands because the Fenians, like the IRA today, planted bombs. A bomb – or 'infernal machine' as they were sometimes called – was found in the left-luggage office at Charing Cross Station in October 1883. It consisted of an alarm clock with the winding handle wired to the trigger of a pistol. When the alarm clock went off, the handle would revolve and tighten the wire. The wire would eventually pull the trigger of the gun. This would then fire into several detonators, around which were packed no fewer that forty-six sticks of dynamite. In this case the alarm clock had gone off and pulled the trigger of the pistol, but somehow the hammer had struck the rim-fire cartridge and the pistol had misfired. It can be imagined how dangerous these early bombs could be. It was essential that the activities of the Fenians therefore be kept under strict surveillance.

In October 1883, a Limerick man named John Daly arrived in England from America. The police immediately placed him under continual surveillance and on 14 May 1884 he was arrested in Birkenhead, possessing three bombs which some people later suggested had been planted on him by the authorities. In fact, the bombs had been supplied to him by a Fenian supporter who was also a long-standing police informer, which is why Daly had been expected and kept under watch on the police. In certain police circles it was thought that Daly's arrest had put an end to the immediate plans of the Fenian bombers, but later that year an anonymous letter was received at Scotland Yard. It contained a threat to 'blow Superintendent Williamson off his stool' and to destroy all public buildings in London by dynamite on 30 May.

Shortly before 9 p.m. that night, a large bomb was placed in a cast-iron public urinal – 'a disgracefully dark place', according to *The Times* – built into the side of Great Scotland Yard and above which were the offices of the Irish Branch. Working late in the office was Sergeant John Sweeney, perhaps one of the best-known early 'Special Branch' officers because of his book of reminiscences, *At Scotland Yard*. He was there until just after 9 p.m. and had just left for home when the bomb exploded. Sweeney's office was completely destroyed and the corner of Scotland Yard which housed the CID was blown completely away, to a height of about thirty feet and a width of fifteen. Considerable damage was also done to the Rising Sun pub across the road and most buildings in the area lost windows. Two other explosions also occurred that night. Half a mile away in St James's Square a bomb exploded in front of Sir Watkin Wynn's house and another wrecked the basement of the Carlton Club. The following morning a bomb was found at the foot of Nelson's Column. It had failed to go off and the detectives were therefore able to quickly establish that it was of the type commonly used by the Fenians.

As so often seems to be the case, the bombers failed to achieve their objectives. Wynn's house and the Carlton Club had been mistaken for Adair House (headquarters of the War Office Intelligence Department) and the Junior Army and Navy Club. Even the landlord of the Rising Sun did not suffer. He charged admission for people to inspect the damage to his establishment and sold them refreshment whilst they did so. And, remarkably, not even a pane of glass was apparently broken in Williamson's office. The only people who were hurt were those caught by flying glass and also a cabman whose injuries sustained in the explosion kept him from work for several months. A policeman was also injured, but not seriously. According to John Sweeney:

> We never discovered how the bomb was ignited ...
> Neither have we ever been certain who the perpetra-
> tors were; but we suspected two men named Burton
> and Cunningham ... This affair caused confusion at
> Scotland Yard for some months; we could not console
> ourselves in the same way as the proprietor of the
> 'Rising Sun'.

Towards the end of the year there was a violent explosion beneath London Bridge. Then came another, which was effectively the last in the series: in January 1885 a bomb went off in the Armoury in the White Tower of the Tower of London, causing a fire and considerable damage. The alarm was sounded, the gates were shut within minutes of the blast and all those who were trapped inside were interrogated by the police. Everyone was asked to give their name and address and these were confirmed before the person was allowed to leave. James Monro has left his personal recollections of the incident:

> ... I was in my office at Scotland Yard when a
> telegram was received of an explosion having taken
> place at the House of Commons in Westminster. I was
> just putting on my overcoat to proceed there when
> a second telegram arrived that there had been an
> explosion at the Tower.

Monro sent Williamson to the House of Commons and went himself to the Tower. He noted that the names and addresses of all those there were being taken:

> While this was being done, Inspector Abberline of the

95

H Division, in the charge of which Division the Tower was, brought a man to me saying that he could not quite make him out; that he seemed to be an Irish American; and that his address given was peculiar . . .

Inspector Abberline also left an account of his involvement in the case:

When I arrived at the Tower of London immediately after the explosion I found the gates closed and several hundred people detained there, and it was myself who suggested that every person detained should be interrogated before leaving which Supt. Arnold approved and we fixed up a table and writing materials outside the Police Office in the Tower and an Inspector in uniform was told to write down the names and addresses of each person and anything I considered necessary they said in reply to my questions.

It was by this means that I discovered the presence of Cunningham alias Gilbert through the hesitation in his replies and his general manner.

All but two people were eventually cleared. One was an old lady who, shocked and flustered, had given her daughter's address by mistake. The other was twenty-two-year-old James Gilbert Cunningham, who gave himself away by his vagueness and by offering a false name and address. When his true address was learned, and searched, the police found a detonator. Inspector Abberline completes his story thus:

Up to that time we had absolutely no knowledge of the man whatever, it will there be seen that his detection there brought about his arrest and afterwards that of Burton his colleague who no doubt caused the explosion at the House of Parliament as both explosions occurred the same day and about the same hour.

The numerous inquiries necessary in this case took me and other officers assisting me a long time to complete and there were many anxieties to contend with in finding out bit by bit the evidence which established the guilt of the prisoners.

There were no less than one hundred and ten witnesses who gave evidence at the trial of this case, which lasted eight days.

So it will be seen how hard we had to work to bring all the various details together and I was especially overworked, as the then Home Secretary Sir Wm Harcourt wished to be supplied every morning with the progress of the case, and after working very hard all day I had to remain up many nights until 4 and 5 am the following morning making reports for his information.

At the close of the trial, however, he ordered me to be given £20 as a reward.

I may add that after the arrest of these two men the explosions in this country ceased. At the close of the trial Cunningham accused the police of causing the Detonator to be put in his box, but some months afterwards the Commissioner of Police, Mr Monro, informed me that a Firm in America had identified it as their make and who no doubt had supplied several of them to the prisoner.

I had never seen a Detonator before it was found.

Monro also commented on the reports sent to Sir William Harcourt. He recalled that they formed the basis for theories constructed by Harcourt and Jenkinson who persistently pestered Monro with demands for clarification on this or that point, especially if it seemed to be contrary to their ideas. Monro wrote:

> The fact is, that Sir William Harcourt, able man as he was, simply went off his head when there was any talk of explosions . . . Throughout this case he (Jenkinson) and Sir William Harcourt nearly drove me frantic . . . attempting to direct a police inquiry instead of letting the responsible police officers do the duty.

Monro also described how during his questioning of Cunningham he received three increasingly angry telegrams from Sir William Harcourt demanding Monro's presence at the Home Office. On arrival Harcourt, greatly agitated, was furious that Monro had not been at Scotland Yard and had not sent detectives to cover the ports. Monro replied that men already stationed at the ports had been sent messages furnishing them with all the available information; that his own men knew no more and could do no more than those police officials and that they were in any case needed in London. This logical reply cannot have appeased the frantic Harcourt because he went to Scotland Yard himself and ordered fourteen of Monro's men to the ports. Monro accordingly had to call them back and remained angry at Harcourt's action for years.

The police learned that Cunningham often met a man named Harry Burton at Aldgate Station in East London. Burton was arrested and, with Cunningham, was charged and found guilty of conspiring to blow up certain public and private buildings. They were sentenced to life imprisonment. Yet even after the capture of Burton and Cunningham, relations between Monro and Jenkinson continued to deteriorate. In his memoirs, Monro devotes excessive space to repetitious complaints about Jenkinson (as, indeed, Jenkinson did about Monro and Harcourt in letters to his friend Earl

Spencer) and even complains that Jenkinson was: 'found out in having established in London a regular school of private detectives under a scoundrel of the name of Winter for the express purpose of thwarting the action of Scotland Yard'.

According to Patrick McIntyre's reminiscences published in *Reynolds News* in 1895, a man came to Scotland Yard and explained that he had replied to an advertisement for Roman Catholic Irishmen to be employed as porters. Along with twenty other men he had been employed by someone named Winter who told them that, although ostensibly employed as porters, their real job was to help tracing dynamiters. It seems therefore that Winter used some of his men to keep surveillance on CID officers and, according to McIntyre, this was the final straw for Monro. Winter (also known as Dawson) was later tried at the Old Bailey for obtaining a divorce from his wife under false pretences and for committing perjury but Monro refused Jenkinson's request to 'protect' Winter from prosecution.

It is clear that Jenkinson was mostly at fault for the friction, though in fairness it has to be said that he believed the Yard to be grossly inefficient, unable to trace suspects whom he himself was able to locate quickly and without difficulty, and either inactive when supplied with infor-mation or inclined to move too soon, thereby alerting the conspirators and/or endangering the lives of Jenkinson's informants. Jenkinson also believed that the Yard was riddled with corruption. In July 1885 he wrote to Earl Spencer: 'There is hardly a man among them who does not take money.' No wonder Jenkinson tried to act on his own, wouldn't pass his information on to Monro and wanted a watch kept on the Yard's men.

Harcourt, also, was not as supportive of Monro over Jenkinson as Monro seems to have thought. Harcourt's problem was that Jenkinson had no constitutional right to act on the information he received. The Metropolitan Police were the only people who could act on that information. This was not entirely what Jenkinson had been told when he was brought over from Ireland for he seems to have been led to understand that he had authority over all Britain's mainland anti-Fenian agencies. Changing circumstances now resulted in Harcourt appreciating the political disadvantages in the liberties he had initially granted Jenkinson. Harcourt's support of Monro was therefore motivated by reasons other than agreement with Monro's opinions. Nevertheless, Jenkinson's determined secrecy put a strain on his relationship with everyone, including Harcourt, whose temper eventually flared. Harcourt told him: 'It is all jealousy, nothing but jealousy, you like to get information and keep it to yourself. You are like a dog with a bone who goes into a corner and growls at anyone who comes near him.'

The root cause of the differences between Monro and Jenkinson and which lay behind the latter's criticism of the police was their opposing opinions about how anti-Fenian 'policing' should be conducted. Monro and Williamson attempted to preserve the Peelite policy of open policing while Jenkinson possessed an 'espionage orientated' mentality: a preoccupation with secrecy and a devotion to almost any underhand trick to obtain his aims. The difficulties with Jenkinson eventually led Monro to consider tendering his resignation. In his memoirs he wrote:

I made up my mind that I could and would no longer tolerate such a mischievous system. I made up my mind to resign if no relief was afforded and in the Autumn of 1886 we looked at lodgings in Edinburgh, intending to go there for the winter and leave the Met Police. In the Autumn of '86 I was sent for by Mr Matthews, the new Secretary of State, and had an interview with him which lasted for more than three hours. I laid the whole of the circumstances before him and told him very plainly that I could not consent any longer to work with Mr Jenkinson. He had constantly interfered with police action and to me personally on more than one occasion he had lied in such a disgraceful manner that I declined to have any dealings with him.

Briefly the end was, after a short time, that Mr Jenkinson was dismissed. He got a month's notice and resigned, but everybody knew the Under Secretary of State, Sir Godfrey Lushington, termed his resignation – dismissal.

Who was to succeed him? . . . [I] . . .recommended another officer, not in the Met Police at all*, to succeed Mr Jenkinson. This officer was however not considered suitable by the Secretary of State and in the end, at the urgent request of Government, I consented to act as Chief of the Secret Department as regards intelligence, and at the same time to retain my office as Asst Commissioner.

The precise reasons for Jenkinson's dismissal/resignation are uncertain, but there were probably many of them. Monro's claim that the Government virtually insisted that he take Jenkinson's place is also likely to be true. As noted, Jenkinson was not constitutionally permitted to act on any information he obtained but was obliged to hand it over to Scotland Yard – just as MI5 agents cannot perform police

* We do not know who this person was. Though not in the Force at the time of Monro's recommendation, the use of the word 'officer' could suggest that it was somebody who eventually did join the Metropolitan Police. It could have been Robert Anderson or Melville Macnaghten, both of whom began their police careers on Monro's recommendation. If either, it is more likely to have been the latter.

duties today but must hand over to the Special Branch. This created problems and those problems would have continued to exist if Jenkinson had been replaced by someone from outside Scotland Yard. The problem was solved by replacing him with Monro, although the solution itself created a clash between Monro and Commissioner Warren, as we shall see.

Monro above referred to himself as chief of the 'Secret Department'. It was generally known as 'Section D' (the Irish Branch was known as 'B'), but also sometimes referred to by other names such as 'Special Confidential Section' and, significantly, 'Home Office. Crime Department. Special Branch'. It was from Monro's new 'secret department', 'section D', 'Special Branch' that today's Special Branch descended, and not section B as is often believed, erroneously, to be the case.

Monro's staff consisted of one chief inspector and three second-class inspectors. The chief inspector was John George Littlechild who was taken from the Scotland Yard 'Irish Branch' and not replaced there. The inspectors were named Pope, Melville and Burke, and all were secretly financed out of Imperial, not Metropolitan Police funds, although Home Office instructions were that they were not otherwise to be ostensibly distinguished from other members of the CID.

The existence of this group was extremely confidential. It operated nationally and, according to a later commissioner, E.R. Henry, the squad was instructed to maintain observation on anarchists as well as Fenians. This was something new and one must wonder which group took priority, especially as Scotland Yard already had Williamson's Irish Branch to keep an eye on the Fenians. Section D was further distinguished by being answerable directly to the Home Secretary, not to the Commissioner of Police, and in due course this would be the cause of friction between Monro and the new Commissioner, Sir Charles Warren.

However, the Fenian bombing campaign throughout most of the 1880s should not be allowed to obscure other events taking place at this time. On Monday, 8 February 1886, for example, the London United Workingmen's Committee held a meeting in Trafalgar Square to protest about unemployment. The LUWC alerted Sir Edward Henderson of their fears that the rival Social Democratic Federation might cause trouble, but Henderson did not take the warning seriously and only stationed a small number of policemen in Trafalgar Square. Command was entrusted to seventy-four-year-old Divisional Superintendent Robert Walker. As the LUWC had feared, there was a riot. Walker was wholly incapable of handling the situation and for a time the rioters held complete control as they surged down Pall Mall leaving wrecked and looted buildings in their wake.

Henderson had, in fact, taken the precaution of having a reserve of over five hundred policemen placed on alert in case of trouble and these men could have quelled the riot but messages were confused and they were sent to the Mall instead of Pall Mall. The disturbance was eventually brought to an end by an Inspector Cuthbert. At Marylebone police station he was in the middle of parading his evening relief of one sergeant and fifteen constables when he received news that the rioters were heading in his direction. In a display of British stiff-upper-lip bravado (or stupidity) in the face of overwhelming odds, Cuthbert took his handful of men to Oxford Street and led a baton-charge. Amazingly, the rioters broke and ran.

Constant rumours of further trouble circulated during the next two days and Henderson this time took them seriously enough to issue precautionary instructions to shopkeepers and other property owners. Nothing happened and as a result he looked foolish, and was heavily criticised. Unfortunately for Henderson there was now a new Home Secretary, Hugh Childers. The latter should have supported

Henderson, who had been a good Commissioner throughout a difficult period, but Childers was weak and inexperienced. His reaction was to order the inevitable Commission of Inquiry. Henderson promptly resigned but would probably have been dismissed if he had not done so. In his place, Childers appointed Sir Charles Warren.

A most important incident during this time was the Jubilee Plot. 'Uncovered' by Monro's Secret Department, the plot consisted of Fenians putting dynamite in Westminster Abbey and detonating it during Queen Victoria's Golden Jubilee thanksgiving service on 21 June 1887.
    According to Monro:

I had undeniable information that every effort was to be made to bring off a dynamite outrage in the Jubilee week. In the beginning of the year two noted Fenians left London for America. One of these was a man, General Millen, who had been a general in the Mexican War, and who had a good deal to do with the earlier Fenian risings in Ireland.

In America, Millen was assigned the job of arranging a bomb outrage in London at the time of the Jubilee. Monro states that he 'had the fullest information' of this mission 'and Millen was closely supervised'. After a short stay in Paris, Millen went to Boulogne. Here he became friendly with an elderly man and his wife. The elderly man was suffering from gout. 'This interesting invalid,' wrote Monro, 'was Supt. Thomson of the Metropolitan Police, whom I had deputed for the purpose.' He continued:

The Jubilee time was now drawing on, and with Millen at Boulogne evidently in expectation of someone, I felt uneasy. I therefore resolved to cripple Millen by letting him see that the London Police was aware of him being at Boulogne for no good purpose. I therefore sent Chief Supt. Williamson, my second in command, to Boulogne with instructions to interview Millen and frighten him. Supt. Williamson went and at the entrance to the hotel, met Millen and his party, including the interesting invalid, going out to take a drive. Both Supt. Williamson and Supt. Thomson were too good policemen to take the slightest notice of each other. Supt. Williamson subsequently interviewed Millen, and talked to him like a Metropolitan Police man. The result was that, as we were informed by the invalid who was intimate with Millen, the latter quickly thought Boulogne was unsafe for him. He therefore returned to Paris.

As Monro had anticipated, Millen returned to the *hotel* he had used earlier where Monro had Inspector Melville already in residence. Millen had been joined by his daughters but none of them had much grasp of French and they seized upon their fellow guest's offer to translate for them. Monro thus continued to be well-informed. Meanwhile, Millen had been writing frequently to England and Monro had kept a close eye on the correspondence. It had so far been so unimportant that he issued instructions for the surveillance to be discontinued. His orders were not carried out however: '. . . This inattention was in the highest degree remarkable. I call it providential,' he wrote. It may be imagined that in other circumstances this act of providence may have been interpreted as sheer negligence.

A letter arrived with an enclosure that was to be passed on to someone called 'Kitty' and given by her in turn to another person. The enclosure consisted of three letters. Each bore a different signature but all had been written by Millen. The letters were addressed to three Irish Members of Parliament: Joseph Nolen, William O'Brien and (Monro was uncertain, but thought it was) a Mr Harris. The letters introduced to their respective recipient a Mr Joseph Melville. 'Kitty' was one of Millen's daughters. She was kept under watch and was seen to visit Joseph Nolen at the House of Commons, presumably to deliver the letters. The police supposed that shortly Joseph Melville would present himself. In due course, Melville and another man called upon Nolen and on leaving were shadowed by two detectives. Unfortunately Melville and his companion entered a large pub with two entrances and the detectives were forced to separate in case Melville and his companion parted and left by different doors. It turned out that they did not separate, which meant that only one detective was available to follow when they departed, the other being left watching the second door. Eventually, however, Melville and his companion did separate and the detective elected to follow the former.

The next day the police called upon Melville and asked him a series of disconcerting questions. A few days later, he left England for Paris and there had a meeting with Millen. On returning to London, Melville was again closely questioned by the police who informed him that details he had previously given about himself appeared to be false and that the police would keep an eye on him. On finding that he could do nothing in England, Melville left for America where, as a result of a tip-off from Monro, he and a lady companion were arrested for smuggling lace. Melville was subsequently identified as John J. Morony, a well-known member of Clan-na-Gael, an Irish–American Republican organisation.

Meanwhile, H Division (Whitechapel) had come across a man within their jurisdiction whom they could not account for and who apparently had nothing to do except visit a sick friend. Monro's Secret Department took over the investigation and the man, whose name was Michael Harkins, was taken to Scotland Yard where he was questioned by Monro. In his pocket was found an extract from the *Daily News* announcing the date on which Mr Balfour was going to Birmingham. Harkins, who claimed to be able to neither read nor write, had no explanation for the cutting. Also found in his pocket was a postbox number in Philadelphia, for which Harkins likewise offered no explanation.

A wire to Philadelphia soon brought Monro the reply that the postbox belonged to a man named Burchell, a well-known Clan-na-Gael member. Harkins subsequently wrote to Burchell asking for money. Further investigation also turned up the fact that Harkins had been Joseph Melville's companion when he visited Joseph Nolen M. P. The sick man whom Harkins had been visiting was called Cohen and he died whilst these inquiries were being conducted. His landlady told the police that Cohen had also received visits from a man other than Harkins. It turned out that Cohen had been the treasurer for the group and that his death had left the others with serious financial difficulties. Ultimately, this led to the identification of Cohen's other visitor, Thomas Scott, whose real name was Thomas Callan. When Callan's lodgings were searched, a note was found written in his hand to say he had been obliged to get rid of the 'tea'. His landlady said that he had thrown something down the toilet, with the result that the drains became blocked and had to be cleaned out. The contents, or 'stuff' as the landlady called it, were found in the dustbin. The 'stuff' was dynamite. A somewhat comical extra to this story is that one very wet day a neighbour had found some of the dynamite and, thinking it was something else for which she had a use, she put it in her oven to dry. Afterwards, she needed a new oven.

It transpired that Callan and Harkins had been the men whom Millen had been waiting for, but their inability to gain passage on a ship from America had delayed them. By the time they arrived, Millen's cover had been blown. They were left in London with dynamite but nobody to tell them what to bomb. They made some plans for themselves, but things had steadily gone from bad to worse. As a result, Callan and Harkins were gaoled for fifteen years. Monro and his men heartily congratulated themselves for having prevented this plot becoming a reality and, even in his memoirs, written for his children, Monro maintained that he had frustrated 'the Jubilee dynamite scheme'. However, it has never been clearly established just how serious the plot really was.

In 1909 Robert Anderson, Monro's successor as Assistant Commissioner of the CID, revealed in his autobiography that one of the conspirators, whom he called 'Jinks', had been in the pay of the British Government. A document written by Monro at the time of the plot and contained among Anderson's papers now held by the Public Record Office confirms that this was indeed the case. 'Jinks' was none other than Millen, the organiser of the plot. Born in County Fermanagh, Millen appears to have been a firm supporter of Fenian ideals but, shocked by and despising the Fenian leaders, whom he thought unfit to rule the free and united Ireland, he began passing information to the British consul in New York. Millen seems to have been passing information to the British for years by the time of the Jubilee Plot and had warned Jenkinson about it. Jenkinson, however, had done nothing to prevent the plot from developing, hoping that he would be able to catch the plotters. Remarkably, however, he had forgotten to tell anyone about it when he was sacked/resigned. Monro only found out about it by accident.

This created a huge problem for Monro. Unlike Jenkinson, who had wanted to uncover and arrest the conspirators, Monro, in the true tradition of a preventative police force, wanted to nip the conspiracy in the bud. However, he could not now arrest Millen for fear that he would tell the world he had already told Jenkinson of the plot, and that Jenkinson's inaction had left him with no alternative but to go ahead with it. Thus, Jenkinson's behaviour came dangerously close to actually encouraging the plot. Monro therefore decided to make it impossible for Millen to make a move without being noticed and so, knowing that he was watched by the police, he was forced back to the United States.

What remains to be seen is how much information Millen had actually provided Jenkinson with and whether he continued to give information to Monro's detectives. From Monro's memoirs it would seem that Millen either told them nothing or that Monro refused to deal with him. Either way, it seems that Monro knew of the plot but apparently did not know who the conspirators were. There was, therefore, a very real danger. To his account of the Jubilee Plot, Monro added a fascinating footnote. The Fenians, he said:

> . . . resolved to inaugurate a system of assassination of eminent persons, Mr Balfour [A. J. Balfour a future Prime Minister but at that time Minister for Ireland in Lord Salisbury's administration] especially, to be carried out by Irishmen, not Irish Americans. The agent chosen for this rascality was J. S. Walsh, resident of Brooklyn, and a well-known ruffian who had been concerned in the Phoenix Park Murder.

Nothing further is known about Walsh. Another man involved in the plot was named Roger Mackenna, who was in Dublin, where the Irish police kept him under surveillance until one day he vanished from sight. Walsh and Mackenna turned up in Paris. Walsh was interviewed by the Prefect of Police and Inspector Melville of the Yard. Mackenna, meanwhile, was tailed by a Sergeant Flood wherever he went. Eventually, as if out of the movies, Mackenna joined his shadow for a drink. Just at this moment Walsh happened along, jumped to the conclusion that Mackenna had 'fingered' him, and a row developed between the two conspirators. Both men realised that their mission was blown and returned to the United States.

There is a small and curious addition to this story which was noted in our *The Jack the Ripper A to Z*. On page 208 of his book *The Rise of Scotland Yard*, author Douglas G. Browne briefly reviewed opinions held by senior policemen about the identity of Jack the Ripper and says that 'Sir Melville Macnaghten, appears to identify the Ripper with the leader of a plot to assassinate Mr Balfour at the Irish Office.'

It is clear that Mr Browne, whose book was published in 1956, had been granted privileged access to the police files on the Ripper case, but neither the files nor any other known source now contain any mention of A. J. Balfour. However, over the years a great many papers are known to have 'gone missing', so it is possible that they did contain a reference to Balfour when Browne saw them.

It is further known that from at least as early as 1894 Sir Melville Macnaghten thought that a barrister-cum-teacher named Montague Druitt was the Ripper.

Did Browne therefore see something in the Ripper files which implicated Druitt with a plot to assassinate Balfour or did whatever Browne saw predate Macnaghten's belief that Druitt was the Ripper and refer to someone else? Could it have had any connection with the Walsh plot or been connected with the cutting mentioning Balfour's visit to Birmingham found in Michael Harkins' pocket? Or did Browne simply make a mistake? It's just another mystery to add to the catalogue of those surrounding Jack the Ripper.

Chapter Eight

CHANGES

The clandestine operations of the Irish Branch and Monro's Secret Department against the Fenian bombers was a dramatic and exciting period for the CID, but other events which in many ways were of equal significance had also been happening at this time. Howard Vincent resigned in 1884, as we have seen, and his successor, James Monro, was given the rank of Assistant Commissioner, CID. Two years later, in 1886, Commissioner Henderson and Area Superintendent Robert Walker resigned following the Trafalgar Square riots fiasco. The former was replaced by Sir Charles Warren and Adolphus Williamson was promoted to Chief Constable, CID. There was also a change of government. Gladstone's Liberal government lost a general election after only seven months in power and Hugh Childers was replaced as Home Secretary by Henry Matthews.

Matthews, who was later elevated to the peerage as Lord Llandaff, was a wealthy sixty-six-year-old bachelor and lawyer (he prosecuted Sir Charles Dilke in the Crawford divorce case). He was not an altogether happy choice for Home Secretary and his poor relations with the Metropolitan Police Commissioner soon became common knowledge. Commissioner Warren had been appointed by Matthews's short-lived predecessor in the Home Office, Hugh Childers and he was generally welcomed. *The Times* described him as 'precisely the man whom sensible Londoners would have chosen to preside over the Police Force of the Metropolis' and even the *Pall Mall Gazette*, a vigorous and outspoken critic of the Metropolitan Police, declared that Warren was 'a man after our own heart'. However, why Warren was chosen from four hundred candidates (according to Warren's biographer) to replace Henderson is something of a mystery, no statement on the matter being preserved in the public records. Warren seems to have believed that he was appointed to reorganise a demoralised Force and to have been promised a free hand in the methods he employed. This seems also to have been the impression of the Press, at least regarding the reorganisation. It was not, apparently, Matthews's understanding of the situation or, if it was, it was not a situation he allowed to continue.

The hostility between Matthews and Warren may to some extent have been due to the rapid decline in Warren's popularity following a series of incidents from 1886–8 and to accusations that Warren was attempting to militarise the Force. Warren strongly denied this charge and there is no real reason to believe that it was true, although he was a military man by training and inclination and his use of military methods would probably have given the impression of attempted militarisation. Warren's star went into a decline following the Lord Mayor's Show in 1886 when a section of the crowd got out of hand and there was a riot in Clerkenwell. Hot on the heels of this came the Miss Cass case, which Warren handled tactlessly; the murder of Miriam Angel by Israel Lipski; a riot in Trafalgar Square remembered as 'Bloody Sunday'; and to cap it all, of course, the infamous Jack the Ripper case, during which he received such widespread publicity that his tenure of office has been seen in a poor light ever since.

The first of these events was the Cass Case in June 1887. Although it did not directly involve the CID, the CID, which was still widely distrusted, was adversely affected by criticism of the police in general, that they were interfering with what today would be described as civil liberties. On Jubilee night, 21 June 1887, PC Bowden Endacott arrested twenty-three-year-old Miss Elizabeth Cass in Regent Street and charged her with soliciting. Outraged friends of Miss Cass strongly declared that she was not a prostitute but an innocent young girl recently arrived in London from Stockton-on-Tees, whose respectability should have been abundantly clear from her general appearance. PC Endacott steadfastly maintained that his attention had been drawn to Miss Cass on previous occasions and that his action in arresting her had not been on the spur of the moment or ill-considered.

The case against Miss Cass rested on PC Endacott's account. At the Marlborough Street Magistrates' Court the magistrate, Mr Newton, found the charges unsupportable and dismissed them, but he concluded his judgement by warning Miss Cass: 'If you are a respectable girl, as you say you are, do not walk Regent Street or stop gentlemen at ten o'clock at night. If you do, you will be fined or sent to prison. Go away and do not come here again.' Newton's remarks clearly show that he believed PC Endacott's account and they branded Miss Cass as a prostitute even though the charges against her were unproven. Feelings for and against Miss Cass ran high, even in the House of Commons, where there was a fierce debate which the Government lost by five votes, largely the result of an inept performance by Home Secretary Henry Matthews.

In fact, Matthews was censured in the House for having refused to set up an inquiry. He tendered his resignation as a result but, as on previous occasions, Lord Salisbury refused to accept it. However, the Press and the public were unforgiving and Matthews was strongly criticised, especially by W.T. Stead, editor of the influential *Pall Mall Gazette*, who made something of a hobby out of attacking Matthews and, indeed, the police.

An inquiry *was* held. Miss Cass was presented as a snow-white innocent and the police responded by producing evidence garnered by Superintendent Ball of the Stockton police which amounted to no more than that Miss Cass had enjoyed the company of several men friends and had spent some time alone in a hotel room with a married man who had given her a diamond ring. This evidence suggested that Miss Cass was not as innocent as her friends and her defence wanted everyone to believe but it did not corroborate the charge that she was a prostitute. On the face of it the action of the police and prosecution was morally underhanded as well as irrelevant. The more so since PC Endacott's own innocence of character was also the bastion of the prosecution's argument, yet his sexual knowledge and habits were not paraded before the public. By continuing to insist that he had previously had his attention drawn to Miss Cass, Endacott invited a charge of perjury. He was duly so charged by Miss Cass's legal representatives, suspended from duty and tried at the Old Bailey.

The case against him was ultimately reduced to the question of whether or not he had lied when claiming to have seen Miss Cass in Regent Street on previous occasions. Since nobody could prove that he had not done so, the judge expressed the opinion that the charges against Endacott were unsustainable. The case was dismissed but Endacott was *not* cleared. There was simply insufficient evidence against him, just as there was insufficient evidence to prove his contention that Elizabeth Cass was soliciting. He was reinstated but he spent the rest of his police career on special duty at the British Museum.

A few days after the arrest of Miss Cass, a murder took place in the East End of London which also became the focus of national Press attention. On 28 June 1887, Miriam Angel was found dead in her bedroom at 16 Batty Street, a small side street running off Commercial Road. Nitric acid had been poured down her throat and a twenty-two-year-old Polish immigrant Jew called Israel Lipski was charged with her murder. Fifteen people lived at 16 Batty Street and, among these, Miriam Angel lived with her husband in a small room on the second floor while Israel Lipski lived alone in the attic. When Miriam Angel did not turn up at her mother-in-law's for breakfast, as was her custom, inquiries were made and her body was found. Lipski was discovered beneath her bed with traces of nitric acid in his mouth. He was alive, but unconscious.

The murder was investigated by Inspector Final and Sergeant Thick of the local H Division. They spoke to a shop manager, a Mr Moore, who identified Lipski as the man who had bought an ounce of nitric acid from him on the morning of the murder. Lipski was charged with the murder but insisted that it had been committed by two workmen named Rosenbloom and Schmuss. Lipski was tried but his story was not believed and he was sentenced to death. The evidence was inconclusive and many people believed that the guilty verdict was brought in as a result of the summing up by the judge, James Fitzjames Stephen, who suggested to the jury that Lipski's motive for killing Mrs Angel was lust. In fact, no motive had been suggested by the prosecution during Lipski's trial and the defence had not been afforded the opportunity to refute such an allegation. Lipski's defence counsel, totally convinced of his client's innocence, made the most desperate attempts to save Lipski's life. Apart from arguing that Stephen's plausible speculations were not based on any evidence presented during the trial, he pointed out that the shopkeeper, Moore, had sold only an ounce of nitric acid to Lipski, yet medical evidence showed that at least a full ounce had been administered to Miriam Angel. Another ounce had been spilled on Lipski's coat and some had also been dropped on the bed, which was also marked by acid mixed with

115

blood. The point was that no blood was found on Lipski or his clothing – but he did have abrasions on his elbows which were consistent with his claims of having been knocked on to his back and having been in a violent struggle with Rosenbloom and Schmuss. As for the most damning evidence against Lipski, namely the claim that Miriam Angel's door was locked on the inside, the defence had expert advice from a locksmith who said that the lock had not been fitted properly and could have easily appeared locked when it was not. Moreover, the locksmith said that anyone with the requisite knowledge could easily have locked the door from the outside providing the key was in the lock, which it was. One of the men accused of the crime by Lipski was a locksmith.

The campaigning *Pall Mall Gazette* took up Lipski's case and turned it into a sensation but Henry Matthews and the Permanent Under-Secretary, Godfrey Lushington, in whose hands a reprieve or a pardon rested, assessed the evidence and concluded that there were no grounds for altering the verdict or the sentence. Israel Lipski was hanged but on the eve of his execution he made a full confession. Doubts have since been expressed about its genuineness – not in the sense that Lipski did not write it, but that it might have been a false confession.

The Cass and Lipski cases did nothing to endear Warren and Matthews to either the public or the Press, especially when it became clear that the two men were in dispute with one another and, in Warren's case, with Assistant Commissioner Monro. For Warren to have argued with so many people has been interpreted by almost every commentator as being Warren's fault and he has accordingly received a thoroughly bad press for over a century. Yet it is telling that quieter and more observant contemporaries held rather different views. Evelyn Ruggles-Brise, Matthews's Private Secretary, for example, later wrote:

Pennefather [the Receiver of the Metropolitan Police] was a very able man, but disagreeable to deal with; he rubbed everybody up the wrong way. Warren was the finest man we had in Whitehall, but probably the worst appointment, because he must be independent, and the Commissioner of Police is held in very tight bonds by the Home Office. Matthews was an exceedingly able lawyer, but quite incapable of dealing with men; he was a regular Gallio in his attitude to Warren's complaints. Later on he quarrelled with Bradford [Warren's successor as Commissioner], and if you couldn't get on with Bradford you could get on with nobody.

Robert Anderson, who cannot be counted among Warren's supporters, also did not attach all the blame to him. In his memoirs, *The Lighter Side of My Official Life*, he indicated that the Permanent Under-Secretary, Godfrey Lushington, not merely failed to apply a soothing balm to the disputes but rather exacerbated them:

As several of the men concerned are still with us, I cannot speak freely on this subject. But this much I may say, that if Sir Adolphus Liddell had still been in office [Sir A. O. Liddell was Permanent Under-Secretary from 1867–85 and was Lushington's predecessor], and influence of Whitehall had savoured of a plaister rather than of a blister, the course of events would have been different ... With his many excellent qualities Godfrey Lushington's intervention and influence as Under Secretary were generally provocative and his manner was irritating.

As for his own working relationship with Warren, Anderson wrote: 'My relations with Sir Charles were always easy and

117

pleasant . . . I always found him perfectly frank and open, and he treated me as a colleague.'

The cause of the problems was undoubtedly Warren's relations with James Monro. Warren believed that Monro's independence and direct access to the Home Secretary in his capacity as head of the Secret Department imperilled 'the safety of the Metropolis'. Monro's opinion, on the other hand, was that Warren interfered with the operation of the CID to an unprecedented degree and seriously affected its efficiency. By June 1888, he had washed his hands of all responsibility and written to the Home Secretary:

> With the restrictions now attempted to be imposed on my action as Head of the Department, I must, in justice to myself disclaim all responsibility meanwhile for any unfavourable results, to which the system now initiated will lead.

Monro further claimed that his department was under-manned and over-worked. He said that Williamson's health had broken down in consequence and that his own would soon do so. What Monro wanted was a post of Assistant Chief Constable to be created and he had recommended Melville Macnaghten for the job. The Home Office agreed to the appointment but Warren pointed out that when Macnaghten was a planter in India he had so provoked some mild-mannered natives that they attacked and beat him badly. Warren said that Macnaghten was 'the one man in India who has been beaten by Hindoos' and he also pointed out that Macnaghten had no qualifications for doing the job and that there was no shortage of well-qualified men avail-able. He suggested that Monro could very easily resolve his staff shortage by shedding the Secret Department work. All things considered, Warren made several valid points and the

118

Home Office agreed with him. Macnaghten's appointment was rescinded, much to Monro's embarrassment because he had already assured Macnaghten that the job was his.

Another difference between Warren and Monro was their opposing views of policing. Warren was a disciplinarian and perhaps sorely needed after Henderson's laxity. He was a solid supporter of the original preventative function of the police:

> The whole safety and security of London depends, in great measure, upon the efficiency of the uniform police constable acting with the support of the citizen. . .And it cannot be too strongly impressed upon the mind, at a time when the detective efficiency of the police is being called in question, that it has always been held as a police maxim that 'the primary object of an efficient police is the prevention of crime, the next that of detection and punishment of offenders if crime is committed . . .'

Warren clearly had no time for the detectives. He wrote in an article entitled *The Police of the Metropolis*: '. . . the value of the detective branch is but a drop in the ocean' and also somewhat foolishly declared that detective work was not suited to the 'genius of the English race', thus implying that police work should be visible, open to inspection and abide firmly by rules. Few, would disagree with policing being visible and open to inspection, but the wish to play by the rules overlooked the fact that criminals don't honour them – and that often they can only be caught if the opposition cheats as well.

Essentially, Monro held the opposite view to Warren, that you can't catch sewer rats by staying out of the sewer. So divergent were these visions of the police that both men can rarely have seen eye-to-eye. It might be worth observing that other commentators viewed the heads of the Metropolitan Police as men obsessed: Warren with efficiency gained through military discipline and Monro with bombing conspiracies. Both probably had a common bond in their opposition to 'subversives', but neither would have agreed with the other about the best way of dealing with them. In the end, Monro's views prevailed, largely because they were shared by his successor as head of the CID, Robert Anderson. As a result, the CID became an elitist department which was looked upon as superior to the uniformed branch instead of simply doing a different type of police work.

Both the Miss Cass and Lipski cases reflect the underlying social tensions which boiled over in the mid-1880s. The ordinary individual was seeking to establish or otherwise protect his rights and this is reflected in many major events of the period, such as the growth of labour movements and the large number of people who began to voice, or otherwise support, revolutionary ideas. A major contributory factor to the growing social unrest were the cyclical fluctuations in the economy which every nine years or so produced a downswing and consequent unemployment. One such recessionary period struck in the late 1880s and people found jobs hard to get. In fact, the situation faced by the working man was so bad that 1882 saw the first use of 'unemployed' as a noun and, in 1888, the introduction of the study of 'unemployment' in economics. Previously the working man suffered his privation in silence, except for the odd riot through the streets. In the 1880s things changed: the working man began to stand up for himself. There was a growth in socialism and trade unionism – in 1888 there were strikes by the gas workers led by Will Thorne and the Bryant and May matchgirls, and in 1889 the dockers downed tools. The spokesmen for the various groups which emerged during this period often held widely divergent opinions but, nevertheless, links were forged between liberals, the labour movement, anarchists and even Fenians. The authorities – the Establishment – became concerned and public order was soon the issue of the day.

In the autumn of 1887, Sir Charles Warren took the unprecedented step of prohibiting the use of Trafalgar Square for the large open-air meetings which radicals and socialists were in the habit of holding there. On 13 November, a demonstration was organised to be held there in defiance of Warren's instructions. A huge crowd duly amassed and Warren sent in the police. There was bitter conflict with the demonstrators and eventually the Foot Guards and mounted Life Guards were called in to clear the square. Over two deaths and a hundred casualties resulted and bitter memories lasted for more than twenty years in working-class districts. Apart from anything else, Warren's action alienated that segment of the population from the police and caused him to be a hated figure among the working classes. At the same time, Matthews was pilloried by the large and influential liberal and radical press. The plight of the poor and the working classes became the focus for extensive press attention and the responses of Warren and Matthews to the needs of these ordinary people were scrutinised. All that was needed was an event which would unite both liberal and radical critics against the government and the police, whatever their differences of opinion. That event turned out to be a madman in the slums of Whitechapel in the East End of London: Jack the Ripper.

Chapter Nine

JACK THE RIPPER

By 1888, when Jack the Ripper began prowling the streets of the East End, relations between Assistant Commissioner James Monro and Commissioner Warren had deteriorated to the point where Monro felt compelled to resign. While one can sympathise with Monro's problems, surviving documents give the impression that he was the kind of man who was unwilling to play a game unless everyone else played it according to his rules. In his (unpublished) memoirs, Monro wrote:

> Assistant Commissioner, Sir C. Warren made life so intolerable for me that I resigned. What the Home Secretary thought of the merits of the matter at issue between us may be gathered from the fact that he retained me as Chief of the Secret Department...

Monro left Scotland Yard and moved to the Home Office, where it is known that he continued to be consulted by Henry Matthews and was replaced as Assistant Commissioner, CID, by Dr Robert Anderson, the former Adviser on Matters Relating to Political Crime. By this time, Warren had won the full support of the uniformed branch but there was no love for him within the CID. Monro's 'departure' was deeply resented and matters were not helped by the refusal of the Home Office to give advance notification of who his replacement was going to be. Feelings ran so high that, according to Anderson: 'I had some difficulty in preventing Chief Superintendent Williamson from sending in his resignation.'

The date of Monro's departure and Anderson's appointment was officially 31 August 1888. One of Anderson's first acts as the new assistant commissioner was to take a month's sick leave. In his memoirs, *The Lighter Side of My Official Life*, Anderson explained that he was 'physically unable to enter on the duties of my new post' and that his doctor had insisted that he take at least two months' complete rest:

> This, of course, was out of the question. But I told Mr Matthews, greatly to his distress, that I could not take up my new duties until I had had a month's holiday in Switzerland. And so, after one week at Scotland Yard, I crossed the Channel.
>
> But this was not all. The second of the crimes known as the Whitechapel murders was committed the night before I took office, and the third occurred the night of the day on which I left London. The newspapers soon began to comment on my absence. And letters from Whitehall decided me to spend the last week of my holiday in Paris, that I might be in touch with my office. On the night of my arrival in the French capital two more victims fell to the knife of the murder fiend. . .

Jack the Ripper was never publicly identified (if, indeed, his identity was ever known) and the mystery of who he was has fascinated thousands of people around the world. A great many books have been written about the Ripper and his crimes, most of them offering inventive and often plausibly argued theories about who he was, but the crimes were significant on another level because Scotland Yard treated them as equal in importance to the Great Scotland Yard Scandal and the Fenian bombing outrages. The reason for this is probably because of the attention being given to the Yard by the Press and public. The Cass Case and the Trafalgar Square riots had done nothing to enhance the reputation of the police. At the same time, their efficiency was under close scrutiny both nationally and internationally; it can hardly have pleased anyone when the *New York Times*, for example, pulled no punches in its declaration that London had the most stupid detectives in the world!

Dr Robert Anderson believed that the Ripper's first victim was Martha Tabram. She was found lying in a pool of blood on the first-floor landing of 37 George Yard Buildings at 4.45 a.m. on Tuesday, 7 August 1888. She had been stabbed thirty-nine times. The previous evening she had been in the company of a friend named Mary Ann Connelly, nicknamed 'Pearly Poll', and a couple of soldiers. They had been drinking in various pubs and had separated with their respective soldier companions at 11.45 p.m. Nobody is known to have seen Martha Tabram alive after that time. Martha's companion was the most obvious suspect and the police held several identity parades in an effort to identify him. 'Pearly Poll' would not or could not pick out either of the men they had been with on the night of the murder. Gradually the inquiry ground to a halt.

The East End was a notoriously violent district and although Martha Tabram had been savagely attacked the inquest into her death attracted little interest. Only the authorities, witnesses and a few journalists were present. While Martha Tabram is not generally accepted as a victim of Jack the Ripper, Robert Anderson, in his memoirs, stated that 'The second of the crimes known as the Whitechapel murders was committed' on the eve of his taking office on 31 August. This is a reference to Mary Ann Nichols, and indicates that he followed the opinion of the contemporary press that the first victim in the series was Martha Tabram. It is Mary Ann Nichols who most people believe to have been the Ripper's first victim. She was found at about 3.40 a.m. on 31 August in Buck's Row, a short, narrow road situated behind the present-day site of Whitechapel tube station. Her throat had been cut and she had been savagely 'ripped' in the abdomen. One week later, on 8 September, as Anderson embarked on his recuperative holiday, Annie Chapman was found murdered and mutilated in the yard of 29 Hanbury Street. The police had no doubts that Mary Ann Nichols and Annie Chapman had been killed by the same person.

Inspector Frederick George Abberline, who had been involved in the investigation of the Fenian bombs at the Tower of London, knew the East End well, having served for years with H Division which covered Whitechapel. Born in 1843 in Blandford, Dorset, he had spent from 1873–87 with H Division and in November 1887 had been transferred to the Criminal Investigation Department at Scotland Yard. He can hardly have anticipated that without even having had time to brush the dust of the East End from his shoes, he would be returned there – but his special knowledge was needed. Overall charge of the investigation was given to Chief Inspector Donald Swanson who was relieved of all other duties so as to be able to devote his entire time to the case. Swanson, who in 1881 had arrested Percy LeFroy, was born in Thurso, Caithness, the youngest son of John Swanson, a brewer. He had been a schoolmaster before moving to London and joining the Metropolitan Police Force. After serving in several divisions he was transferred in November 1887 to Central Office. Here, he would achieve the rank of superintendent before resigning in July 1903. He was described as possessing 'an originality in method quite unusual' and to have viewed 'his work as a decidedly secret service', being 'much opposed to public "reminiscences".'

The murder and mutilation of two women in a week aroused considerable press interest and public alarm. This intensified when two women were murdered within an hour of each other on the night of 30 September 1888. Elizabeth Stride was found in a passage leading from the road to the rear yard of 40 Berner Street. This was the International Workers Educational Club, a well-known meeting place for Jewish socialists. In the yard at the rear of the building was the editorial office of the important Jewish Radical journal *Der Arbeter Fraint*. The club steward, Louis Diemschutz, hawked cheap jewellery as a sideline and had been at market all day. He returned to the club at about 1 a.m. and discovered Stride's body. He was horrified to find her throat had been cut and that blood was still oozing from the wound. A meeting held in the club had finished shortly before the discovery of the body and plenty of people were inside the building, either eating supper or singing. Nobody had seen or heard anything suspicious.

Less than an hour later in Mitre Square, just inside the jurisdiction of the City of London Police, a policeman discovered the body of Catharine Eddowes. Unlike Stride, Eddowes was appallingly mutilated. The panic now reached fever pitch. There was considerable criticism of both the police and the politicians and Dr Robert Anderson was compelled to return to London:

I spent the day of my return to town, and half the following night, in reinvestigating the whole case, and next day I had a long conversation on the subject with the Secretary of State and Chief Commissioner of Police. 'We hold you responsible to find the murderer,' was Mr Matthews' greeting to me. My answer was to decline the responsibility. 'I hold myself responsible,' I said, 'to take all legitimate means to find him.'

One cannot help but wonder how thoroughly Anderson could have reinvestigated the case within a day and half the night. He presumably meant only that he read and digested the available documentation. Anderson says that he took certain measures. Whether or not these had any effect is not certain, but a month passed without Jack the Ripper claiming another victim. People began to relax a little but the Ripper was merely waiting in the wings to make his awful and horrific curtain call. By all accounts, Mary Kelly was an attractive young woman but her butchered corpse was barely recognisable as that of a human being. She was found on 9 November in her small room at 13 Miller's Court, off Dorset Street.

Kelly is the last accepted victim of Jack the Ripper. With Kelly's death the killer vanished as suddenly as he had appeared, leaving the mystery of his identity as his legacy. Several people saw or claimed that they had seen the victims in the company of a man shortly before the bodies were found.

A Mrs Darrell said she had been walking along Hanbury Street and had seen a woman whom she was sure was Annie Chapman talking to a man on the pavement outside number twenty-nine. George Hutchinson claimed that he had seen Mary Kelly shortly before the estimated time of her death. He said she had been picked up by a well-dressed man whom she had taken back to her room. Hutchinson gave a very detailed description of the man – perhaps too detailed – and no doubt helped to foster the impression that the murderer was a 'toff'.

Yet two 'witnesses' have in recent years assumed considerable importance, largely because of a reappraisal of some comments by Anderson and the comparatively recent 'discovery' of papers belonging to Chief Inspector Swanson. The first, a Hungarian immigrant named Israel Schwartz, claimed that he had seen Elizabeth Stride assaulted outside the gates leading to the passage where her body was found. He claimed that he had entered Berner Street at about 12.45 a.m. Ahead of him was a man. A woman was standing on the pavement outside the gates to the club and, as the man came abreast of her, he assaulted her, apparently without provocation, and threw her to the ground. Schwartz, alarmed, crossed the street. At that moment a man came out of a public house and someone, Schwartz thought the man who had assaulted the woman, yelled out: 'Lipski!' Schwartz believed the remark had been directed at him. ('Lipski' was a reference to Israel Lipski, whose name had come to be used as a derogatory expression directed at Jews.) Schwartz fled. He thought that the second man pursued him.

Schwartz later identified the woman he had seen assaulted as Elizabeth Stride and documents in the police files on the case show that his story was accepted by the police. If Schwartz's story of the assault is true – and its acceptance by the police at the time must weigh heavily in its favour – then there can be little doubt that the woman was Elizabeth Stride. It is possible that she could have been someone else, but it seems to be flying in the face of probability to argue that two women could have been assaulted, or that the same woman could have been assaulted twice, in the same place, within a space of fifteen minutes. So, if the woman was Elizabeth Stride, the man who assaulted her also probably killed her. But was Elizabeth Stride really a victim of Jack the Ripper?

As far as we know, all the Ripper's victims were extensively mutilated. Stride was not. On the face of it the attacker seen by Schwartz would have had ample time in which to mutilate Stride and the absence of mutilation makes a convincing case for Stride not having been a Ripper victim. Equally, however, the killer could have been frightened away for any one of several reasons, not the least being his encounter with Schwartz.

The question therefore remains open, though the police must surely have reviewed the same issues and their conviction that Stride was a Ripper victim must tip the scales.

The other important witness was a man named Joseph Lawende. At 1.35 a.m., Joseph Lawende and two friends were passing the entrance to a short alley called Church Passage which led into Mitre Square. There, Lawende saw a man talking with a woman whom he later identified as Catharine Eddowes. Ten minutes later, PC Watkins of the City of London police found the terribly mutilated corpse of Eddowes. The timings in this murder are considerably less questionable than with Stride but Lawende only identified the woman as Eddowes by her clothing. She was fairly distinctively dressed with a green and black velvet-trimmed black straw bonnet and an imitation fur-trimmed black cloth jacket. Thus few, if any, researchers have seriously doubted that the woman seen by Lawende was indeed Eddowes. The timings also make it very unlikely that she could have been murdered by anyone other than the man seen by him. The extensive mutilation also makes it certain that she was a Ripper victim. As with almost everything about this case, nothing is certain. The woman may not have been Eddowes and her companion may not have been the person who killed her, but the City Police appear to have attached considerable weight to Lawende's evidence.

So who was the Ripper? A great many suspects have been advanced over the years, each often supported by well-reasoned but highly speculative argument. The most famous is Queen Victoria's grandson, Prince Albert Victor, but he has to be eliminated because he was demonstrably not in London at the time of any of the murders. The other is the Royal Physician, Sir William Gull, alleged to have committed the murders as part of a Government-inspired Freemasonic conspiracy to kill Mary Kelly because she knew about an alleged secret marriage between Prince Albert Victor and a Catholic shop-girl. This theory also lacks factual support. The main suspects – and in truth they are the only ones which, on the basis of available evidence, can be seriously entertained – are three men named in a document written by Sir Melville Macnaghten in 1894 and preserved in the Scotland Yard papers on the case. In that year a newspaper alleged that the Ripper was a Broadmoor patient. It did not name the patient but it is known from Macnaghten's memorandum to have been Thomas Cutbush, the nephew of Superintendent Cutbush of the Executive Department at Scotland Yard. Macnaghten wrote his memorandum to refute the allegations. It is not known, however, for whom the document was written, although the Home Secretary seems probable, and it was not intended that the contents become public knowledge. In the course of the paper, Macnaghten named three Ripper suspects: Montague John Druitt, Michael Ostrog, and a Polish Jew called Kosminski. These men were described by him as being 'of a type more likely than Cutbush to have been the murderer' and several authors have argued that Macnaghten's words should be taken literally, that the three men should be regarded as representing the type of person that the Ripper was likely to have been, not that they were ever suspected of having been the Ripper.

We believe this interpretation is wrong. Macnaghten thought one of those named was the Ripper. Swanson, and apparently Anderson, believed the Ripper was another of the three. And, of the third, Macnaghten says that his whereabouts at the time of the murders could never be satisfactorily ascertained. If two of those named were believed by senior investigators to have been the killer, it is reasonable to accept that all three were serious suspects, not just men 'of a type'.

The first of those named, and Macnaghten's favoured candidate, was Montague John Druitt. He is the most fully researched of all Ripper suspects but so far no evidence has been forthcoming to suggest why he should even have been suspected, let alone that he was the Ripper. A barrister-cum-teacher, Druitt appears to have had no money worries and to have enjoyed an active social life. In late November 1888 he was dismissed from his teaching job because of an unspecified 'serious offence' and the following month he drowned himself in the Thames. He left a note in which he referred to fears that he was 'going to be like mother', his mother having recently been committed to a mental institution. Macnaghten did not say why he believed Druitt was the Ripper, only that he had received information from a private source sometime after June 1889. Druitt's suicide could explain the sudden cessation of the crimes and the social standing of his family could explain why his identity as the Ripper was never made public, but the most determined research has so far failed to throw any light on the reasons for Macnaghten's conclusions. This is not to say that no evidence existed, and the Macnaghten memorandum offers good reasons for putting him in the frame.

Michael Ostrog was a con man and sneak thief who used some twenty-five aliases or more. The earliest record of him so far traced is in 1863 when he received ten months' imprisonment for swindling various business people in Oxford. Several other known offences followed. He got seven years in 1866 for theft and in 1874 he conducted his own defence against charges of theft, and was reportedly chagrined when he received a sentence of ten years. In 1887 he was committed to the Surrey Pauper Lunatic Asylum, from where he was discharged in March 1888. He appears to have been on ticket-of-leave but he failed to report monthly to the police and was consequently described by the *Police Gazette* as a wanted and 'dangerous man'. So far nothing has been forthcoming to explain why Ostrog was deemed a Ripper suspect, although Macnaghten claimed that he was 'unquestionably a homicidal maniac . . . habitually cruel to women . . . known to have carried about with him surgical knives . . .' This probably constitutes sufficient reason for making him a candidate.

The third suspect was called 'Kosminski' and, like Ostrog, he was a mystery until 1987 when identified in a book by the crime historian Martin Fido. Macnaghten described Kosminski as a Polish Jew who hated women, especially prostitutes, became insane through 'solitary vices' (masturbation) and was committed to an asylum. The only person named Kosminski ever committed to an asylum was an Aaron Kosminski, a Polish Jew living in Whitechapel who was sent to Colney Hatch asylum in 1891. Dr Robert Anderson, who wrote several times that the identity of Jack the Ripper was known to the police, said in his book, *Criminals and Crime*, that the Ripper 'had been safely caged in an asylum'. Then, in his memoirs, *The Lighter Side of My Official Life*, he wrote that the Ripper lived in the immediate vicinity of the crimes and:

> the conclusion we came to was that he and his people were certain low-class Polish Jews, for it is a remarkable fact that people of that class will not give up one of their number to Gentile Justice.
>
> And the result proved that our diagnosis was right on every point . . . the only person who had ever had a good view of the murderer unhesitatingly identified the suspect the instant he was confronted with him, but he refused to give evidence against him.

In saying that he was a Polish Jew I am merely

stating a definitely ascertained fact. And my words are meant to specify race, not religion. For it would outrage all religious sentiment to talk of the religion of a loathsome creature whose utterly unmentionable vices reduced him to a lower level than those of the brute.

Given that many people have misunderstood what Anderson was saying, it is important to appreciate that he did *not* say the police in 1888 knew who the Ripper was. He only said that in 1888 the police constructed a profile of the Ripper and that at a later date this profile proved to be correct on every point. He did not indicate how long after the murder of Mary Kelly this was. Then, in his posthumously published introduction to a book called the *Police Encyclopedia*, he wrote: '. . .there was no doubt whatever as to [the] identity of the criminal.'

Anderson is a difficult man to assess but there is no evidence that he was a liar. His memoirs contained other revelations – such as Jubilee Plot conspirator Millen being in the pay of the British – and where these can be checked they prove to be true. The only sensible conclusion is that Anderson genuinely believed the essential details of his story and accepted that the suspect, Kosminski, was Jack the Ripper. The surprising thing is that Anderson's statements were ignored for almost half a century, it being assumed that his candidate was a Jew named John Pizer who was briefly suspected and exonerated in 1888. However, in recent years evidence has become available which shows that Pizer was never committed to an asylum. Furthermore, late in 1987, some writings by Chief Inspector Swanson were found which tacitly support Anderson. The Swanson marginalia are some notes pencilled by Chief Inspector Donald Swanson in the margins and on the endpapers of his personal copy of Anderson's memoirs. These notes expanded on what Anderson had written and named Anderson's suspect as 'Kosminski'.

The authenticity of material so important to Ripper studies, emerging 100 years after the event, has understandably been questioned and doubted but the provenance of the marginalia was established in 1987 and an expert handwriting analyst at the Home Office Forensic Science Laboratory confirmed they were written by Chief Inspector Donald Swanson. This book is not the place to go into the complex arguments surrounding the interpretation of these documents, but Aaron Kosminski is the only person who could have been the 'Kosminski' named by both Macnaghten and Swanson and identified by the latter as the unnamed Polish Jew said by Anderson to have been the Ripper. He fits all the criteria needed to be Anderson's suspect: he was male, a Jew, he was Polish, he lived in the immediate vicinity of the murders, he had 'people' (presumably a family, though it has been suggested that Anderson merely meant people with whom Kosminski lived) and, in 1891, he was committed to an asylum. His medical records also give the cause of insanity as self-abuse (masturbation; not now a credible cause of insanity but widely believed in Victorian times to be the cause of many ills, including death), which seems to match the 'utterly unmentionable vices' spoken of by Anderson in connection with his suspect and with the 'solitary vices' which Macnaghten attributed to 'Kosminski'.

So, was Aaron Kosminski Jack the Ripper? His medical records make him look an unlikely Ripper. He seems harmless and there is no hint that he was sadistic in any way. Yet the surviving records are brief bi-annual statements about his general health and mostly do not extend to more than a line or two. They, by no means, tell the whole story. The main problem with the identification of Aaron Kosminski with Anderson's suspect, however, is

135

that he does not fit some of the details given by Swanson – and also that Swanson's account conflicts in part with what Anderson says. This led Martin Fido, who originally discovered Aaron Kosminski, to suggest that he had been confused with someone else, someone who *was* Anderson's suspect. Unfortunately, his argument has proved unconvincing to most serious researchers. This means that, until the problems with the sources can be resolved, the mystery remains unsolved – but perhaps solvable.

On the day that the body of Jack the Ripper's last victim was found it was announced that Sir Charles Warren had tendered his resignation and that it had been accepted. It was widely assumed at the time, and has been repeated ever since, that Warren's resignation was forced upon him by the failure of the police to catch the Ripper. The real reason was that Warren had written for a magazine an article defending the police. He had not first submitted the manuscript for vetting by the Home Office, as he was obliged to do, and was accordingly reprimanded by Home Secretary Matthews. Warren responded by declaring that he would never have accepted the position of Commissioner if he had known that he needed Home Office permission to defend himself and his Force in print. He consequently tendered his resignation and, into his shoes, hot from the Home Office, stepped James Monro who soon discovered that the view from behind the Commissioner's desk was very different from what he had been used to in the CID. Like Warren, Monro would soon clash with Matthews and Lushington.

Passing reference may here be made to another scandal, the Maybrick case. Florence Elizabeth Chandler came from Alabama. In 1881 she married a wealthy and hypochondriacal Englishman, James Maybrick. Six years later she discovered that her husband kept a mistress and that he was in serious financial problems. Florence sought solace with a friend of her husband. When James learned of the liaison there was a violent row during which he hit his wife. During the following week Florence purchased three dozen arsenic-based flypapers and a short time later, James Maybrick died. Traces of arsenic were found in his body and Florence was tried for murder. Although a damning quantity of evidence was marshalled against Florence Maybrick, there was also evidence that James Maybrick self-administered large doses of arsenic which he believed acted as an aphrodisiac. Traces of strychnine, hyoscine and morphine were also found in his stomach and were the remains of a 'medicine' he had been taking. Despite the evidence that James could have overdosed, there was considerable prejudice against the unfaithful Florence and the judge summed up heavily against her. She was found guilty of murder and sentenced to death, the sentence being reduced to a prison term of fifteen years. She was released in 1904 and died in the United States in 1941. Scotland Yard had no involvement in the case, but the judge who so damned her was James Fitzjames Stephen, who in 1887 had summed up too heavily against Israel Lipski. It was now discovered that he was mentally ill and he was committed to an asylum.

To round off the decade, there was another scandal which began with a theft of money from the General Post Office in St Martin's-Le-Grand in the City of London in 1889. Charles Thomas Swinscow, a fifteen-year-old messenger boy, was the prime suspect. He had been seen leaving the room from which the money had been taken and was also found to possess more money than he could legitimately have earned. Confronted by PC Hanks, Swinscow explained that he had got the money doing private work for a Mr Charles Hammond who lived at 19 Cleveland Street. Pressed as to what kind of work he did which paid so well, Swinscow replied, 'I got the money for going to bed with gentlemen at his house.' It transpired that other telegraph boys had also supplemented their wages in this way, among them Henry Newlove, George Alma Wright and Charles Ernest Thickbroom. Newlove and a boy named Hewitt immediately went to Cleveland Street to tell Charles Hammond what had taken place and the following day Hammond left London.

Meanwhile, the statements taken by PC Hanks were forwarded to Monro, who deputed Abberline, now chief inspector, to obtain warrants for the arrest of Hammond and Newlove for inciting and procuring Wright and others to commit 'buggery against the peace of Her Majesty the Queen'. Abberline, of course, found that Hammond had flown the coop but he arrested Newlove. On the way to the police station Newlove said to Abberline: 'I think it is hard that I should get into trouble while men in high positions are allowed to walk about free.' With these words what was to become known as the Cleveland Street scandal began. Pressed by Abberline, Newlove claimed that regular visitors to Cleveland Street included Lord Arthur Somerset, Lord Euston and Colonel Jervois. Further evidence was then gathered against Lord Arthur Somerset, Thickbroom and another boy named William Perkins identifying him as a man who had 'behaved indecently' with them.

The investigation had now taken a different course. Newlove and an associate of Hammond's named Veck, who had also been arrested, were defended by Arthur Newton, who also acted for Lord Arthur Somerset. On 16 September 1889 Hamilton Cuffe, the Assistant Public Prosecutor, wrote to his chief:

I am told that Newton has boasted that if we go on a very distinguished person will be involved (PAV). I don't mean to say that I for one instant credit it – but

138

in such circumstances as this one never knows what may be said, be concocted or be true.

'PAV' stood for Prince Albert Victor, grandson of Queen Victoria, heir presumptive to the throne. The rumour that Prince Albert Victor had visited the house in Cleveland Street seems to have been known to other visitors there. Lord Arthur Somerset certainly seems to have heard and believed it, and a letter he wrote suggests that the Prince went there with Lord Euston. The upshot of this case was that Lord Arthur Somerset fled the country to escape prosecution and lived in self-imposed exile on the French Riviera until his death in 1930. Lord Euston stayed in London and successfully sued Ernest Parke, editor of the *North London Press*, for criminal libel, admitting that he had once visited the house in Cleveland Street in the belief that it offered 'poses plastique' (a Victorian strip-tease), but had left and not returned when offered boys instead. He died in 1912.

However, we have found Lord Euston's name in a document among Chief Inspector Swanson's papers. It appears, along with several distinguished people, among them vicars, military men, civil servants, a QC and an MP, in a list of those connected with what appears to have been an extensive blackmailing operation. Letters were sent by the blackmailers to a great many people demanding money in return for their acts of 'unlawful and gross indecency' not being made public. Whilst this does not constitute proof of the Cleveland Street charges against Lord Euston, many of those named were known homosexuals of some notoriety and included Alfred Taylor and Charles Parker, later involved in the Oscar Wilde libel case. Whether or not the charges against Prince Albert Victor were genuine remains to be seen.

That same year, 1889, marked the end of an epoch.

Adolphus Williamson died in December of that year. He had seen the Criminal Investigation Department through many trials and tribulations, among which were Whicher's downfall over the Constance Kent case, the Great Scotland Yard Scandal, Fenian bombings and the Jack the Ripper case. Sadly, he left no personal observations behind.

Chapter Ten

NEW SCOTLAND YARD

The 1880s had been a bad decade for the police and the CID. A quieter period was no doubt looked forward to but the 1890s was a decade heralding dramatic changes in almost every area of life and therefore in the work of the CID. In fact, notwithstanding all the excitements of what was nearly half a century of existence, in comparison with what was to come, the life of a detective had been comparatively placid. There were quite a few names to take the Force into a new century: Melville Macnaghten replaced Adolphus Williamson as Chief Constable; John Shore and then Donald Swanson occupied the Superintendent, CID's chair and John Littlechild and his successor William Melville took charge of Special Branch. To the regret of hardly anyone, Home Secretary Henry Matthews departed the Home Office following the collapse of the Salisbury administration in 1892 and was replaced by Herbert Asquith.

Motor cars were first seen on the roads in the 1890s; big-time fraud commenced, requiring investigation by detectives with special talents; scientific aids were introduced into the art of detection with Bordet's discovery of reliable blood tests, Bertillon's anthropometric system, and Galton's fingerprint system; then, to be discussed later in this chapter, the fallibility of eye-witness identification was also revealed in the case of Adolf Beck. Yet there were other changes too. The police moved to an impressive new building designed by Norman Shaw. It almost immediately proved inadequate to meet the needs of the growing Force but in the succeeding decades, particularly following the development of the cinema and detective films, it would symbolise the British police. A. P. Herbert described it as a 'very constabulary kind of castle', but Commissioner Monro more prosaically called it New Scotland Yard. Despite a subsequent move the headquarters of the Metropolitan Police has been known by this name ever since.

During the course of the 1890s, Britain appeared to pull out of the economic depression which had struck in the 1880s. Crime statistics also declined and in 1896 reached the all-time low of 18,536 offences, with convictions rising by 18%. Despite this, though, the 1890s were a time of social uncertainty. Many people felt threatened by the growing economic and military might of other nations and the evil Asiatic hordes. Ever since the Boxer Rebellion it was feared the latter would sweep across the Western world. Fiction reflected these fears with arch-villains such Dr Fu Manchu. Others worried about 'racial degeneracy' and that the nation's moral fibre was being sapped. This was blamed on just about anything you could put a name to: steam trains, Jewish immigration, capitalism, socialism, democracy, weak government, strong government, sex (particularly homosexuality), Ibsen, penny dreadfuls – and anarchism. Anarchists as a whole did not advocate violence but a minority thought that a campaign of indiscriminate murder was a good way of encouraging people to accept political change. Anarchist bombs and violence exploded in America, Russia, France and Spain, and kings, presidents, government officials, military men, policemen and judges were killed or seriously wounded.

Britain was not greatly affected by what the *Review of Reviews* described as an 'epidemic' of terrorism, although a few incidents made the headlines. An anarchist bomb-making factory was discovered in Walsall, near Birmingham, in January 1892. Four men, Fred Charles (he had changed his name by deed poll from Fred Charles Slaughter), Victor Cails, an Italian shoemaker named Battola, and an unnamed fourth man, received long prison sentences. On 15 February 1894, a Frenchman named Martial Bourdin unintentionally killed himself when crossing Greenwich Park. He tripped over a tree root and a bomb he was carrying exploded. It was fortunate that the bomb, which used acid as a time-fuse, had not gone off earlier when Bourdin was travelling with it by train from Central London. Joseph Conrad based *The Secret Agent* on this event. Also, in 1894 eighteen-year-old Francis Polti, an admirer of Bourdin, was arrested in Farringdon Road with a bomb wrapped in brown paper. He had planned to cause an explosion in the Royal Exchange.

The few genuine incidents fostered an atmosphere of fear among the general public and led to frequent scares, mostly caused by hoaxers or misidentification. For example, a new design of baby's feeding bottle and egg-shaped rabbit exterminating bombs destined for Australia were among the devices thought to be bombs. Some explosions were caused by copy-cat bombers rather than anarchists, such as the bomb at Aldersgate station in 1897. It was against this background that Commissioner James Monro suddenly resigned. During his brief tenure of office he won the support of the uniformed and plain-clothed policeman, managed to establish policing as a professional career, handled social tensions with tact and efficiency and also won a measure of sorely needed public respect for the Force. Yet he, too, clashed with the Home Office. Although something of a mystery, the reason usually given for his resignation is that he was dissatisfied with the Government's attitude towards police pensions. It is known that Monro battled to improve the pension rights of the police and that the Government was, or seemed to be, unwilling to accede to significant but reasonable increases. However, he submitted his resignation on 12 June, five days before the Police Pensions Bill was to be published. In the event, it offered a generous scheme and won general approval. Why didn't anyone tell Monro what the bill offered? Why did he not wait to find out? According to Monro's all too brief account, his resignation:

> was a sacrifice of my interests on behalf of those of the Police. This is absolutely true. There was absolutely no necessity for my resigning my post had I chosen to remain. All that I had to do was to tell my men that I had done all I could for them in the way of getting their pensions, but that government would not comply with their demands ... I was asked to be a party to wrong doing towards men whose interests I was bound to protect and whom I was under an obligation to shield to the utmost of my power ... Every effort was made from all quarters to induce me to withdraw my resignation – the highest in the land, our present King, who was then Prince of Wales, used his personal influence to get me kept in my post – but for me, so far as I could judge, there was but one course which was consistent with right and honour ... Had I not resigned, I have no hesitation whatever in saying that the men would not have got their pensions – when I did resign, and when it was known why I did so, the feelings in Parliament was so strong that the unjust proposals of the Home Secretary as to pension were swept away in indignation, and in the end the men got almost what they asked for.

It is known that Home Secretary Matthews initially proposed less than what the police wanted and from what

Monro says it would seem that Matthews wanted Monro to approve the offer and that Monro refused and resigned. Monro seems to have believed that his resignation forced a revision of what was going to be offered. But only a week separated Monro's resignation from the publication of the Pensions Bill. Could the proposals in a Government bill have been altered within a week? And even if they could, even if Matthews was prepared to consider a compromise, given the influence of the people involved in attempting to get Monro to withdraw his resignation, why wasn't Monro simply told that Matthews was willing to reconsider? The mystery of Monro's resignation is deepened by the speed with which the notoriously indecisive Matthews announced the name of Monro's successor. Within forty-eight hours it was revealed that the new Commissioner would be Colonel Sir Edward Ridley Colborne Bradford.

Bradford was a distinguished cavalry officer, a veteran of the Indian Mutiny and active in the suppression of the Thuggee and Dacoitee. He was also missing his left arm, which had been amputated (without anaesthetic!) following a dispute with a tiger. He was a proven leader and administrator, had been many years a political agent in India and, since 1887, had been head of the Political and Secret departments of the India Office in London. His commissionership has been described as one of 'military firmness combined with infinite tact and diplomacy'. He certainly enjoyed harmonious relations with the Home Office, though Matthews soon vacated the office, which may in part explain it.

Yet Bradford did not have a wholly restful tenure. Within a few weeks of taking office he had to deal with a police strike, the second in the history of the Force which, in this instance was caused by general ill-feeling generated by the delayed Pensions Bill. Morale hit a new low and seems even to have extended to senior officers. In 1895 the *News of the*

World reported 'considerable friction among the heads of the service' and that Sir Melville Macnaghten, Chief Constable of the Detective Force, had applied for the position vacated by Colonel Roberts as head of the uniformed service, although the latter position was considered inferior. The article went on to say that the friction was the cause of an Inspector Tonbridge resigning at a time when he was next for promotion to replace Chief Inspector Shore and in 'one well-known Officer declining to go on duty' and consequently being brought before the Bow Street magistrates where he was fined £5.

The rank and file of the CID, which was now 800 strong, were also dissatisfied with the way men of the 'special service' [the Irish Branch and Secret Department] were returning to regular police work and being showered with preferments. The CID also had to contend with several cases which did not improve its poor reputation with the public. Yet, outside the Force, life and death went on as normal and several people were taking steps towards the gallows and into the criminal history books. One of them was Mrs Eleanor Pearcy. She is always known as Mrs Pearcy but seems never to have been married. Her real name was Mary Eleanor Wheeler and she took the name Pearcy from a man who had lived with her for a while. On 24 October Mrs Phoebe Hogg took her eighteen-month-old son, Jeffrey, out in his pram. The following day her body, the head almost severed, was found in Hampstead. Jeffrey's body was later found discarded on some waste ground.

Clara Hogg (Phoebe's sister) and a family friend, twenty-four-year-old Mary Pearcy, went to the mortuary to identify the bodies. Mrs Pearcy's over-hysterical reaction drew police attention to her. It was discovered that she had been having an affair with Frank Hogg, the victim's husband. When her house was searched – throughout which Mrs Pearcy played the piano – considerable evidence in the

146

way of bloodstained clothing, knives and an axe were found. Witnesses also came forward to say that they had heard a woman screaming in Mrs Pearcy's house on 24 October and had seen Mrs Pearcy wheeling a perambulator on that day. Mary Eleanor Pearcy declared her innocence but was found guilty. She missed Christmas, being sent to the gallows on Monday, 23 December 1890 and apparently displayed great calmness to the end.

Another murderer of the period whose memory has endured was Glasgow-born Thomas Neill Cream. He was a doctor, having graduated in medicine from McGill University in Canada. While practising in Chicago he poisoned a man named Stott with strychnine and was sentenced to life imprisonment. He was released from prison in 1891 and in July of that year came to London. Cream had a personality quirk. He could not help poisoning people and, in London, he compulsively poisoned a succession of prostitutes. He was also determined to incriminate himself and it must be said that his inability to attract the attention of the CID was not due to any lack of diligence or effort on his part. For some reason the police just seemed to ignore him but the CID finally saw what had been staring them in the face and after the necessary legal proceedings he was executed on 15 November 1892. It has been alleged that, on the scaffold, just as the trap opened beneath his feet, Cream said, 'I am Jack the . . .' However, Cream was safely locked in Joliet Prison on the other side of the Atlantic when the Ripper murders took place.

Murder was not the only crime during this period. Fraud was becoming fashionable and the notorious fraudster of the day was Jabez Balfour. In 1870, at the age of twenty-seven, Jabez Spencer Balfour became managing director of the Liberator Building Society, a very successful business which financed the building of housing estates, a pioneer block of flats (Whitehall Court), and a couple of hotels.

Balfour became a Member of Parliament in 1880 and Mayor of Croydon in 1883, was a prominent churchman and a wealthy, successful businessman who had a London home as well as a country estate in Oxfordshire. Precisely what went wrong is uncertain but the Liberator Building Society became financially unstable and in 1892 it crashed, owing £7 million, most of it money which Balfour had encouraged small savers to invest in the ailing company. Advised by a legal friend to flee the country, Balfour went to the Argentine and it took the police two years to get him back to England where he was sentenced to fourteen years in prison.

The officer who went to the Argentine to collect Balfour was Inspector Frank Froest. Most descriptions of him refer to his excellent dress sense, grooming, charm and 'delicate hands and pink nails'. One expects a bit of a dandy, not the bull-headed, Teutonic-looking individual who stares out from the photographs. Balfour later wrote about Froest in his book *My Prison Life*:

> The great detective was not at all an unkindly man, but he had come from England with the fixed impression in his mind, amounting to an absolute obsession, that I was bent on committing suicide . . . [he] could not drive from his brain that he might arrive in England minus his prisoner.

Froest would go on to become one of the most famous detectives of his day. Meanwhile, the last surviving link with the old days of policing died. In January 1894 Peter Schonfeld, reputed to be the last Bow Street Runner, died at the age of eighty-five. In his day he was apparently as famous as Goddard and Townsend, and had open access to the Royal Family.

1894 was also the year of the Oscar Wilde libel case.

The previous year John Littlechild had resigned as head of Special Branch and set up business as a private investigator. One of his first commissions was to procure evidence for the Marquess of Queensberry when Oscar Wilde brought the infamous libel case against him. The Marquess of Queensberry had left a card at the Albermarle, Wilde's club, addressed: 'To Oscar Wilde posing as a Somdomite [sic]'. Wilde was livid and despite good advice from friends to forget about it, he elected to sue Queensbury for libel – and Queensberry was arrested.

Edward Carson, with initial reluctance because he recognised that Queensberry had a weak case which he seemed likely to lose, agreed to defend the Marquess. Private detectives, among them Littlechild, were hired to find such supportive evidence as they could. They found enough. Various boys were discovered who were willing to testify that Wilde had committed sexual acts with them. In court Edward Carson, perhaps unintentionally, but possibly with the intention of making Wilde over-confident, engaged in an exchange about literature. Carson quoted from *Dorian Gray* and asked Wilde, 'Have you ever adored a young man madly?'

'I have never given adoration to anybody but myself,' replied Wilde, much to the delight of the court.

Again reading a passage from *Dorian Gray*, Carson asked, 'Is that a beautiful phrase?'

'Not as you read it, Mr Carson. You read it very badly.'

With exchanges such as these, Wilde's wit and the apparent discomfiture of Carson was winning the approval of the jury. Wilde was perhaps carried away by his success so that, when asked if he had ever kissed a boy called Grainger, he replied that the boy was ugly; he had not done so. This attempt at wit was miscalculated and thereafter Wilde squirmed like a caught fish under Carson's relentless questioning. The rest is history. It was obvious that Littlechild and the detectives had done their job, that Carson had witnesses to support Queensberry's defence and that Wilde would lose his case. Wilde sensibly withdrew the libel charges, at which point there seemed no alternative but for a warrant to be issued for his arrest. At 6.30 p.m. two policemen knocked on the door of the Cadogan Hotel and Wilde was ruined.

Newspaper reports of sensational cases like the Oscar Wilde one were by now generating public interest in the police and the judiciary, and some detectives and barristers were beginning to acquire a status which today is reserved for pop stars. One case which made headlines was the Muswell Hill murder and indirectly it introduces one of the most famous detectives of all time. Muswell Lodge was a rather isolated house which backed on to Coldfall Wood near Muswell Hill. The house had been built to the designs of Mr Henry Smith who, aged seventy-nine and widowed, lived there alone. His only help about the place was a gardener named Webber. On the morning of 13 February 1896, Webber went to Muswell Lodge as usual but his knocking at the front door failed to get an answer. Webber ran to the nearest house, the home of a Major Challen, and on returning to Muswell Lodge they forced an entry and found old Mr Smith dead on the kitchen floor. His legs had been bound, a towel had been forced into his mouth and a rag tied over it. His head had been severely injured. Upstairs, his rooms had been ransacked and his safe opened.

The murder inquiry was placed in the hands of two CID detectives, Inspector Marshall and Inspector Nutkins, the latter of whom had been involved in the Thomas Orrock and Mrs Pearcy investigation as well as several others of note. Marshall and Nutkins immediately fixed on two known criminals named Albert Milsom and Henry Fowler. A few inquiries resulted in a bull's-eye lantern and tobacco-box, both found at the scene of the murder, being identified as Milsom's. Both men were eventually traced to Bath, where they had joined a travelling circus, the powerful Fowler playing the part of the strongman Ajax. The two men were arrested.

At the Old Bailey, Milsom tried to save his neck by incriminating Fowler, and the latter was so angry that he brushed aside the efforts of half a dozen warders attempting to restrain him. He was eventually pulled off but the enmity between the two men was such that, at their execution, they had to stand either side of another murderer, William Seaman.

It is Seaman, a brutal fellow whose real name was possibly William King, who introduces us to the most famous of detectives: Frederick Porter Wensley. Wensley was then a young detective sergeant, but he achieved the distinction of being the first policeman from the ranks to become Assistant Commissioner.

In 1896, Seaman murdered John Goodman Levy and his housekeeper Sarah Gale at the former's home in Turner Street, a road running off Whitechapel Road, near the London Hospital. Seaman was still in the murdered man's house when Wensley entered and noticed a hole in the bedroom ceiling. Standing on a chair and peering through he saw another hole in the roof and a man disappearing through it. It was Seaman, who jumped from the roof, hoping that some bystanders below would break his fall. They didn't. He fractured an arm and a thigh, as well as sustaining other injuries.

The primary detective task in this case was to identify this man, who refused to answer any questions, but the H Division detective inspector, Stephen White, recognised him as Seaman, a violent thief of long standing. Wensley later observed that he had had extensive experience of the underworld but that Seaman was 'the most truculent and

151

repulsive desperado with whom I ever came in contact. I think he is the only man I ever met of whom I could honestly say that he had no single redeeming trait.'

Seaman was tried at the Old Bailey, found guilty and hanged between Milsom and Fowler. He is alleged to have remarked: 'Well, this is the first time in my life I've ever had to act as a bloody peacemaker.' The hangman on this occasion was James Billington and he was evidently anxious to send Fowler and Milsom into eternity before their brawling caused him any problems. Billington's assistant, a man named Warbrick, was pinioning one of the victim's legs and was hidden from the view of Billington, who, thinking everything was all clear, pulled the lever. The three murderers plunged through the trap, Warbrick followed head-first. He was lucky, and was able to grab the legs of the body nearest him and so save himself a nasty injury. He also presumably hastened the end of the criminal in question. The execution of Fowler, Milsom and Seaman was the last triple hanging to be carried out at Newgate. The following day, Billington hanged Amelia Dyer who, at fifty-six, was the oldest women to be hanged in Britain since 1843. No woman older than Dyer would be hanged in Britain again.

For various reasons the most important case of the 1890s was that of Adolf Beck. It should never be forgotten. In 1887, a man calling himself Lord Willoughby (or sometimes Lord Winton or Lord Winton de Willoughby) conned a woman out of her jewellery and passed a bogus cheque. He was caught, gave his name as John Smith, was sent to Portland prison and, in 1894, was released on licence. Then, in the summer of 1895, a French woman named Ottilie Meissonier was conned in a similar fashion. Madame Meissonier identified the perpetrator of this crime as Adolf Beck and he was taken into custody.

The case was placed in the hands of Inspector Frank

Froest who noted the strong similarity between the crime of which Beck was accused and that for which 'John Smith' had been convicted. Despite Beck's claim to be a Norwegian citizen who had been resident in Peru prior to 1885 (that is to say, he had not been in Britain when the 'John Smith' crimes took place), a series of identify parades were held and ten out of twenty-three people identified Beck as the man who had swindled them. A hand-writing expert named Gurrin declared that specimens of Beck's handwriting were identical to that of 'John Smith' and a PC Eliss Spurrell, who had arrested 'John Smith' in 1877, stated positively that Beck and 'Smith' were the same person. The evidence was therefore conclusive that 'John Smith', with his many aliases was up to his old tricks again.

Beck/Smith stood trial in 1896 and the indictment against him contained fourteen counts, four in the name 'John Smith', and ten in the name of Beck. The defence case was that Beck was not 'John Smith', but would prove that he was in South America when the four offences were committed by 'Smith' – and that it was 'Smith', not Beck, who had committed the remaining ten counts on the indictment. The four counts against 'Smith' were largely irrelevant to the prosecution's case against Beck but if the defence had been able to introduce its plea of mistaken identity it would have thrown doubt on the ten charges against Beck. Thus, there was a good chance that Beck would leave the court a free man. The prosecution therefore dropped the four 'Smith' counts and scuppered the defence case by preventing the mistaken identity plea from being raised. This was a clever and perfectly legal, if underhand, piece of outmanoeuvring by Horace Avory, the prosecutor, and Beck was convicted. Moreover, although it was never proved that Beck was 'Smith', the judge passed a particularly stiff sentence – seven years imprisonment – because he believed Beck was Smith and therefore an old offender. For once, justice was

153

achieved despite the efforts of an unscrupulous con-man and the planned clever trickery of his defence. Sent back to Portland prison, Beck was made to feel at home again. He was even given 'Smith's' old number: D. W. 523.

The only glitch in this otherwise successful case was that Adolf Beck was *not* 'John Smith'. 'John Smith' was a circumcised Jew and Beck was Gentile. Beck's lawyer, Duerdin Dutton, applied to Robert Anderson to see 'Smith's' file but Anderson refused him access. Dutton then petitioned the Home Office for a re-trial but was turned down. Beck remained in prison.

In fairness, except for the harshness of the sentence which had been based on the assumption that Beck and 'Smith' were one and the same person, the 'John Smith' crimes had played no part in the case against Beck, who had been convicted in his own name for a crime which *prima facie* he had committed. The judgement was therefore just. Beck was released in 1901 and three years later 'John Smith' was up to his old tricks again. Several women were swindled out of jewellery and money and one of them, a Miss Scott, gave the swindler's name as 'Lord Willoughby', the 1877 alias of 'John Smith'.

Detective Inspector Ward remembered Beck, and Miss Scott immediately identified him as the man who had defrauded her. Beck was arrested and stood trial on 27 June. The situation now was that Miss Scott had been conned by a man using an alias known to be used by 'John Smith'. This suggested that she had been conned *by* 'John Smith'. However, she had identified Beck as the man who had conned her. Thus, 'John Smith' and Adolf Beck were widely believed to be the same person. Yet the Home Office knew for certain that 'John Smith' and Beck were not the same – but the Home Office saw no reason to tell anyone.

Beck was tried and found guilty but the trial judge, Mr Justice Grantham, postponed sentence. Ten days later

Chief Inspector Kane was making an inspection at Tottenham Court Road Police Station when a man called William Thomas was brought in, having been arrested when he tried to pawn some jewellery. Kane immediately recognised him as 'John Smith'. In due course Beck was released and was given a free pardon and £5,000 compensation. He died in 1909, a broken man.

The police were exonerated of any blame for wrongful arrest, although Anderson's decision not to let Beck's lawyer see 'John Smith's' file seems questionable. The judge at Beck's first trial was also criticised for passing a sentence based on the unproven assumption that Beck was 'Smith', and the Home Office officials were hauled over the coals. It transpired that Charles Murdoch, the Assistant Under-Secretary of State at the Home Office, knew (presumably from prison documents) in 1898 that Beck and Smith were not the same person but had not thought it important to inform the police, even though he had the opportunity to do so. Also, C. E. Troup, Murdoch's successor, told a Commission of Inquiry in 1904 that although he, too, was aware that Beck was not Smith, he had not apprised the police of this fact at the time of Beck's second arrest because he had not known that Beck had been arrested. Given that the newspapers were full of the arrest and that it was the talk of London, Troup seems to have been grossly ignorant of current affairs.

The importance of the Beck case is twofold. It dramatically illustrated the unreliability of eye-witness identification and it was instrumental in bringing about the acceptance of the fingerprint system.

Chapter Eleven

ALL CHANGE

The new century opened with the return of an art treasure which had been stolen twenty-six years earlier. Georgiana Spencer, the Duchess of Devonshire, acclaimed as the most beautiful woman in England, was painted by Thomas Gainsborough in 1783. The painting passed into the hands of an elderly spinster, Miss Margaret Maginnis, who trimmed the canvas so it would fit a smaller frame and hang above her fireplace. She later sold it to a dealer named Bentley and, in turn, the picture was sold to a collector called Wyn Ellis. Some seventy years later the portrait was sold at auction for £10,500 to Agnew and Co., of Bond Street. This made it, at that time, the highest valued painting by an English artist.

On 26 May 1876 the Gainsborough portrait was stolen from the gallery of Agnew and Co. The theft was committed by a clever and successful thief named Adam Worth, better known by the alias Harry Raymond, and regarded during his lifetime as the greatest thief of the nineteenth century. Born in 1844 in Cambridge, near Boston, Massachussets, to a German immigrant family, he had received a reasonable education but during the Civil War had fallen in with a bunch of rogues and thieves. He became a pickpocket and graduated to bank robbery, first as a 'banker', furnishing the capital to pay the expenses of the robberies, then as

157

a participant, and finally as an organiser. He executed big-time robberies. In the 1860s he teamed up with 'Big Ike' Marsh, Bob Cochran and Charles 'Piano Charley' Bullard, and robbed the Boylston Bank in Boston, Massachusetts, of $1 million in money and securities.

Worth and Bullard sailed to Liverpool where they adopted false names, Worth taking for the first time the name 'Harry Raymond' after the editor of the *New York Times*. Bullard took the name 'Charles Wells', under which he would later become a celebrity in Paris as the owner of the lavishly furnished American Bar. Worth, however, quickly resumed his criminal career by robbing a Liverpool pawn-broker of jewellery valued at £25,000. He then moved to London and his expensive apartment at 198 Piccadilly became the meeting place for the leading thieves of America and Europe, Worth himself acting as receiver for most of the big robberies. In 1875–6, one of Worth's friends was extradited to London from Paris and held in Newgate while awaiting trial. Worth planned to gain him his freedom. With a notorious English thief named Jack 'Junka' Phillips and Joseph 'Little Joe' Reilly (also known as Frederick Elliott), Worth gained entry to Agnew's gallery and cut the Gainsborough from its frame, escaping under cover of a thick fog.

The plan was that a shady solicitor acquaintance of Worth's should visit Worth's friend in Newgate and give him a small square of canvas cut from the Gainsborough. The solicitor was then to visit Agnew's and say that a client of his had information about the painting and that he would reveal its whereabouts if his release was arranged. The irony was that, meanwhile, the charges against Worth's friend were dismissed because of a legal technicality. This left Worth and his confederates in possession of a valuable and by now perhaps the best known and most undisposable painting in the world. Also, by some means unclear, the

London police knew who had committed the robbery but lacked the evidence necessary to make an arrest. In April 1887 'Little Joe' was arrested in America. He disclosed the whole story of the robbery to Robert Pinkerton, of the famous Pinkerton detective agency, and offered to have the Gainsborough restored in exchange for being released from prison. These facts were communicated to Superintendent Shore at New Scotland Yard, confirming what the CID already suspected, but 'Little Joe' was unable to fulfil his end of the bargain and the whereabouts of the painting remained a mystery.

Adam Worth had by now become a wealthy man: he owned a steam yacht called *Shamrock* with a crew of twenty men, and also a sailing yacht, but he continued in criminal endeavours and was eventually caught and sentenced to a prison term. He emerged with failing health. In January 1899, for uncertain reasons, Worth met 'off the record' with Pinkerton in America and promised the return of the Gainsborough if no charges were brought against him. The deal was communicated to Superintendent Donald Swanson (who had headed the Jack the Ripper investigation) and he contacted the solicitors acting for Agnew's. Eventually, through an intermediary named Sheedy, a deal was struck in which the Gainsborough would be restored if Agnew's allowed Sheedy to make and have sole control of steel engravings of the painting. In January 1901, Swanson cabled Pinkertons to arrange the return of the Gainsborough and the painting was restored to Mr Agnew in Chicago, in perfect condition after having been missing for twenty-six years.

The return of the Gainsborough was in some ways a watershed for the CID, the ending of a link with the past, with 'Dolly' Williamson, who had first investigated the theft, and through him with the Detective. The twentieth century came like a new broom to Scotland Yard and old

159

faces disappeared into retirement. Robert Anderson went in 1901 and was replaced as Assistant Commissioner, CID by Edward Henry, who in 1903 became Commissioner. Melville Macnaghten then became head of the CID, being replaced as Chief Constable, CID, by F. S. Bullock. In that same year, 1903, Donald Swanson retired as Superintendent, CID, and was succeeded by Arthur Hare.

Society also changed. Queen Victoria died and was succeeded by Edward VII, and so began an era as distinctively Edwardian as the previous near-century had been distinctively Victorian. Society gradually became less restricted, more vocal, and science and technology increasingly began to play a part in the commission of crimes and in crime detection. For centuries, the Chinese had used thumb impressions to sign documents but it was not until 1880 that Dr Henry Faulds, a Scottish physician working in Japan, suggested that fingerprints might be employed in crime detection. His interest in fingerprints resulted from the thought that they might have a relationship with race or ethnic origins. Faulds made copies of the prints of sooty fingers which were discovered on the whitewashed walls of a neighbour's recently robbed house. He compared these with the fingerprints of a man who was later arrested for the crime. Faulds declared that the prints did not match. On the other hand, when a second man was arrested and Faulds was allowed to take his fingerprints as well, they were found to match.

Fauld's published an account of these events in the prestigious science journal *Nature* and among those who read it was Sir William Herschel. Herschel wrote to *Nature* and described how, as an administrator in India, he had for years used thumb impressions to identify illiterate prisoners. Yet it was Sir Francis Galton, a cousin of Charles Darwin, who established that each fingerprint was individual and permanent. He also laid the foundations of the classification system which sorted fingerprint impressions into the three most commonly observed features of arches, loops and whorls. In 1892 Galton published a book called *Fingerprints*.

Meanwhile, in Argentina, Juan Vucetich, head of the Police Statistical Bureau, had read and been impressed by Galton's work and had devised his own system of fingerprint classification in the face of opposition from his superiors. In 1892 he achieved the distinction of gaining the first conviction in history through fingerprint identification. Twenty-five-year-old Francesca Rojas murdered her two children (because her lover did not like them) and accused a peasant neighbour of the crime, but she had left a bloody fingerprint and on being confronted with this evidence she confessed.

The task of fingerprint classification was completed by Sir Edward Henry who, in 1896, employed fingerprinting in India where he was serving as Inspector-General of Police in Bengal. Henry did much to have fingerprinting employed at Scotland Yard. The first conviction directly attributable to fingerprints was that of Harry Jackson, a professional burglar, who left a palm print on some wet paint at the scene of the crime. Edward Henry was a man of outstanding calibre and on appointment set about creating what was virtually an entirely new department, the Central Finger Print Bureau, and remodelling the Register of Habitual Criminals, thus creating the Criminal Record Office (CRO) in the process. He chose three experienced CID officers to head the new bureau: Inspectors Stedman, Collins and Hunt.

In 1901 there were 93 fingerprint identifications recorded; in 1902, 1,722; 1903, 3,642; 1904, 5,155. In 1902, Henry also began a small training school for detectives at New Scotland Yard and this led in 1907 to the opening of the first Police Training School at Peel House in Westminster.

The following year, 1903, saw the last steam train chug its way through the London underground and a private telephone line was installed at Central Office to keep in touch with the Divisions. A possibly more significant change at Scotland Yard was the appointment of Henry to the commissionership when Bradford retired. Henry proved to be one of the five outstanding occupants of that office.

Meanwhile, a fingerprint was to prove the conclusive evidence in a murder case and for the first time sent a man to the gallows. Elderly Thomas Farrow and his wife, Ann, lived in a flat above his paint shop in Deptford, south-east London. On 27 March 1905, he was found dead in the parlour with his wife unconscious in one of the bedrooms. She died four days later. Both had been savagely beaten with a jemmy. Inspector Collins searched the place and eventually found a thumb-print on a cash box which had been forced open. Everyone known to have handled the cash box, including the dead couple, were fingerprinted but none of the prints matched.

A witness, Ethel Stanton, had that morning seen two men running along Deptford High Street. She knew one by sight as twenty-two-year-old Alfred Stratton. Another witness, a milkman, had seen two men leaving Farrow's shop but although he could not recognise the men again there existed the possibility that one of them was Stratton. Alfred Stratton was therefore arrested and Collins took his fingerprints. Alfred's right thumb was found to match perfectly the one on the cash box. So he, and his twenty-year-old brother Albert, were charged and tried at the Old Bailey in May 1905. The fingerprint evidence was contested by the defence but the jury brought in a verdict of guilty and the brothers were hanged.

The use of forensic aids, training, and the wide variety of crimes investigated by the CID began to increase the number of requests for assistance the Yard received from the provincial Forces, few of which had detectives. Over the years, the calls for aid were predominantly in cases of murder and, as a result, the officers of Central Office Criminal Investigation Branch who were deputed to assist became known as the 'Murder Squad', though this was never a formal title. Superintendent Frank Froest was appointed to head the new squad of officers readied for detachment. At first there were only four men with him: Detective Chief Inspectors Fox, Arrow, Kane and Dew. The last named was to become the most famous.

However, aside from domestic issues, the greatest concern was with anarchists and Communists. Investigation of these groups was handled by the Special Branch and it is clear from autobiographies and other writings that some members of the Branch almost regarded themselves as the saviours of the nation. In fact, the threats were more imagined than real but the general atmosphere of concern led to Special Branch detectives doing things which a few decades earlier would not have been tolerated, such as disguising themselves in order to spy on those whom they believed to be subversives. For example, in 1905 Detective Constable Herbert T. Fitch hid in a cupboard and heard what he regarded as an inflammatory speech delivered by 'a smooth-haired, oval-faced, narrow-eyed, typical Jew' – the speaker was Lenin. A little later he dressed as a waiter in a restaurant where Lenin was dining with a secret society called the 'Foreign Barbers of London'. He claimed that the information he gathered caused the Russian Revolution to be delayed for twelve years.

Espionage was also becoming an issue in Britain. This was largely because of novels by the likes of William Le Queux, who was obsessed with the idea of German agents infiltrating the Establishment and all levels of society. He later became convinced that his writings so damaged espionage networks in Britain that enemy agents kept him under constant surveillance and threatened his life almost daily. He requested police protection and even threatened to 'pull' powerful strings if his requests were not satisfied but no evidence for his claims was forthcoming and his threatened string-pulling earned him a severe reprimand. Nevertheless, Le Queux did succeed in convincing and gathering the support of several influential people. Among them was Major James Edwards, who in 1908 became head of the Army's secret service and largely on whose initiative M15 was formed.

Looking back, not so long before, to the days when every level of society found the idea of spies thoroughly repugnant, it is clear that public attitudes were now changing. This largely imagined threat from without prepared them to accept, and indeed want, the police to act in a way which only a few decades earlier would have caused national uproar. The extension of police powers which this provoked is still with us today and was undoubtedly sanctioned by changing public attitudes. The fears of espionage which existed in Britain during the latter half of the first decade of the new century are illustrated by an article in the *Daily Mirror*, dated 27 January 1909. A short report headlined, 'German Spies in Britain', reported: 'Remarkable allegations as to the activity of German spies in England', and were made by Major A. F. Reed, secretary of the Primrose League for Perthshire, and William Le Queux, at a meeting at Bickford. They claimed that in Scottish industrial centres there were no fewer than 1,500 people in the employ of the German General Staff and that there were as many as 5,000 in Britain as a whole!

The allegations were spurious, of course, but it is interesting that on the same page the newspaper carried an article about a more important incident which was described as the 'Tottenham Outrage'. In Chestnut Road, off Tottenham High Road, was Schnurmann's rubber factory and, opposite,

164

was a police station. On Saturday, 23 January 1909, twenty-nine-year-old Joseph Wilson and seventeen-year-old Albert Keyworth arrived in a car with the Schnurmann workers' wages. Waiting for the car were two men, immigrants from Latvia named Paul Hefeld and Jacob Lepidus (or Lapidus). Keyworth got out of the car with the wages bag and was attacked by Lepidus. There was a struggle, which Wilson joined. Hefeld, meanwhile, drew a gun and fired repeatedly at Wilson. Bullets riddled his long overcoat and a glancing shot even sliced his vest but, as Superintendent Jenkins of the local Division later reported, 'In a miraculous and unaccountable way he escaped injury'.

A gas stoker named George Smith now joined the fray. He was shot in the stomach by Hefeld. Then, Hefeld and Jacob managed to grab the money and they made off towards Tottenham Marshes followed by two policemen, PCs William Tyler and Albert Newman, the latter being picked up by Joseph Wilson in the car. Other officers followed. In Mitchley Road, Hefeld fired a fusillade of shots at the car, which was rendered useless. PC Newman was slightly wounded and a ten-year-old schoolboy named Ralph Joscelyne received a bullet in the right breast, from which he very soon died. Tyler and Newman now pursued Hefeld and Jacob but Hefeld turned, took careful aim and shot Tyler in the head. Tyler lived for long enough to reach hospital but died five minutes after admission. Newman did not continue the chase but remained with his fallen comrade.

The pursuit, taken up by other policemen and members of the public, resulted in other casualties. Eventually Hefeld and Jacob reached the bank of the River Ching. It was bounded by a fence which Jacob managed to climb but Hefeld, unable to do so, yelled, 'Go on, save yourself, I've only got two left.' He then sank to the ground and shot himself in the head. Amazingly, he did not succeed in killing himself and was promptly taken into custody, but the wound proved fatal and he died nineteen days later. Jacob ran on and eventually took shelter in Oak Cottage, the home of coal porter Charles Rolston. Mrs Rolston saw him and ran out crying, 'Oh, my children.' (They appear to have been in a lean-to and were safely brought out by a Walthamstow baker named Charles Schaffer and PC Dewhurst.)

Superintendent Jenkins wrote: 'He [Jacob] first ran to the front room, where judging from the amount of soot which was found lying in the room, he had made an attempt to climb into the chimney.' Jacob then fled to the upstairs front bedroom and cautiously peered out of the window. He was seen by his pursuers, many of whom were armed and who at once poured a volley of shots into the room, wrecking almost all that was inside. PCs Charles Eagles, Charles Dixon and John Cater now entered the building and cautiously climbed the stairs. Dixon had earlier managed to secure a ladder and had climbed to the window of the rear bedroom, having seen Jacob in the front one. The policemen fired three shots through the door of the room. A fourth shot was fired by Jacob: he killed himself.

Eagles, Dixon and Cater were awarded the King's Police Medal for Gallantry (only instituted that year) and were promoted to sergeant. A public subscription for PC Tyler's widow raised £1,055 and provided her with a police pension of £15 per annum. The father of the murdered boy received £1. Joscelyne tended to be forgotten amid the extensive publicity surrounding PC Tyler's death and funeral but his schoolfriends erected a fine monument over his grave. It was rediscovered, untended for decades and overgrown, in the 1980s by a group of local schoolchildren.

While the police continued investigations into the Tottenham Outrage, political agitation was surfacing elsewhere. Just to add to what many perceived as dramatically declining social standards, women now wanted the right to vote.

Mrs Pankhurst's Women's Social and Political Union was formed in 1903 and its members were called suffragists. Two years later, the more militant among them began a campaign of annoyance and became known as suffragettes. By 1908, their strategy of physically assaulting government ministers had turned them into a 'problem' and, when some women attacked Home Secretary Herbert Gladstone's car, he was sufficiently impressed by the suffragettes' effectiveness to recommend that a separate section of the Special Branch be set up.

Duties in the Suffragette Section required that the senior Special Branch officers involved exhibit exceptional tact and diplomacy since they often had to put up with considerable abuse. A report by the head of the Special Branch, Patrick Quinn, dated 29 April 1913, remarked in connection with a visit to Mrs Pankhurst that he and his men had been called various names including 'Cowards', 'Pigs', 'Brutes', 'Syphilis' and 'Gonorrhoea'. The actual amount of damage caused by the suffragettes was disproportionate to the large number of Special Branch officers tied up in the investigations. By 1914 the personnel of the Special Branch had increased to seventy, most of them engaged in saving Britain from spies, anarchists and women.

Elsewhere, sex was the cause of another name entering the criminal history books: Hawley Harvey Crippen. He perhaps ranks with Christie and Jack the Ripper as one of Britain's most notorious murderers and though his was a sordid domestic crime, it was in some respects instrumental in creating a superstar detective out of Inspector Walter Dew, whose race across the Atlantic in pursuit of Crippen gripped newspaper readers. On 2 February 1910, a letter was delivered to the committee of the Music Hall Ladies' Guild. It was from Cora Crippen or to use her stage name, Belle Elmore, and explained that the sudden illness of a relative had necessitated her hurried departure for America and that in the circumstances she had no alternative but to resign her position with the guild.

About a month later her husband, Hawley Crippen, told friends that Cora had contracted pleuro-pneumonia in America and was in a critical condition. On 24 March he announced that she was dead and a little later the theatrical weekly newspaper *Era* carried an obituary. Hawley's behaviour aroused the suspicions of Cora's friends and eventually, on 31 March, Mrs Louis Smythson reported Cora Crippen's disappearance to New Scotland Yard. Other similar reports reached the police and eventually Walter Dew was assigned to undertake some inquiries. He called at Crippen's home, 39 Hilldrop Crescent in Holloway, and met Crippen's girlfriend, Ethel Le Neve. He later visited Crippen at his office in New Oxford Street, and later they dined together at an Italian restaurant. Crippen openly admitted that his story about his wife's death was a lie. The marriage had failed, he said, and Cora had gone off to America to live with an old flame named Bruce Miller. He explained that he had invented the story of her death to protect her reputation and at the same time save him from the embarrassment of his failed marriage becoming common knowledge.

The following Monday, Dew visited Hilldrop Crescent again. Crippen and Le Neve had flown the coop. Dew searched the house thoroughly and finally, in a small coal cellar, buried under six inches of clay and the brick floor, found the lime-covered remains of a body, later identified as Cora Crippen. The story was an age-old one. Crippen loved and was loved by his secretary, Le Neve, and was unhappy and humiliated by Cora Crippen who drank, flirted outrageously and made no secret of her attachments to other men. Eventually Crippen murdered her. On 20 July, he and Le Neve – who was dressed as a boy – boarded the *Montrose* at Antwerp and sailed for Quebec. Unfortunately, the papers had been full of stories about the police hunt for

Crippen and he was recognized. On 22 July Captain Kendall sent a radio message that Crippen and Le Neve were on board and the next day Dew left aboard the *Laurentic* and set off in pursuit, the newspapers at home covering the race in detail, avid readers following the story like modern television viewers follow a soap opera. This vessel overtook the *Montrose* and on 31 July Dew arrested Crippen and Le Neve at Father Point, Canada. They were gaoled until extradition could be arranged.

Back in London, Crippen's defence was handled by a crooked solicitor named Arthur Newton, who saw in Crippen a means of settling a few outstanding gambling debts; and Arthur Tobin was appointed as Crippen's defence counsel following an argument between Newton and the clerk of possibly Britain's most gifted barrister, Edward Marshall Hall. Crippen, who displayed a cast-iron nerve in the witness box, consistently denied that the body was that of his wife but Bernard Spilsbury, the renowned pathologist, who was then embarking on his career, showed that the body was indeed that of Cora. Crippen was unable to explain how a body in his coal cellar had come to be wrapped in a pyjama top which could only have been acquired at a date after he and his wife had moved into the house. It took only twenty-seven minutes for the jury to find Crippen guilty and he was sentenced to death. 'I still protest my innocence,' he declared.

Crippen's guilt is unquestioned, but his motive for murdering his wife at that particular time has remained a mystery. Cora Crippen comes across as a drink-ridden, nagging, domineering woman. Did the worm in Crippen finally turn? Was it a burning hatred which finally led him to murder? Or was it his love for Le Neve and what he perceived as the social stigma of divorce which compelled him to kill? An alternative theory was advanced by Edward Marshall Hall and was based on the fact that

Cora Crippen had been poisoned with hyoscine. Hall suggested that he had been administering the drug as an anti-aphrodisiac but a variation on this idea is that he had administered it as a sedative, putting Cora to sleep so that he could entertain Le Neve. Both arguments propose that Crippen had that night accidentally given Cora too much.

Whatever his reasons, Crippen took them with him when he went to the gallows. He never admitted his guilt. On 5 November 1910, the day that Crippen's appeal was turned down, Walter Dew tendered his resignation without giving a reason. He died in Worthing in December 1947. Ethel Le Neve was acquitted. She adopted the name Ethel Nelson and later married an accountant named Stanley Smith and had two children. Her husband died in 1943 and, incredibly, he never knew Le Neve's true identity. She herself died in Dulwich in 1967.

While Dew was grabbing the headlines, Special Branch investigators had been continuing to inquire into the wages theft, also known as the Tottenham Outrage, and were convinced that it had been organised by one Christian Salnish, who at this time they knew only by the name Jacob Fogel. They also knew that he had taken part in several bank raids and committed at least five murders. Salnish had come to England to undertake the organisation and transportation of arms and literature into Russia. He financed these activities by expropriation, a Robin Hoodish activity of robbing the rich to finance the cause – otherwise known as violent robberies.

One such robbery had been the Tottenham Outrage and another was the attempt to rob the jewellery shop of Mr H. S. Harris at 119 Houndsditch. During the day of 16 December 1910, strange noises had been heard coming from the shop and eventually a neighbour, Max Weil, went in search of a policeman. In Bishopsgate he found a young City constable,

Walter Piper. Piper agreed that the noises sounded suspicious, made a few inquiries among other neighbours and, from the furtive behaviour of some men he encountered he felt convinced that something was up. Back in Houndsditch he called Constables Walter Choate and Ernest Woodhams from adjoining beats. Messages were sent to Bishopsgate Police Station and additional policemen began to arrive. These included Sergeant Robert Bentley, two plain-clothes constables named James Martin and Arthur Strongman, and Sergeants Bryant and Tucker.

Inside the house were George Gardstein, Yorka Dubof, Max (Smoller), Jacob Peters, Fritz Svaars, and Nina Vassilleva. They decided to come out shooting. As Donald Rumbelow has written in his excellent account of these events:

> None of them had any scruples about shooting a policeman. Peters had had his finger nails torn out by Tsarist police and Dubof his back torn by Cossack whips. In their own country policemen had killed, tortured and condoned the most outrageous brutalities, and there was no reason to assume that the English police were any different. Why assume they were unarmed? Fritz and Gardstein both had special pockets for concealing their guns so why shouldn't the police? Any chance of removing their fears, which were common, not only to them but to most of the East End's immigrant population at this time, was completely destroyed by their ignorance of the language.

Bentley was shot. He lived long enough to reach hospital, coherently answer questions and talk to his wife, who was expecting his child. Tucker was also killed. Bryant and Woodhams were wounded. As the men made a break from the house, Constable Choate managed to grab the hand of one of the men, Gardstein, but the others turned their guns on him and shot repeatedly. Choate, with eight bullets in him, refused to release his grip and Gardstein was accidentally shot by one of his comrades. The expropriators finally managed to free Gardstein from Choate and get him back to lodgings at 59 Grove Street (a few streets away from Berner Street where the Ripper victim, Elizabeth Stride, was murdered). Gardstein later died there. Walter Choate underwent surgery but died on 17 December 1910.

By Thursday, December 22, three of the men who were believed to have some connection with the crime had been found. They were Yorka Dubof, Jacob Peters and Osip Federoff. Others were arrested over the next few weeks: John Rosen, Karl Hoffman and Nina Vassileva. Federoff and Hoffman were discharged at the police court; Peters, Dubof and Rosen were acquitted at the Old Bailey; Vassileva was convicted and sentenced to two years' hard labour, but on appeal the conviction was quashed on the ground of misdirection by the judge. Then, on Monday, 2 January 1911, an informer, Charles Perelman, told the police where they could find Svaars. He was with a man called 'Joseph' and was staying in the room of a Russian woman, Betsy Gershon, at 100 Sidney Street. The police surrounded the house. Then the shooting started and, in the course of it, four policemen were wounded: Detective Sergeants Leeson and Chesham, Sergeant Digby and Constable Dyer. Leeson was reported to have told his superior: 'I am shot. Mr Wensley, I am dying. They have shot me through the heart. Give my love to my children. Bury me at Putney.' He did not die, however, but lived to write a highly colourful account of his career.

The weapons of the police were outmatched. A detachment of Scots Guards were summoned from the Tower of London and a number of big-wigs also added their largely unnecessary presence. These included Deputy Commissioner Woodhouse, Assistant Commissioner Melville Macnaghten and Home Secretary Winston Churchill. There was a great deal of firing, a greater deal of confusion and much excitement then, shortly before one o'clock, it was realised that the house was on fire. When the blaze was eventually extinguished the bodies of Svaars and Joseph were found among the debris. Joseph, it seems, had at some time been shot through the head by a rifle bullet and Svaars had bravely fought on alone.

Christian Salnish, who is thought to have planned the Tottenham Outrage and who may be regarded as having started the whole episode, emigrated to America in 1913, then went to Russia in 1917 where he became a senior soldier. In 1939 he was shot on Stalin's orders. Nina Vassileva remained in Britain and later worked for the Soviet Trade Delegation at 49 Moorgate. She spent her last years in a small flat in Brick Lane and died in St Bartholomew's hospital in 1963.

Many people at the time, and since, have thought that in some way the murder of an East End immigrant named Leon Beron was connected with the events surrounding the siege of Sidney Street in 1911. On New Year's Day, 1911, Leon Beron was found dead in some bushes on Clapham Common. He had been dealt some severe blows to the head and there were several knife slashes on his face. Initially, the police seem to have suspected two Frenchmen who had been noticed in Beron's company but from inquiries in Whitechapel, where Beron lived, the police soon learned that he had been seen shortly before his death with a man named Stinie Morrison, a burglar and thief of long standing, who had apparently not been seen in his usual haunts since about the time of the murder.

Morrison was on ticket-of-leave and had failed to report

himself to the authorities. His description was therefore circulated in *Police Informations* and a watch was kept on a house in Newark Street where he had lodgings. A week after the murder he was seen to enter the lodgings in Newark Street. He left after a short time and went to Cohen's restaurant in Fieldgate Street. Detective Inspector Wensley of H Division, with officers Brogden, Dessent, Jeffery and Bellinger made for the restaurant and Morrison was arrested.

A case was soon built up against Morrison. It was shown that he had frequently been much in Beron's company during the week preceding the murder and that they had left a restaurant together just before midnight on 31 December. He was seen with Beron in Whitechapel Road at 1.45 a.m. and in Commercial Road some time after 2 a.m. A taxicab driver named Arthur Castlin claimed that Morrison was one of two men he had driven to the neighbourhood of Kennington Church at 3.30 a.m. It was also learned that at 11.00 a.m. on New Year's Day Morrison had left a parcel at St Mary's Railway Station, Whitechapel, which contained a gun and ammunition. Morrison was charged and stood trial. Despite a spirited defence by Edward Abinger he was convicted and sentenced to death. The sentence was later commuted and Morrison gained a reputation as a troublesome prisoner. He died in prison in 1921.

The case exercises considerable fascination for three reasons. Firstly, Beron's face was marked in a way which suggested a ritual killing by a secret society; secondly, the police behaved very strangely; and thirdly, it has been suggested that Beron may have been connected with the Houndsditch gang.

His cheeks had been marked with what looked like the letter 'S' and, in the words of Dr Joseph Needham, the then Divisional Police Surgeon at Balham: 'They could not have been produced accidentally. No mere coincidence could have

174

produced them ... I think there was a meaning to them.'
However, in his memoirs Wensley stated:

> There was, it was true, a wound on one cheek that very
> remotely resembled the letter 'S'. On the other was
> another slash that might have been an 'S' in reverse.
> I shall adopt Mr Justice Darling's words. 'Anyone who
> sees the letter "S" in either of these scratches has
> either better eyes or a more vivid imagination than I
> can possibly claim to possess.'

The refusal of the police and the judge to even acknowledge
that the wounds were 'S'-like has remained one of the
more curious and enticing aspects of this case. Beron's
face had also been deliberately framed with a black silk
handkerchief. Many people then and since have found it
difficult to avoid the conclusion that, despite claims to the
contrary, these things had some arcane significance.

At the trial, much weight was attached to Morrison's
behaviour once he arrived at Leman Street Police Station.
According to Wensley, Morrison asked to see him:

> 'You have accused me of murder,' he declared. 'I
> want to make a statement.' I replied that I had done
> nothing of the sort, and the significance of his remark
> at once flashed across my mind. Why should he have
> associated his detention with a murder charge?
>
> In view of what followed I should like to make it
> plain that none of the officers had been told the man
> was suspected of murder, although it is possible that
> they may have drawn the inference from my presence
> at the arrest that the capture was one to which I
> attached importance.

One might observe that Morrison, who had been in Beron's
company on the night of the murder and in the course of

the following week, would probably have heard about it and could easily have drawn the same inference from Wensley's presence. Also, as he was frog-marched to Leman Street Police Station a crowd, estimated, perhaps overestimated, by the police to number 3–4,000, had followed, calling out to Morrison in Yiddish, German, French and Russian. It is barely conceivable that no one mentioned murder, referring either to Beron or the Houndsditch case, both of equal local importance and likely to spring to mind. At the trial, a constable named Greaves stated that he had heard Detective Sergeant Brogden tell Morrison that he was suspected of murder. Greaves, however, had previously been suspended for making untruthful statements about his superior officers and had been reprimanded by Wensley 'for writing wild letters to me making utterly unfounded accusations against certain people in connexion with the Sidney Street business'.

The police also behaved a little oddly with regard to Beron's antecedents. He was generally represented as a respectable businessman, although Wensley acknowledged in his memoirs that Beron 'was believed to be fond of the society of women (it has in fact been suggested that he was a pimp), and there was an impression that he was not unwilling, under favourable conditions, sometimes to dabble in stolen property'. These were guarded words by Wensley. Equally guarded were statements by journalists. The *People* described Beron as having 'queer ethical standards' and of conducting a flourishing business 'under cover of darkness'; and Basil Thomson, a future head of the CID, years later in the *Sunday News* similarly observed that Beron 'might have had an occupation which he preferred to keep to himself, and that that occupation was the receiving of stolen property'. It is therefore hard to escape the conclusion that Beron's character was suppressed during Morrison's trial.

There was also the question of an accomplice. As Wensley wrote in his memoirs:

It was always our view that Morrison was not alone in the murder – indeed this was clearly indicated in the case for the prosecution. We knew the other man, also a criminal, and there was at one time a possibility that we might arrest him ... Ward, however, feared that to put him on trial would add fresh complications to an already difficult case, and thought that a jury might become so bewildered that both murderers would escape ... the man left the country some time after, and I heard that he had been executed for a murder and robbery in the United States, though I never troubled to verify the report.

This raises another slightly curious point, particularly as Wensley says that Morrison's subsequent behaviour could be explained if he believed himself innocent because the accomplice had in fact murdered Beron. Morrison, of course, would probably still have been guilty of murder (all those party to a criminal act which results in death are deemed to be equally guilty). But why would the arrest of the accomplice have added greater confusion to the case? And why, if the accomplice was the one who actually killed Beron, was he allowed to go free?

One suggestion has been that Leon Beron was in some way connected with the Gardstein gang and was murdered because it was believed that he was going to inform the police about something he knew. Alternatively, it has been suggested that he had some dealings with French criminals. Wensley, however, was emphatic: Beron 'was not a spy, an agent provocateur, a member of any secret society, or an informer'. The question mark remains, however, and the mystery of Leon Beron's death and the extent of Stinie Morrison's involvement remains unresolved. The final word, however, should go to Wensley who presumably knew all the secrets: 'I am, I think, the only living person who knows every circumstance of that case, and after twenty years I am still convinced that Stinie Morrison was convicted as justly as any murderer I have ever known.'

Science at this time was coming on apace and another murderer was about to step on to the gallows as a result of forensic evidence. In 1832, eighty-year-old farmer George Bodle died. Evidence suggested that he had been poisoned by a grandson, John, who could not wait for old age and natural causes to deliver him his inheritance. A young and impoverished chemist named James Marsh was asked to see if he could find evidence of arsenical poisoning. He did find arsenic in George Bodle's intestines and in the remains of coffee he was known to have drunk but unfortunately the jury found Marsh's scientific evidence insufficient and Bodle was found not guilty.

Marsh spent the next few years trying to find a way in which the presence of arsenic could be clearly demonstrated to even the most stupid juror. He succeeded. His technique proved capable of detecting arsenic in quantities of a thousandth of a milligram and in October 1836 he published his findings in the *Edinburgh Philosophical Journal*. There was only one problem. Arsenic proved to be a very common element, minute traces of which could be found in the bones of people known to have died of natural causes and even in samples of soil taken from a graveyard. This did not invalidate Marsh's test but meant that it had to be conducted very carefully with, for example, samples of grave soil being tested in cases of exhumation. However, it was not until 1912 that the Marsh test was used in a court of law – and the test could hardly have faced a greater ordeal because it was challenged all the way by Marshall Hall.

Forty-nine-year-old Miss Eliza Barrow had a great deal of money. In July 1910, she took lodgings in the Islington home of the Seddon family: Frederick Henry Seddon, District Superintendent with the London and Manchester Industrial Assurance Company, his wife, five children and aged father. During the next few months Seddon acquired all her assets, then Miss Barrow became ill with vomiting and diarrhoea. Despite the ministrations of a doctor she died in 1911 and Seddon had her buried in a common grave, even gaining a commission from the undertaker for putting some business his way.

A cousin of Miss Barrow, a man named Frank Vonderahe, learned about her death and visited the Seddons. Made suspicious by evasive answers and the fact that Seddon had acquired Miss Barrow's money, Vonderahe went to the authorities and Miss Barrow's body was exhumed. It contained traces of arsenic. Seddon was arrested on 4 December, along with his wife some weeks later, and was tried at the Old Bailey in March 1912. The prosecution amply demonstrated that Seddon had motive, method and opportunity, and the evidence of Dr William Willcox, an outstanding forensic scientist who was Senior Analyst at the Home Office, showed that Barrow's body contained an estimated 131.57 milligrams of arsenic – ample proof of fatal poisoning. The jury found Seddon guilty.

However, both Seddon and the judge were Freemasons and Seddon, making a Masonic sign, stated: 'I declare before the Great Architect of the Universe I am not guilty.' The judge replied, 'You and I know that we both belong to one brotherhood . . . But our Brotherhood does not encourage crime.' Seddon's remark has generally been interpreted as a plea for leniency on the basis of common brotherhood but it might in fact have been an oath of innocence. Indeed, Seddon may not have been guilty at all. Nevertheless, he was executed at Pentonville on 18 April 1912.

Chapter Twelve

THE WAR YEARS

Melville Macnaghten retired as Assistant Commissioner, CID, in June 1913. He was succeeded by Basil Home Thomson. Thomson was the son of the Archbishop of York. After completing his education at Eton and New College, Oxford, he enjoyed a varied career with the Colonial Service in Fiji, Tonga (where he was Prime Minister) and New Guinea. He was tutor to the sons of the King of Siam. Later he became Inspector of Prisons, Secretary to the Prison Commissioners, and Governor of Cardiff, Dartmoor, and Wormwood Scrubs prisons. By 1913, war was widely expected but some people anticipated serious civil unrest if war did not come. Thomson recalled in his book *Queer People* that 'unless there was a European war to divert the current, we were heading for something very like revolution'. Many feared the consequences of the latter rather more than the former.

People like Thomson were also concerned about espionage. Espionage had become an issue largely through the efforts of journalist/writers like William Le Queux who claimed to possess evidence that Britain was riddled with German spies. If Le Queux was to be believed it was barely possible to lift a pebble without finding half a dozen German agents hiding beneath it. The fears thus generated can be said to have led directly to the creation of MI5, to the

Aliens Act, the introduction of a general warrant for the interception of mail, and the passing of a new Official Secrets Act all in the early years of the new century. Of the latter, Bernard Porter has observed: 'It was presented as a measure aimed solely at foreign spies, and as "nothing novel", which was not strictly – or even remotely – true.'

Largely because of an uncritical acceptance of Le Queux's often risible 'evidence', the authorities suspected the existence of a large number of saboteurs in Britain. The attitude of the police to this spy-mania was considerably less excitable. Commissioner Henry, for example, regarded Le Queux as a person 'not to be taken seriously'. In fact, Le Queux even lost the interest of MI5, which he bombarded with warnings to which, as he later complained, he received no reply but 'a mere *printed acknowledgement*'. This naturally convinced Le Queux that the enemy had penetrated the highest echelons of the British security service and government. The only problem lay in finding these enemy agents.

During the first months of the war something in the region of 120,000 separate inquiries were undertaken by the Special Branch. No saboteurs were found but, in 'MI5-think', this only proved how good the saboteurs' cover was. Therefore, more men were accordingly drafted into Special Branch so the inquiries could be extended. The 'evidence' of Le Queux and Kell (the first Head of MI5), however, was magnificently wrong, though it was acted on to a ludicrous extent. The spy situation in Britain was small and quickly neutralised on the outbreak of war. Only thirty German spies were arrested in Britain between 1914–18. Twelve were executed. The best known of these was Carl Hans Lody who was tried in November 1914 and executed by a firing squad at the Tower of London on 6 November. One committed suicide, the rest were imprisoned. S. Theodore Felstead, a former MI5 officer, claimed in his book *German*

182

Spies at Bay that 'None of the German spies in Britain ever picked up much that could not have been read in our newspapers, most of which went to Holland and so found their way into German hands.'

The long-term impact of the spy-fever was the inability of many people to distinguish between a spy and someone who merely expressed alternative ideas, especially ideas different from the ones held by those in authority. The war caused surveillance to be maintained on liberal-minded groups, the Labour Party (which became involved in anti-war activity) and labour movements. The latter were a particular worry because a number of members of the government were convinced that the labour movement was being liberally funded by the Germans and, after the October Revolution in 1917, by the Russians.

Basil Thomson was deeply fearful of 'subversion'. This was probably a result of being impressed as a child by several pictures of scenes from the Paris Commune. He became increasingly involved in the work of the Special Branch and his memoirs make it clear that he defined 'subversive' fairly broadly. It embraced almost everyone who thought differently from the way he did and included everyone from suffragettes and socialists to trade unionists and pacifists. Thomson even went so far as to 'persuade' the newsagents W. H. Smith not to sell the magazine *Suffragette*. Again one must wonder what people only a generation earlier would have made of the Establishment attempting to prevent the free circulation of a magazine. Civil liberties in Britain would never be the same again.

Basil Thomson's taking of liberties was a habit shared by a man named George Joseph Smith, who took some liberties too, mostly with his wives, of whom he had four: Beatrice Thornhill, Beatrice (Bessie) Munday, Alice Burnham and Margaret Lofty. Each drowned whilst taking a bath. The death of Margaret Lofty, the last of Smith's unfortunate wives, received some press coverage and the father of an earlier bath victim, Alice Burnham, became suspicious. A landlady who had also suspected Smith of having murdered Alice Burnham also saw the newspaper reports and went to the police. She told them how she had heard violent splashing coming from Smith's bathroom on the night that Bessie Munday died and afterwards Smith playing 'Nearer My God to Thee' on the harmonium. The investigation was entrusted to Chief Inspector Neil, and Bernard Spilsbury, now the Home Office pathologist, was brought in. Smith was arrested, tried for murder, and despite being defended by Sir Edward Marshall Hall, was found guilty and hanged at Maidstone prison on 13 August 1915.

War had now broken out, of course, and the press and public were less interested in domestic trivia, even murder, and the police, too, were occupied with wartime matters such as espionage. This brought into Scotland Yard one of the most interesting spies of all time, a beautiful woman named Margerette Zelle. Few people today know who Margerette Zelle was, though many would know her by the name she used when she became the toast of France as an exotic dancer: 'Mata Hari'. Whether or not Mata Hari was in fact a spy is questionable. She was convicted by the French courts of spying for the Germans and on 15 October 1917 executed by a firing squad, but the evidence suggests that in fact she had done no more than associate with a large number of people among whom were some German spy masters.

The beautiful, seductive and naïve Mata Hari came into contact with Scotland Yard on one occasion. The Yard had received what was believed to be reliable information stating that a known German spy named Clara Benedix had travelled from Madrid to England aboard the SS *Hollandia*. When the ship docked, Mata Hari was arrested in the belief that she was Benedix and on 13 November 1916 she was taken to Scotland Yard where she was interrogated by

Basil Thomson himself. Mata Hari, who was famous in France, although her star was in decline at the time, not unnaturally objected to being identified as someone she was not. Her indignant denial of being Clara Benedix left Thomson with a problem. He had three choices: one, his 'reliable' information was correct and the woman was Clara Benedix; two, the woman *was* Mata Hari and Mata Hari was also Clara Benedix; or three, his information was wrong.

Needless to say the third alternative was *not* the one Thomson accepted, especially when records produced a further complication. Whether or not Mata Hari was Clara Benedix, Thomson was presented with a Yard file concerning a suspected spy named Mata Hari. The problem for Thomson now became even more complex. Mata Hari stated that the French had asked her to spy for them and she described Georges Ladoux, the head of the French counter-espionage service, so well that Thomson was convinced beyond question that she had certainly met him. Was Mata Hari simply a naïve woman caught up in a game which she barely understood (as Thomson was now possibly beginning to suspect); was she a calculating and clever German spy; was she a French agent; a German double-agent; or a French double-agent?

Next, Thomson received three messages. From Spain he was told that Clara Benedix had not left the country; Ladoux cabled from France to say that he had never heard of Mata Hari; and the Dutch replied that Mata Hari was a bona fide Dutch citizen. What was Thomson supposed to do? He took the most expedient route and sent Mata Hari back to France where she could be Ladoux's problem. This was Scotland Yard's only dealing with a lady who has remained one of the most controversial figures in espionage history. Many stories came to be told about Mata Hari, the 'sinister Salome'. She is supposed to have been responsible for the death of 50,000 French soldiers, the death of Lord Kitchener, for mutinies in the French army, and for the success of Ludendorff's submarine campaign against Allied shipping. There were even stories that she had not died at all. One tale claimed that, as the firing squad were about to fire, she swept apart her fur coat to reveal herself completely naked and the sight of her beautiful body caused the soldiers to miss their target!

Less exciting was a wartime murder investigated by Frederick Wensley. On 2 November 1917 a roadsweeper in Regent Square, Bloomsbury, found a bundle done up in a meat sack marked 'La Plata Cold Storage'. It contained the torso and arms of a woman wrapped in a sheet. The legs were later found in another parcel. With the remains was a piece of paper bearing the words: 'BLODIE BELGIAM'. A laundry mark found on the sheet helped to identify the torso. It was that of a Frenchwoman named Emilienne Gerard who had been missing for a month. A search of her room resulted in the discovery of an IOU for £50 signed by Louis Voison.

Chief Inspector Wensley asked Voison to write the words 'BLOODY BELGIUM' five times. On each occasion Voison spelt it 'BLODIE BELGIAM'. Many traces of blood were found in the house. In Voison's cellar the head and hands of Emilienne Gerard were found. Voison and the woman with whom he was living, Bertha Roche, were charged with murder. Bernard Spilsbury, the pathologist, was able to produce evidence which suggested that Emilienne Gerard had been struck several times with a poker, probably by Bertha Roche, but that these had not been fatal. Death had been caused by strangulation, the work of Voison.

Voison was convicted and hanged at Pentonville on 2 March 1918. Roche, charged with being an accessory after the fact and sentenced to seven years penal servitude, became insane and died just over a year later on 22 May 1919. The interest in this case centres on the fact that one of the grounds on which Voison lodged an appeal was that Wensley had tricked him into writing 'Blodie Belgiam' and that it was therefore inadmissible as evidence. The judge took the view that 'the mere fact that a statement was made in answer to a question put by a police officer was not in itself sufficient to make it inadmissible in law'. He went on to say that as the statement was made voluntarily it was admissible.

The post-war years saw a development of political and industrial struggles. In 1918 there were 1,252 strikes with a loss of 6 million working days. 1919 saw more than 1,400 strikes involving 2.5 million workers and the loss of 34 million working days. People continued to believe that Russian money was financing these industrial disputes, although Basil Thomson repeatedly reported to the Home Office that his men could find no evidence for this. The decision was nevertheless made to sever the Special Branch from the CID. Thomson was appointed head of the new 'Branch' and was given or adopted for himself the grand title of 'Director of Intelligence'. His task, as George Dilnot succinctly put it in his book *Scotland Yard*, was to 'save England from "Red" machinations'. Thomson remained in this position from May 1919 – when the Special Branch was returned to the CID, albeit largely independent and still acting as the police wing and public face of MI5.

Although some would say that little has changed today, in 1919 policemen were grossly overworked, seriously underpaid, pensions were insufficient and the Victorian caste system ensured that good men did not achieve senior rank (the much mentioned Frederick Wensley was the first to do so). It was not surprising then that when police pensions again became an issue the Government adopted a cheapskate attitude. All of this meant that, in 1919, the unthinkable became a reality and many policemen went on strike.

187

Inspector John Syme had been involved in a minor disciplinary breach. Treated with soaring ineptitude by his superiors, he reacted strongly and was dismissed. Syme was probably suffering from some sort of persecution mania – he was eventually certified insane and committed to Broadmoor psychiatric hospital where he died – but his sense of grievance on this occasion was largely vindicated by an inquiry which awarded him a modest sum in compensation. The inherent legitimacy of his claims combined with the mental problems which may have contributed to the determination with which he waged a long and heated campaign against the Commissioner meant that he won support from militants within the police, including some members of the CID. The agitation brought about dramatic changes, including the creation in 1912 of the National Union of Police and Prison Officers – and also ultimately the resignation of Commissioner Henry.

Chapter Thirteen

THE FLYING SQUAD

The internal organisation of the Metropolitan Police did not always work in favour of catching criminals. One of the problems was that Divisional detectives could not easily operate outside their Division. Divisional Superintendents and Detective Inspectors were often unwilling and resentful of men from other Divisions 'poaching' on their territory. There was also the more serious question of which Divisional Superintendent should give the orders. This problem was overcome to a certain extent by appointing a detective from Scotland Yard to supervise any major investigation in a Division. This had happened, for example, when Inspector Abberline was sent from Scotland Yard to oversee the Ripper investigation in H and J Divisions, or when Chief Inspector Fox and a small team of men from the Yard were able to move across Divisions when assigned to investigate coin counterfeiting.

In 1916 Frederick Wensley first mooted to Basil Thomson two proposals which eventually became headline-grabbing realities. The first was intended to overcome the inter-divisional rivalry. Wensley suggested that the Metropolitan Police District should be divided among a group of senior officers, each coordinating the activities of the divisions under his jurisdiction and liaising closely with each other. The second suggestion concerned the creation of a mobile, roving body of detectives who could be assigned either to the investigation of a particular widespread crime or sent into a division which was experiencing an epidemic of criminal activity.

The war and Thomson's preoccupation with the Special Branch caused the suggestions to be forgotten but in 1919 Wensley and Chief Inspector Francis Carlin presented the scheme to the new commissioner, Nevil Macready, who liked the idea and authorised the appointment of four area superintendents. The Press nicknamed them the 'Big Four' and the police themselves used the nickname in a propaganda film which portrayed them sitting around a table in earnest discussion. The original 'Big Four' were Wensley, Albert Hawkins, Arthur Neil and Francis Carlin.

Another feature of the post-war years was the change in criminal activity. One of the most dangerous after-effects of war is the cheapening of the fighting man's attitude towards life, both his own and others. Ex-soldiers also have the ability to use guns, which in post-war years are easier to obtain. One man who earned considerable notoriety in his day as a killer was Francis Percy Toplis. He did not directly involve the CID, other than that they along with everyone else were keeping an eye open for him during what was then one of the most sensational man-hunts that Britain had ever known. Yet Toplis represented the type of man the police now had to deal with. Little seems to be known about Toplis himself. We understand that the account given here is accurate.

Toplis, a deserter from the army, was thirty-four years old, rather good looking with a small moustache and fair hair, and he sometimes wore a monocle to give the impression of being a respectable gentleman. In fact, he had been imprisoned many times. On 25 April 1920, the body of a chauffeur named Sidney Edward Spicer was found hidden in some undergrowth at Thruxton Down, near Andover. He had been shot in the head. The police learned that a man fitting Toplis's description had engaged Spicer to drive him to Andover. From there, he had then gone on to Bulford Army Camp in Spicer's car, picked up a soldier named Fallows and together they had driven to Swansea. There, on 26 April, Toplis had bought a newspaper and read about the discovery of Spicer's body.

Toplis made his excuses to Fallows, who returned to Bulford by train, and then got rid of the car in a lane where it was found a couple of hours later by the Swansea police. Toplis remained at liberty for five weeks. It was now, in Banffshire, that he encountered Constable Greig of the Banffshire Police, a gamekeeper named John Mackenzie, and a farmer named John Grant. Toplis shot the policeman in the left lung and Grant was shot in the back. 'Cheerio! Goodbye!,' shouted Toplis, as he took a bicycle belonging to one of the three men and pedalled off. Next, on 6 June, Toplis, dressed in a Royal Air Force uniform, was confronted by Constable Fulton of the Cumberland constabulary.

'Where are you making for?' asked Fulton, suspicious.

Toplis told the policeman he was on duty, had been on leave and was a few days late getting back to camp. He knew this was technically desertion, but he was heading back to barracks. Fulton, less than satisfied, asked to see inside Toplis's kit-bag. Toplis threw the bag to the ground, took a few steps back and looked dangerous. Fulton was now certain that the airman was Toplis. He therefore employed a clever ruse. With a smile, he said, 'Why, you might be the likes of Toplis. Go on, get on with your journey.'

Toplis mounted his cycle and pedalled off. Fulton issued various warnings to local police stations and was with Inspector Ritchie and Sergeant Bertram when later that day they caught Toplis, who fired several shots at them but was eventually shot and killed by the police. He had remained at liberty for seven weeks and had gone from one end of the country to the other, travelling mostly by car.

The increase in mass-produced motor vehicles at the end of World War One not only gave criminals greater and more secure mobility than ever before, but it also resulted in a new type of crime. The Press dubbed it 'smash and grab' – raids in which the thieves would smash the window of a jeweller's shop, grab what they could, and make their escape in a car. The police didn't have any cars and had to give chase on foot. Needless to say, without any measurable success. The car was also in part responsible for the proliferation during the 1920s of racecourse gangs who forced bookmakers to pay protection money, attacked, robbed and terrorised racegoers, and sometimes engaged in inter-gang fights with razors and other weapons.

These developments created a new challenge for the CID and after several meetings the 'Big Four' decided to form a new mobile, motorised section. In the early summer of 1920 the Metropolitan Police purchased two ex-RAF Crossley tenders (vans), to patrol both the north and south sides of the Thames. The small squad was headed by Walter Hambrook, who was responsible for its organisation and direction and who also had charge of one of the 'cars' as they were known. The other vehicle was in the care of Inspector C. Cooper. The squad further consisted of two inspectors, four sergeants, eight detective constables, and two drivers. It became known as the Flying Squad, or in rhyming slang as the Sweeney (=Sweeney Todd, Flying Squad). According to Walter Hambrook, the first head of the squad, the name 'Flying Squad' was coined by a journalist, G. T. Crook, and was so named not so much because they were mobile but because their first vehicles had formerly been used by the Royal Flying Corps. The number of vehicles was gradually increased, wireless was fitted in 1922 and the vans were replaced by Lee-Francis cars.

Originally under the direct charge of the district superintendents (the 'Big Four') the Flying Squad was reorganised in 1920 and became part of the CID. In the same year a *Police Order* was published:

> In the event of an officer receiving information or seeing anything that leads him to believe that persons with a motor car or other vehicle have committed or are suspected to be committing crimes and have decamped, he should at once communicate the available information to C.1. giving the nature of the crime or suspected crime, description of persons and car and direction in which they are proceeding ... It will be appreciated that the object of the information so sent to C.1. is to have the officers patrolling in motor cars warned by wireless.

1922 saw several murders make the headlines and in some cases have a lasting influence.

The Spencer Hotel (today called the Mostyn) in Portman Street was a hotel for the 'right people'. Among the 'right people' who stayed there was Lady White. During the night of 14 March 1922, the eighteen-year-old pantry boy, Henry Julius Jacoby, took a hammer and smashed Lady White's head. Jacoby did not take anything. He just cleaned the hammer, returned it to the workman's toolbag from which he had taken it, and went to bed.

Investigation of the crime was assigned to George Cornish. There were no clues and the crime would probably have remained unsolved had Jacoby not drawn suspicion on to himself by volubly and aggressively advancing various theories concerning the murder.

Chief Superintendent Neil of the 'Big Four' and Cornish searched Jacoby's things and found two bloodstained handkerchiefs. Confronted with these things, Jacoby confessed.

The jury found Jacoby guilty but strongly recommended mercy on account of his youth. In itself this illustrates how society had changed since, a century earlier, nine-year-old arsonists were hanged. The judge agreed and assured the jury that he would endorse such a recommendation to the Home Secretary. The Home Secretary did not carry out the recommendation and Jacoby was hanged at Pentonville Prison on 5 June 1922.

The Jacoby case aroused special interest because it coincided with the trial of Ronald True, who was upper-class and murdered a prostitute. True was declared insane and sent to Broadmoor. To many, the contrast between his fate and Jacoby's smacked of one law for rich men who murder the poor and another for poor men whose victims are rich.

True had served in the Royal Flying Corps in 1914 but was invalided out after a serious crash. He began talking about another 'self' who was impersonating him and forging his cheques. He also began to tell lies like claiming to be a fighter ace and to having achieved military ranks far higher than he had actually achieved. Then, in March 1922, he murdered twenty-five-year-old Gertrude Yates (also known as Olive Young).

Although arrested, tried, convicted and sentenced to death, True was granted a reprieve by the Home Secretary on the grounds of his obvious insanity.

He was committed to Broadmoor and died there aged sixty in 1951.

Although True's reprieve looked odd at the time, he was unquestionably insane. The real controversy was (and is) whether Jacoby was unquestionably sane. Even George Cornish, who arrested Jacoby, voiced doubts, saying that Jacoby's behaviour when under arrest was distinctly odd. But the controversy which developed around the cases of Jacoby and True are otherwise significant because they show that people were beginning to look carefully and critically at the judiciary and were more inclined to question the judgements of those in authority. However, it should not be imagined that people were altogether more tolerant. Offending the moral standards of the day, if associated with a crime, could still lead you to the gallows, as Edith Thompson discovered.

It was a dismal October day in 1922 when Wensley left Scotland Yard at the request of Detective Inspector Francis Hall of K Division to assist in what appeared to be the murder of Percy Ernest Thompson. Wensley would not normally have been directly involved, K Division being Arthur Neil's patch, but Neil was on leave. At the police station Wensley questioned the victim's wife, Edith Thompson. 'She could scarcely have been called a pretty woman, but she had a distinctly attractive personality. She carried herself well, was dressed tastefully,' wrote Wensley in his memoirs, adding that she 'spoke with an air of culture. In moments of animation she must have been a woman of considerable fascination.'

According to Edith Thomson, she had been with her husband to see a play at the Criterion Theatre. They caught the train home to Ilford and were walking to their house at Kensington Gardens when someone leapt from the shadows and attacked Percy Thompson and, it was learned a little later, stabbed him. No suggestion was made that Edith knew the assailant and although the police found it 'difficult to conceive why any person should kill another without any motive', Wensley acknowledged that in the post-war years there were 'a few cases of people doing extraordinarily motiveless things'. After further questioning of relatives, Wensley learned that Edith Thompson had very likely (and as it turned out had indeed) had an affair with a younger man named Frederick Bywaters. Wensley's suspicious nose started to twitch and he went so far as to call in the Flying

Squad to check out every place known to be frequented by the man.

That evening Bywaters was arrested and sometime later Inspector Frank Page of the Squad brought Wensley a packet of letters found in Bywaters's bedroom and which Edith Thompson had written to him. As Wensley later observed: '. . . as I read them I could not fail to remark a sinister under-current in some passages'. Such as: '. . . be jealous, so much so that you will do something desperate . . .' The following day, Edith Thompson caught a glimpse of Bywaters and for the first time learned that he was also in custody. According to Wensley: 'In an instant her nerve had deserted her. "Oh, God! Oh, God, what can I do?" she moaned. "Why did he do it? I did not want him to do it . . . I must tell the truth."' Edith Thompson poured out her story. She had recognised Bywaters as her husband's murderer. When told that both he and Edith Thompson would be charged with murder, Bywaters said: 'Why her? Mrs Thompson was not aware of my movements.'

The police later uncovered further letters from her to Bywaters and these contained passages which strongly suggested that the couple had planned to murder Percy Thompson and that Edith had tried to poison him (although no trace of poison was found in Thompson's exhumed body) and put broken glass in his food. The case against Bywaters was a simple one. He admitted his guilt, though he seems to have viewed Thompson's death not as murder but as an execution for the 'crime' of treating Edith disrespectfully. The case against Edith was different. Curtis Bennett, Edith's counsel, later tried to convince the jury that Edith lived in a world of romantic make-believe, that many of the references suggestive of murder in fact referred to a suicide pact made with Bywaters, and that those that did mention murder were fantasy.

The question was, however, whether Edith had knowingly encouraged Bywaters to murder Percy Thompson and whether she knew that he planned to do so that night. The jury believed that she had, and brought in a verdict of guilty against both of them. Bywaters continued to maintain Edith's ignorance of his intentions and, from the dock Edith Thompson cried, 'Oh, God, I am not guilty!'

On 9 January 1923, Bywaters was hanged at Pentonville Prison and Edith Thompson at Holloway. The trial cannot be said to have been perfect by any means. The use of the letters was questionable, the joint trial was prejudicial to both parties, and the judge delivered a grossly misleading summing up which has since been interpreted as ensuring that Thompson was hanged for adultery as much as for complicity to murder. 'They hanged her,' said Curtis Bennett, 'for her immorality.' Edith Thompson's last days were an anguish of despair but accounts differ. Some say that she was dragged hysterical and screaming to the noose, others, including John Ellis the hangman, said that he thought her doped as she was carried by two prison officers to the trap. The chaplain who witnessed her end had a nervous breakdown and resigned. Other prison officials did the same. At Pentonville, Frederick Bywaters told Governor Blake that Edith Thompson was completely innocent. Blake believed him and he expressed this opinion in his reminiscences published in the *London Evening News* in 1926. He was promptly charged with an offence under the Official Secrets Act.

In the meantime, in 1923 Johann Schober, President of Police in Vienna, with the support of the Austrian government, hosted the Second Congress of Criminal Police. At this meeting, the statutes of the International Criminal Police Commission were established and Vienna became its headquarters. Following the Second World War, the headquarters moved to Paris and the name was changed to the International Criminal Police Organisation. The ICPO – Interpol – is not an international police force, but an organisation for the collection and dissemination of information about international criminals. Investigations are undertaken by the police of each member country and conducted according to the laws of that country. The British headquarters are based at Scotland Yard and form part of the CID, its officers being directly responsible to the Detective Chief Superintendent of Central Office. As with the Flying Squad, the creation of Interpol in 1923 reflected the growing sophistication of the police force and its readiness to adapt to changing social conditions and criminal behaviour.

But the 1920s were still dominated by headline-making murder cases. Some were solved by accident. Some were discovered by accident. Mrs Mahon, for example, knew that her husband was a philanderer, so when he began regularly to stay away from home at weekends her suspicions were aroused and she searched his clothes. She found a ticket for the cloak-room at Waterloo Station and, uncertain about what to do with this discovery, she consulted a friend, a former divisional detective inspector named John Beard.

Beard went with Mrs Mahon to the railway station and in proffering the ticket he received a bag which proved to contain a large knife and some bloodstained silk. Beard told Mrs Mahon to go home and put the ticket back where she had found it. He then telephoned 'Savage of Scotland Yard'. Percy Savage was almost born a policeman. His father Frederick Savage had been with the Metropolitan Police and Percy Savage had, in fact, been born in a room above the cells at Acton police station in 1878. It was almost inevitable that he would also join the Force, which he did in January 1900. Eventually, he was to become

198

Superintendent of the CID at Scotland Yard and would become one of the 'Big Four'.

When Mahon went to collect his bag from the railway cloak-room, the police were waiting for him and he was taken to Kennington Road Police Station, where Chief Inspector Savage was waiting for him.

'Chief Inspector Savage? I've heard about you,' greeted Mahon.

Savage already knew that the blood on the items in the bag was human, so he was able to refute Mahon's original claim that the blood was from dog meat.

'You seem to know all about it,' said Mahon.

'It's not for me to tell you what I know,' replied Savage, who knew nothing about Mahon's affairs, in either definition of the word.

Several hours passed, the silence only broken by the ticking of a clock. Mahon was deep in thought, considering his position. Then he stood up. 'I suppose you know everything. I will tell you the truth.'

He claimed to have begun an affair with a woman named Emily Kaye. They had argued, she had fallen and struck her head. He had panicked, bought a knife and a saw and dismembered her body. It was a boringly unoriginal story told many times by many murderers. Patrick Mahon had been charged many times for crimes such as fraud, embezzlement and robbery with violence. He had been helping himself to Emily Kaye's savings and decided to kill her. He bought a knife and a saw, killed Emily and dismembered her body. This at least was the conclusion of the court in what was described as 'the most cruel, repulsive and carefully planned murder'. He was sentenced to death and hanged at Wandsworth Prison on 2 September 1924.

The importance of this case resulted from the horror with which the pathologist observed Savage handling putrid flesh at the scene of the murder with his bare hands. Savage replied that he had no alternative, not having been provided with rubber gloves, or for that matter any equipment with which to pick up and preserve clues such as hair, soil, dust and so on. This resulted in the introduction of what became known as the 'murder bag'.

A small breath of scandal broke the catalogue of distressing murders when, on 12 December 1925, Sir Basil Thomson, the former head of the CID, was arrested in Hyde Park on a charge of 'violating public decency' with a young woman named Thelma de Lava, 'described as an actress', according to *The Times*. PC Frederick Hancox noticed a man and a woman sitting together. The newspapers veiled precisely what made Hancox suspicious with vague references to Thomson's lap and 'some movement of a hand [which] attracted his attention'. Hancox and PC Lawrie went over to the couple, where PC Hancox said that they were under arrest.

Thomson pleaded not guilty, then failed to turn up in court claiming, apparently truthfully, that he had gone to the wrong court on the appointed day. This only attracted greater publicity, especially when allegations were made to the effect that Thomson had tried to use his former position to have the charges dropped. Thomson's determined defence seems in retrospect to have been a rather futile endeavour (unless, of course, he was telling the truth and was innocent), since Miss de Lava, who from her photographs was an attractive young woman, had pleaded guilty and been fined 40 shillings. It was further revealed that she had previously appeared before the court for similar offences. Yet there is an irony that this should have happened to Thomson, one who had earlier played a role in police efforts to combat moral degeneracy.

Another well-known case of this period was that of the murder of PC Gutteridge. Early on the morning of

27 September 1927, Police Constable Gutteridge, of the Essex Constabulary, was found lying dead on the roadside at Stapleford Abbots. There were two bullet holes in his left cheek, and both his eyes had been shot out. His notebook was on the ground and his pencil was still clutched in his right hand.

On the near side of the road were motor car tyre marks close to the bank, and a trail of blood as if he had staggered backwards after being shot and had fallen against the side of the road.

Chief Inspector Berrett was deputed to take charge of the inquiry. Later that morning a stolen car, which proved later to be the one used by the murderers, was found in Brixton. Among the suspects was Frederick Guy Browne, who was known to carry firearms and had previously threatened to kill rather than be arrested again. Many weeks of searching for Browne proved fruitless.

As so often happens with crime, detection involves a high proportion of luck and patience. In this case, Browne had a car accident in Sheffield. A summons was taken out against him and this was sent to London to be served at the address given on the driving licence. With Browne at the time of the accident was an ex-convict who was able to provide the police with information about him including the fact that Browne was one of the men who had murdered PC Gutteridge. Browne was eventually picked up and found to possess a veritable armoury. His partner in crime, William Kennedy, was arrested in Liverpool. Brought to Scotland Yard, Kennedy claimed that Browne had shot PC Gutteridge. Kennedy's statement was not admissible evidence but in the stolen car found in Brixton was a shell which ballistics expert Robert Churchill was able to show had come from a gun found in Browne's possession when he was arrested.

Browne and Kennedy were vicious criminals prepared

to kill at the drop of a hat. They came to represent the new breed of lawlessness which marked the years following World War One, and would likewise mark the years following World War Two. They were tried and convicted, and executed by Robert Baxter and Thomas Pierrepoint at Pentonville and Wandsworth respectively. The executioner, Thomas Pierrepoint, was the elder brother of Henry Pierrepoint and uncle of Albert Pierrepoint, who together made something of a dynasty of hangmen. Albert has perhaps become the best known, bar earlier ones such as Jack Ketch and Calcraft. Thomas is often credited with having hanged Frederick Bywaters, but this was not the case. He remained on the Home Office list of hangmen for over forty years, one of the longest on record, and never wrote his memoirs, unlike the other Pierrepoints. Thomas executed Jack Field, a nineteen-year-old, who with William Gray had murdered a young typist in 1921; also Albert Burrows, who murdered Hannah Calladine and her three children, sexually assaulting one of them, a four-year-old boy; the poisoner Jean Pierre Vacquier; Patrick Mahon; Dorothea Waddingham; Charlotte Bryant; and many others in a veritable criminal calendar, whose varied crimes perhaps represent the age.

Hyde Park was clearly the place to go if you wanted to be arrested for gross indecency. First was the case of former police commissioner Basil Thomson and Thelma de Lava, and next came the far more serious case of Irene Savidge and Sir Leo Chiozza Money, an aptly named writer on finance and economics. Miss Savidge had been accused of indecency in Hyde Park. The magistrate refused to accept the sworn evidence of the police and dismissed the case but the involvement of Sir Leo led to allegations that there had been a cover-up and the Director of Public Prosecutions asked the CID to investigate. Chief Inspector Collins was given charge of the case and sent a sergeant and a woman inspector to Miss Savidge's place of work to ask her to come to Scotland Yard. This she did. Later, however, she alleged improper behaviour by the male policemen with whom she had be left alone, and undue pressure being placed on her to make a statement. A Royal Commission was appointed to look into the matter and a tactfully phrased majority report exonerated the police officers concerned. The routine for taking statements from women, however, was changed. Henceforward a woman officer would always be present when a woman was being questioned.

The Savidge case caused considerable publicity, most of it anti-police, and brought to the fore again the British distrust of the Force. As a direct result, Basil Thomson's successor, Assistant Commissioner Sir Wyndham Childs and Commissioner Horwood resigned at the end of 1928. Yet the interesting postscript is that not long afterwards Sir Leo was convicted of molesting a young girl on a train.

In October 1928 Vivian Messiter, an agent for Wolf's Head Oil Company in Southampton, was reported missing. Some six weeks later Messiter's body was found behind some wooden cases at the back of a store. It was not a pretty sight since there were plenty of rats in the store. The case was handed over to Chief Inspector J. Prothero of Scotland Yard, a well-known Yard man of the time who later became Superintendent of R Division.

Messiter had an assistant called W. F. Thomas who had left for a better job. The police questioned him and discovered that he was a petty criminal named William Henry Podmore who was currently wanted for alleged fraudulent car deals by the Manchester police. Podmore was gaoled for this crime, was released, committed another theft and sent to prison again. Chief Inspector Prothero now rather belatedly realised that a small scrap of paper – the receipt for a small commission on a sale – held a clue. Inspector O'Brien of the Yard's photographic section was able to show that the receipt contained the pressure marks of something which had been written on top of it. This was a receipt for commission in respect of a firm which did not exist and led to evidence that Podmore had been systematically stealing from his employer. The thefts had been discovered by Messiter and it seemed likely that Podmore had killed him. In December 1929, some fourteen months after the murder had been committed, Podmore was charged and, in March 1930, he was executed.

The General Strike of 1926 had caused headaches all round for the police and done nothing to endear them to the public, who once again came to view the Force as a weapon of authority maintaining the *status quo*. Yet 1928 seemed in comparison to be a quiet year: it was the quiet before the storm. From one perspective the history of the CID can be seen as a leap-frogging from one disaster to another. It owed its origins to a corruption scandal and cases of corruption and alleged corruption seem to have dogged it ever since. Early in 1928, anonymous letters sent to Scotland Yard alleged that the owners of Soho nightclubs and other dubious establishments were paying bribe money to the police, principally to a Sergeant Goddard, the station sergeant at Vine Street police station, who held an excellent record. Frederick Wensley, now Chief Constable, CID, undertook the investigation of the allegations.

To go back in time a little way: a new phenomenon to appear in London following the First World War was the nightclub. By 1924, there were an estimated 200 such clubs in the West End, most owned by foreigners, although Proctors in Gerrard Street and the Silver Slipper in Regent Street were presided over by an Englishwoman, Mrs Kate Meyrick. These two were particularly expensive and often disreputable places which were frequented by prostitutes, gamblers and general riff-raff (from the point of view of acceptable society). They were home to every vice, including drugs, and large sums of money was often paid for cocaine. Girls, notably Billie Carlton and Freda Kempton – who regularly visited another of Mrs Meyrick's establishments, the 43 Club – became addicts and killed themselves.

Billie Carlton, a young actress, was introduced to cocaine by Brilliant Chang, a Chinaman whose real name was Chan Nan and who owned a Chinese restaurant in Regent Street. She was found dead in a den in Limehouse from an overdose and Freda Kempton, who was a young dancing teacher, committed suicide from an overdose of cocaine. Chang was intelligent and clever but also ruthless. He imported cocaine in bulk and had a well-organised distribution network. His main targets were young women. Eventually, in 1924, the police were able to raid Chang's premises in Limehouse Causeway and found a large quantity of cocaine. Chang received an eighteen-month prison sentence (which hardly seems sufficient in the light of the suffering he wantonly caused) and was deported.

Drug trafficking at this time was in the hands of several gangs who were encouraged by the enormous profits and, if caught, by the petty sentences. The CID had difficulty in breaking up the racket but succeeded in doing so under the direction of Detective Inspector Burmby who, prior to the war, had investigated white slaving. The last of the major gangs was the Appleson gang, broken up when it was infiltrated by a detective named Lount who managed to acquire sufficient evidence to have Appleson arrested. Cocaine was a particular menace but opium was also widely available. One dealer alone had £9,000 worth of the drug in his possession. The Government had passed a Dangerous Drugs Act in 1920 and in 1923 alone there were no fewer than 295 prosecutions.

Wensley pursued his investigations of Sergeant Goddard whose £2,000 house and expensive Chrysler motor car had hitherto gone unnoticed, though doubtless unaffordable on Goddard's £6 a week pay. The further discovery that he had £12,000 salted away in various safe deposit boxes shed increasing doubts on Goddard's claim to have made some fortunate investments in business enterprises and at the race track. To cut the story short, Goddard was indeed on the take and together with Mrs Meyrick and another club owner named Luigi Ribuffi, who were on the give, he was tried and sentenced to prison.

The case proved to have an additional complication, however, and it is one which can still exist. When a senior policeman goes bent he is protected by his colleagues' instinctive unwillingness to believe it, and the power he holds over subordinates whom he can subvert. In this case an important witness against Goddard was a detective constable, John Wilkins, who had been under Goddard's wing and also on the take. He had testified on promise of not being punished and obviously could not afterwards be allowed to remain in the Force. He was therefore dismissed but kept his pension rights, a solution which caused questions to be asked in Parliament. However, the point is that, within the Force itself, it was very difficult for anyone to 'inform' on a rotten copper.

The years 1900–14 could be described as stable since the level of crime was more or less constant. Yet, from 1915–30, a period of social upheavals and unrest marked by the General Strike and the beginnings of the Depression, crime increased by about five per cent annually. During the General Strike, the police came to be perceived as the tools of the Establishment instead of the servants of the public. Thus, the 1920s was a difficult decade for the CID.

It is also possible to discern changes in the types of crime, although it is likely that these are partly a reflection of changing social conditions and growing social awareness. The breakdown of the rather rigid social structure of the Victorian period followed by changes forced by the First World War produced a dominant middle class and a youth which tried to break down social conventions. The Twenties saw the introduction of nightclubs, the growth of drug abuse and the beginnings of organised crime. The decade also witnessed an increase in frauds, smash and grab raids and murders. Crime overall became the subject of general interest, largely because the great 'theatrical' barristers such as Marshall Hall turned murder trials into life or death dramas – but the public, who had had some faith in the judiciary, had this shaken by the executions of Jacoby and Edith Thompson.

There were also technological advances which the police had adopted: fingerprinting, photography, motorisation, telegraph and radio, and the scientific expertise of men like Robert Churchill to advise on ballistics and Bernard Spilsbury on forensics. Yet the police, unlike the criminal, had been slow to adopt these advances and, when adopted, slow to learn them.

Chapter Fourteen

THE THIRTIES

All things considered, the prospect for the Thirties was pretty bleak and was made bleaker still by the resignation in 1928 of Metropolitan Police Commissioner, General Sir William Horwood. It cannot be said that there was a cloud of dust in the wake of applicants rushing to get behind Horwood's desk. Quite the contrary. The commissionership was, and continues to be, a thankless job which tarnished the reputations of many who occupied the post. The new commissioner, Lord Byng of Vimy – 'Bungo' as he was generally called – appears to have accepted the position with marked reluctance and only on the clear understanding that he could pack his bags and be out of Scotland Yard within twenty-four hours should he tender his resignation.

Although Byng's appointment was warmly received there was probably a degree of truth in the observation of the *Evening Standard* that it bore 'every mark of having been decided in panic'. The newspaper went on to wonder why the Force itself could not produce a man from its own ranks able to fill the commissionership. It was a valid point. Byng was sixty-five years old and in poor health. He was stolid and stable, yet at the same time alive to technological change, although he hated the telephone and only allowed one to remain in his office on the strict understanding that no calls should be put through. When by accident one day the phone did ring he called his secretary, Miss Drysdale, and complained: 'Drysie, it's gone off. I knew it would.'

Byng was likeable and he won rather than demanded respect. He also had a sense of humour (when Howgrave-Graham – who was Secretary of the Metropolitan Police from 1927–46 – introduced himself as Secretary of Scotland Yard, Byng replied, 'Oh, are you? Why?'). He was also able to delegate, a strength which could be dangerous when a close eye is not kept on those to whom one has delegated. In Byng's case, the delegation of responsibility to others reduced him to the position of little more than a figurehead, the public face of policy decisions. Yet he succeeded in infecting the Force with his own high standard of conduct and it is a measure of the man that he held the Force together through a critical period, and in three short years managed to restore public confidence. He retired on 9 September 1931. His successor, Lord Trenchard, was not so much a new broom as a tornado. Nobody – except possibly Sir Robert Mark and in certain respects Sir Charles Warren – can equal the controversy of Trenchard's commissionership. He was an autocrat. He was intolerant. He was detested by some and loved by others. In a word he was unique.

He isolated three broad categories for reform: (1) poor discipline and conditions, (2) antiquated or non-existent aids to detection, (3) corruption of one sort or another; and he set about a thorough reorganisation. He had an enormous effect on the uniformed police, who are not within the scope of this book, but negligible influence on the CID, which is odd. The CID was in desperate need of reform. There was extensive corruption within its ranks and Trenchard knew about it and wrote about it, yet he did nothing about it. Why is a mystery.

It should be observed that corruption has many faces. It can be great or small and may not even be recognised as corruption even by those involved. It is also pertinent to note

36. Sir Edward Henry, the Commissioner credited with the setting up of the Central Finger Print Bureau and the Criminal Record Office

37. Chief Inspector Charles Stockley Collins, one of the founder officers of the Finger Print Department

38. Two extraordinary studio poses showing detectives 'in disguise' and in their 'Sunday best'

39. The Tottenham Outrage (23 January 1909): in the centre is P.C. Tyler who was killed, around him the other officers who gave chase

40. Wanted poster for Dr Crippen
and Ethel Le Neve, 1910

41. Detectives digging up Crippen's garden

42. The Seddons in the dock at the Old Bailey, March 1912

43. The 'Big Four': (*left to right*) A. V. Hawkins, F. P. Wensley, F. Carlin, A. Neil

44. A Crossley Tender, the first vehicle used by the Flying Squad. This one carries an aerial for telegraphic transmitting (1927)

45. Superintendent George Cornish

46. Percy Savage

47. Police murderers Frederick Browne (*above*) and William Kennedy

48. Viscount Byng, telephone-hating Commissioner

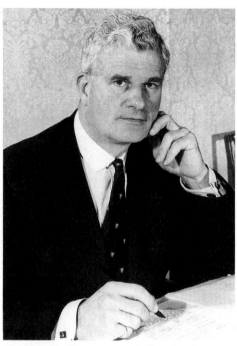

49. John Gosling of the Ghost Squad

50. Joseph Simpson, appointed Commissioner in September 1958

51. Sir Robert Mark, who took office as Commissioner in April 1972

52. Soho pornographer James Humphreys at Heathrow, 9 January 1974, following his extradition from Holland (Press Assoc.)

53. Sir Robert Mark confers with policemen during the Balcombe Street Siege, 8 December 1975 (Press Assoc.)

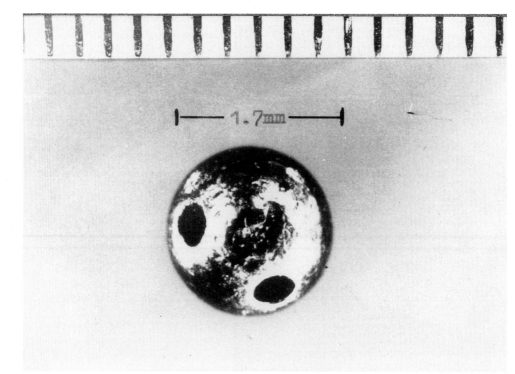

54. Close-up of the iridium pellet found in the thigh of 'poison umbrella' victim Georgi Markov, September 1978 (Press Assoc.)

55. The end of the Iranian Embassy Siege, 5 May 1980; S.A.S. officers storm the building as armed police stand by (Press Assoc.)

56. Ronnie (*below*) and Reggie (*left*) Kray on a rare trip outside prison, at their mother's funeral, 11 August 1982 (Press Assoc.)

57. Sir Kenneth Newman became Commissioner on 2 October 1982

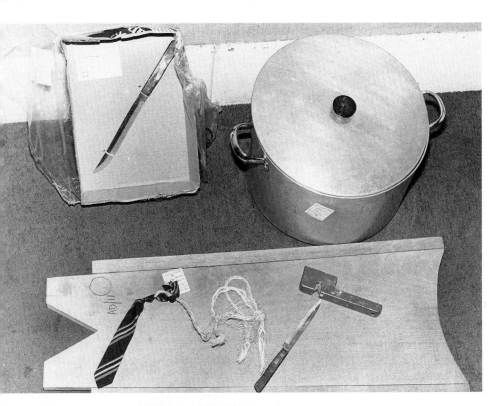

58. Some of the exhibits on display at Dennis Nilsen's trial for murder. Nilsen was sentenced to a minimum of twenty-five years' imprisonment on 4 November 1983 (Press Assoc.)

59. The remnants of the Austin 1100 used in the Harrods car-bomb outrage, 18 December 1983 (Press Assoc.)

60. The three sites of Scotland Yard: the first Scotland Yard (*above*); looking out from Norman Shaw's New Scotland Yard (*below left*); New Scotland Yard in the early 1980's (*below right*)

that between 1919 and 1939 the Metropolitan policeman did not receive a single increase in his basic rate of pay; in fact, pay had effectively been reduced *three* times. Staff welfare arrangements were poor, and conditions were, in Trenchard's own words, appalling. Hardly surprising, then, that some policemen succumbed to temptation.

This is in no way intended to excuse – and certainly not to condone – corruption. A bent policeman is worse than a criminal and deserves the toughest punishment that the law can deliver. Arguably the police service should take steps seriously to reform the procedure for investigating complaints against the police (although there are serious difficulties inherent in this), but it is as well to appreciate that temptation is not always resistible.

The CID, therefore, was desperately in need of reform yet, while Trenchard reformed the Metropolitan Police on almost every level, he hardly touched the CID. After four years he resigned. It is typical of the police that following a reformer comes an anonymous face. Trenchard was replaced by Sir Philip Game. Throughout this period, 1938–45, the Assistant Commissioner, CID, was Norman Kendal, formerly the first Deputy Assistant Commissioner (1918–28). According to Chief Superintendent Greeno, Kendall was 'lean and scholarly, full of school-masterish phrases and scoutmasterish expressions'.

A cause for concern at this time was public order, and specifically the activities of Sir Oswald Mosley's British Union of Fascists, the Communists, and the reappearance of the IRA which in the early months of 1939 was responsible for seventeen bombing incidents in the West End and at main railway terminals. As if Scotland Yard had not got enough serious problems, Adolf Hitler added more. On 19 June 1940 the first bomb fell on the Metropolitan Police district. The Special Branch was kept busy rounding up 'enemy aliens', Fascists and German agents in Britain.

Fortunately there wasn't a William Le Queux around at this time and, if anything, the attitude towards spies of the Security Service and Special Branch was complacent.

One minor point of diversionary interest however is that Guy Liddell was promoted to B Division of MI5, the counter-espionage division. Liddell was a former Special Branch officer who was later claimed by some to have been the 'Fifth Man' in the Philby, Burgess, Maclean and Blunt spy gang. The Branch also continued its usual bodyguarding activities. Neville Chamberlain's bodyguard was Detective Sergeant Arthur Lobb, who had the dubious distinction of meeting Hitler at Berchtesgaden in 1938; Churchill's bodyguard was C. R. Thompson.

Although the number of murders committed during the war remained fairly static, the number of crimes reported in England and Wales rose by nearly 60% between 1939 and 1945. Violent crime showed a marked increase, as did theft, though the latter, perhaps both, was partly explained by black marketeering. The police, understaffed during the war, were consequently stretched to and sometimes beyond their limit.

In one week in February 1942 there occurred the murder and mutilation of four women: Evelyn Margaret Hamilton, Evelyn Oatley, Margaret Lowe and Doris Jouannet. It was obvious that there was, as the pathologist Bernard Spilsbury put it, 'a madman on parade'. The crude mutilations of his victims resulted in comparisons being made with Jack the Ripper. The case was assigned to Chief Inspector Edward Greeno, who would end his career as Chief Superintendent, CID, but like so many before him, had begun it pounding the streets of Jack the Ripper's stamping ground. The 'Wartime Ripper' was a twenty-eight-year-old airman named Gordon Frederick Cummins, handsome, married and known as 'The Count' to his fellow airmen because he claimed to be the illegitimate son of a peer. He was caught when he left his service respirator at the scene of one of his attacks on a woman. A mass of evidence against him was accumulated by Greeno and Frederick Cherrill, premier head of the Fingerprint Branch, who matched Cummins's fingerprints to a set found at one of the murder scenes. Cummins was sentenced to death and was hanged on 25 June 1942.

On 27 March 1945, the 1,050th and last rocket to land in England fell at Orpington in Kent – and on 5 May 1945 Germany surrendered. Between 1939 and 1945, 207 policemen and 1 policewoman had been killed in air raids and 491 policemen had died in the armed forces. In August, the United States dropped atomic bombs on Hiroshima and Nagasaki and the world would never be the same again.

Chapter Fifteen

POSTWAR BLUES

In June 1945 Harold Scott became Commissioner. Scott lacked both imagination and powers of leadership and is described by David Ascoli in *The Queen's Peace* as an 'administrative robot'. A civil servant, his chairmanship of the prison commissioners and position as Permanent Secretary at the Ministry of Aircraft Production was a career background which hardly seems recommendation for the position of Commissioner during the difficult postwar years. Home Secretary Herbert Morrison's reasons for appointing him are neither known nor easily discernible.

The post-war years saw a series of brutal murders, including those by Heath, Haigh, Setty and Christie, and an increase in large-scale fraud which in 1946 caused the creation of the Fraud Squad. There was also an unprecedented increase in the use of firearms by criminals and a dramatic increase in juvenile crime. Much of this crime was caused by the usual post war reaction but also by the continuation of rationing and consequently of black marketeering. Numerous small gangs set up in London and by the standards of the day they were ruthless and well organised. They hijacked lorries carrying rationed goods, forged ration coupons and undertook housebreaking on a large scale. They were a headache for the overburdened Metropolitan Police and to combat them the Yard created a new squad of undercover detectives which became known as the 'Ghost Squad'.

This squad existed from May 1945 to September 1949 and it may have been with a man named 'Squibs' Dance in mind that Chief Constable Percy Worth conceived the idea. 'Squibs' Dance was the brother of Flying Squad leader Alf Dance and according to the chief of the Ghost Squad, John Capstick, 'Squibs' worked almost permanently 'under cover', mingling with the villains and being regarded as one of their own. In January 1946, Percy Worth summoned John Capstick to his office and told him that he was to head a special undercover team which was to get out among the villains and gather information. This information was then to be handed on to local divisional officers or the Flying Squad.

'They will make the arrests,' said Worth. 'Neither you nor your men will give evidence in court. As far as the underworld is concerned, you will have no more material existence than ghosts.'

Capstick's original team, which was to undergo several changes, consisted of Detective Inspector Henry Clarke (known as 'Nobby'), the almost always trilby-hatted Sergeant John Gosling and Sergeant Matt Brinnand. Over the next couple of years the team members changed and only Gosling stayed throughout, eventually becoming its head. Although it would have disgusted Sir Robert Peel, the squad was a revolutionary idea at the time and was enormously successful. In 1946 it made 171 arrests. In 1947 it made 186 arrests and solved 402 cases. In 1948, 252 criminals were arrested and 560 cases solved. And 1949 saw 180 arrests and 400 cases solved.

Towards the end of the Ghost Squad's life, Interpol was restarted in Paris and Neville George Clevely Heath was executed. Heath murdered and savagely mutilated two women, thirty-year-old film extra Margery Gardner and twenty-one-year-old Doreen Marshall. Heath did not make it difficult for suspicion to fall on him since Gardner's body was found at the Bayswater hotel where he had registered as Colonel and Mrs N.G.C. Heath. This made short work of turning up his criminal record but he had also left his fingerprints at the murder scene.

However, Heath contacted the police by letter and denied murdering Gardner, offering as an explanation a variation of the 'it wasn't me, I panicked' story. He said that he had given the hotel room key to Miss Gardner, who was expecting a male friend. On returning to the room he found the body but did not inform the police because he was wanted for fraud. There now occurred a problem, the solution to which may have caused Doreen Marshall to lose her life. The police had circulated a wanted poster containing a photograph of Heath to all police stations. It was learned that a newspaper intended publishing this photograph but while this would have alerted the public – and especially potential victims – that they were consorting with a suspected murderer, the Assistant Commissioner, Crime, Ronald Howe, urged Commissioner Scott to attempt to persuade the newspaper not to publish it. He believed that Heath's defence could have weakened the testimony of all witnesses by claiming that they did not recognise Heath from memory but from the published photograph. Scott's view was that there was 'no reason to suppose at that time that Heath would commit further murders' and the photograph was not published.

On the face of it Scott's conclusion seems extraordinary. The mutilation of Miss Gardner should have indicated that Heath was a dangerous sadistic murderer likely to kill again unless stopped. Neville Heath possessed perverted sexual tastes to which Miss Gardner may have responded and if the police were aware of this then they may have thought Miss Gardner's death an accident caused during sex play.

Heath's sadistic tendencies may not have been regarded as homicidal.

Heath was eventually arrested when he visited a police station. He was convicted but there was some question about his sanity and his defence counsel argued memorably that 'Life led by young airmen . . . may bring to the surface a defect of the mind. The human frame is not built to fly and to be shot at.' Heath's plea of insanity was unconvincing and he was executed.

In April 1947, Robert Fabian temporarily took charge of No. 1 District when Chief Superintendent Tom Barratt took his annual holiday. On 29 April, three armed men held up a jewellers in Charlotte Street but the staff foiled the robbery and the men made a hurried exit, only to find that their getaway car was blocked by a lorry. They did not hang about but fled the scene on foot. At this moment Alec de Antiquis manoeuvred his motor cycle around the parked lorry and saw the gunmen. He skidded his machine into the path of the would-be robbers, and one of them shot him in the head.

Fabian did all that was possible to assemble some clues but even the assistance of Fred Cherrill, Bernard Spilsbury, Robert Churchill and other experts was of no help. However, a taxi driver provided a lead which Fabian and his team determinedly followed up. This led to the discovery of a raincoat which had unquestionably been worn by one of Antiquis's killers. The coat was traced to a twenty-three-year-old Harry Jenkins who admitted nothing, but by his behaviour convinced Fabian that he was guilty. Further patient detective work finally established that Jenkins, twenty-one-year-old Christopher Geraghty and seventeen-year-old Terence Rolt had committed the crime, Geraghty shooting and killing Antiquis. All three were found guilty, Jenkins and Geraghty being hanged at Pentonville on 19 September 1947 and Rolt, being below the age for the death penalty, was sent to prison. According to Fabian, 'For weeks after the hanging of Jenkins and Geraghty we began to find guns . . . The men of the underworld had decided to think twice about using guns in London. So whenever I think of Antiquis these days it is as one good life lost – but also as a thousand lives saved.'

This case is significant for several reasons. It illustrates the seriousness of juvenile crime in the immediate post-war years and, as noted by Fabian, the effect of the hanging of Jenkins and Geraghty on the armed robber, many of whom evidently thought about the cost of carrying firearms and decided that it was too expensive. It is also memorable for the public outcry against the execution, rather than imprisonment, of the two thugs, amidst which the death of the brave if perhaps foolhardy Antiquis was forgotten. It was an outcry which also attached itself to the case of Craig and Bentley which, in his book *Scotland Yard*, Sir Harold Scott called 'an affray such as had not been seen in London since the Battle of Sidney Street in 1910 . . .' This is perhaps an overstatement but several books have been written about the case, or prominently feature it, and there has also been a television film documentary and even a movie about it. The general view is that there was a gross miscarriage of justice and that Derek Bentley should not have been hanged. It has even been argued that Bentley, in the argot of the underworld, was 'stitched up' by the police and condemned by a judge who derived sexual satisfaction from passing the death sentence.

Briefly, the story is as follows. At 9.25 on the night of Sunday, 2 November 1952, Croydon Police Station received a telephone call telling them that two men had been seen climbing a gate into Barlow and Parker's warehouse in Tamworth Road. About ten minutes later the police arrived at the warehouse in *two* vehicles. In a van were Detective Constable Frederick Fairfax, PCs Norman Harrison, Claude

Pain and Allan Beecher-Brigden;* and in a wireless car were PCs Leslie Miles and James McDonald. The suspected thieves, two youths, were on the flat roof of the warehouse. They were sixteen-year-old Christopher Craig and nineteen-year-old Derek Bentley.

DC Fairfax examined the ground floor doors and windows but could find no sign of forced entry. He then told Harrison, Pain and Beecher-Brigden to separate and position themselves around the warehouse. Meanwhile, PCs McDonald and Miles had learned that the two youths were on the roof. McDonald told DC Fairfax, who scaled a drainpipe to the roof and went to within six feet of Craig and Bentley saying: 'I'm a police officer. Come out from behind that stack.' Fairfax moved forward and grabbed Bentley, the nearest of the youths. Bentley then pulled away and called out: 'Let him have it, Chris!'†

There was a gunshot and Fairfax was hit in the shoulder. He managed to drag Bentley behind a roof light and rapidly searched him, finding a knife and a knuckleduster. Bentley made no attempt to resist and said, 'That is all I have got – I have not got a gun.' Fairfax told Bentley he was going

---

* Beecher-Brigden is called 'Bugden' in several sources, including Sir Harold Scott, *Scotland Yard* and David Yallop, *To Encourage the Others*.

† John Parris, Bentley's solicitor, and William Bentley, Derek Bentley's father, say that Bentley never called Craig 'Chris' but always called him 'Kid' or 'Kiddo'. David Yallop in *To Encourage the Others*, without giving his source (which must have been Craig, whom Yallop interviewed), says that Bentley called Craig 'Kid', 'Kiddo' and 'Chris' indiscriminately. Yallop is probably correct. In an interview with Yallop, Craig quoted an exchange between himself and Bentley in which he twice referred to the latter addressing him as 'Chris'. Also, nobody seems to have disputed that Bentley yelled out, 'Look out, Chris. They're taking me down.' There seems no basis for therefore supposing that Bentley could not have cried, 'Let him have it, Chris' because he did not address Craig by that name.

to work him down to a doorway to get cover from the shots. Bentley made no effort to resist as the wounded policeman used him as a shield to get under cover – which arguably saved Fairfax's life. PC James McDonald, who had also climbed a drainpipe but was unable to haul himself on to the roof, called out. Fairfax left Bentley to help McDonald. Bentley did not try to go to Craig and when joined by the two policemen he volunteered information that Craig's gun was a .45 with plenty of ammunition. 'I told the silly b – not to use it.' By this time PC Harrison had gained the roof but found himself a sitting target. Craig fired at him once, possibly twice, and Harrison crept back the way he had come and climbed down.

About fifteen minutes had now passed and more policemen had reached the scene. One of them had the key of a door to the stairway leading to the roof. Several policemen went up. The first to reach the roof was PC Sidney Miles. Christopher Craig immediately shot him dead. DC Fairfax used Bentley as a shield and manoeuvred him to the stairway. Bentley yelled, 'Look out, Chris. They're taking me down.' Fairfax reached the stairway and they began to descend. By now guns had been issued. Fairfax got one and went back to the roof. He fired several shots. Craig, out of ammunition, jumped from the roof but his apparent suicide bid failed.

Christopher Craig and Derek Bentley were tried for murder but the case against Bentley rested on a fine point of law. As we have seen several times in this book, if two or more people commit a crime, the action of one is regarded in law as the action of all. In other words, in law Derek Bentley was held to be as guilty of shooting PC Miles as if he had pulled the trigger himself. Moreover, it was believed that by allegedly shouting, 'Let him have it, Chris', Bentley incited Craig to shoot and therefore started the sequence of events which led to PC Miles's death. Bentley denied yelling these words. Craig claimed that he never heard them. At the trial the judge in the course of his summing up said that of the police testimony:

> ... if their evidence is untrue that Bentley called out, 'Let him have it, Chris', those three officers are doing their best to swear away the life of that boy. If it is true it is, of course, the most deadly piece of evidence against him. Do you believe those officers have come into the box and sworn what is deliberately untrue ...?

Derek Bentley was mentally subnormal. He made contradictory statements to the police and in the witness-box issued denials by the handful. He denied knowing that Craig was armed. He denied that Craig had shown him the gun. He denied warning Craig not to use the gun. He denied saying: 'Let him have it, Chris.' He denied telling Fairfax and McDonald that Craig had a .45 with plenty of ammunition. He denied being under arrest when the fatal shot was fired. The meaning of the words, 'Let him have it, Chris' is ambiguous – was Bentley telling Craig to shoot DC Fairfax or hand the gun over to him? Unfortunately, since Bentley denied shouting 'Let him have it, Chris,' he could not be questioned as to what he meant. In the event, Derek Bentley was convicted of murder and executed at Wandsworth Prison in January 1953. The irony is that Craig, who had actually murdered PC Miles, was too young to hang. He was imprisoned and released ten years later.

The controversy surrounding whether or not Bentley was a victim of a miscarriage of justice has raged ever since. At its simplest level, Craig and Bentley were regarded as hardened criminals who had gone to the warehouse armed (Craig with a gun and Bentley with a knife and knuckleduster) and presumably prepared to resist arrest. The fine legal question which has concerned commentators

222

on this case is whether or not Bentley had, by word or action, severed his partnership with Craig and from that point ceased to be mutually responsible for Craig's actions. There was an interval of fifteen minutes between Bentley allegedly shouting 'Let him have it, Chris' and Craig shooting PC Miles. During that time Bentley made no attempt to rejoin Craig or resist the police, he volunteered information to them and at some risk to his own safety allowed himself to be used as a shield. The inference has to be that he had ceased to condone or otherwise support Craig.

However, it seems unacceptable for Bentley to be freed of responsibility for the outcome of what he began when he allegedly shouted 'Let him have it, Chris', and incited Craig to start firing. Yet whether the words were shouted or not, Craig denied hearing them. If Craig did not hear them then he was not incited by them and Bentley cannot be held responsible for beginning the sequence of events which led to PC Miles being killed. If the charge of incitement cannot be brought against Bentley then the issues surrounding the words would seem to be irrelevant and the central question would instead be whether or not during those fifteen minutes Bentley had, by his actions, severed his partnership with Craig and abrogated his shared responsibility for Craig's actions.

We have seen undisputed police testimony concerning Bentley's behaviour during those fifteen minutes which implies a termination of his partnership with Craig. Additional information on this question is to be found in an interview given by Craig to author David Yallop who published it in his book *To Encourage the Others*:

To me one of the most terrible things that happened was Bentley turning against me. Helping the police like that. They got him to come over to me to persuade me to give myself up. Bentley walked towards me and called

223

out, 'For Christ's sake Chris, what's got into you?' I realised what he was up to and I told him to stop or he'd get it too. Bentley stopped for a moment, then he started to move towards me again, not in a straight line, but as if he was trying to work his way behind me. I told him that I knew what he was up to, and that he was trying to get behind me to get at the gun. Again he asked me, 'What's got into you, Chris?' I told him to 'get back or I'll shoot you. Get back or I'll shoot you.' For a moment I thought he was still going to come on. Then he turned and walked back to the police.'

It appears that this incident took place *after* PC Miles was shot. If Craig's story is true then Derek Bentley had clearly ceased to support Craig's actions and in fact, at considerable risk to his own life, had tried to persuade Craig to surrender to the police. To the extent that we understand the facts and the questions raised, it would seem that Derek Bentley did not incite Craig to begin firing and had demonstrably ceased to support Craig's actions. It seems possible that the court did not have all the facts because the right questions were not asked. It also seems that while the judge clearly and probably correctly directed the jury to accept the evidence of three policemen that the words 'Let him have it, Chris' were shouted by Bentley, he incorrectly inferred that these words incited Craig to shoot. That they did so was not established in court. Craig in fact denied hearing them.

We are not lawyers and therefore cannot comment on fine legal questions and points of law. It is for those who are qualified to decide whether at this late stage the Craig and Bentley case should be officially re-examined. That the case should be reopened has been the motivation behind several books. Various reasons have been put forward for this, one maintaining that PC Miles was shot by a police marksman, not by Craig, but apparently no guns had been issued to the police at the time he was killed and the police were satisfied beyond doubt that the fatal bullet did come from Craig's gun.

Perhaps the most serious allegation is that advanced by M.J. Trow in his book, *Let Him Have It, Chris*. According to Trow, PC Claude Raymond Pain, who had travelled with PC Fairfax to the warehouse, used a rickety ladder provided by a neighbour to climb to the roof of the warehouse. He alleges that he was there throughout the exchanges and alleged exchanges and denies that Bentley said, 'Let him have it, Chris.'

Trow suggests that PCs Fairfax, Harrison and McDonald invented 'evidence' to ensure that Craig and Bentley were found guilty; that PC Pain made a written statement which contradicted the Fairfax, Harrison and McDonald story and that this was suppressed; and that the Metropolitan Police are still operating a cover-up. He has also cynically suggested that when the Craig and Bentley case papers are opened to public inspection the deposition by PC Pain will be missing. Trow's enjoyably cynical view of the police force actually puts him and PC Pain in an 'every which way win' situation whatever the files are found to contain when they are opened.

In *Let Him Have It, Chris* Trow attacks the fact that the Craig and Bentley case papers are closed to public inspection and asks: 'If a case is closed (as that of Craig and Bentley is) then what can be the harm in making its entire contents open to the public? To do otherwise could imply that there is some pressing need for such files to remain dormant.'

Case papers contain documents generated at the time of, and sometimes subsequent to, an investigation. They might, for example, give the name of an informer whose life could be endangered if his identity was made public. More prosaically, the files contain suppositions, theories

225

and speculation. They sometimes contain criminal records as well as documentation about suspects and general information which could cause distress. Such information needs to be retained in the event of the case being reviewed. For these reasons case papers are kept, closed to public inspection, generally for a period of anything between 30 to 100 years. Scotland Yard is currently reviewing files and in many cases recommending earlier opening. Closure of files is provided for by law and determined by Public Record Office guidelines, not by the police, and can be frustrating not only for writers and historians but also for the police who cannot use the contents of such files to refute damaging allegations such as those levelled by PC Pain and Trow – if, of course, the files contain refutation!

There is no evidence we know of to support Pain's claim that he was on the roof at any time. As far as is known he was on the ground throughout. On the other hand, there is no obvious reason why Pain should now claim to have been on the roof if in fact he wasn't.

It is curious, however, that Trow does not mention the alleged attempt by Bentley to get Craig to surrender (as described by Craig to David Yallop). This information does not appear to have been given to the court. This may be because the police were never asked to give it, but equally because it was deliberately withheld. *Prima facie* the second possibility could be interpreted as supporting Pain/Trow's contention of a conspiracy to misrepresent what happened on the roof.

While it is possible that Pain forgot to mention it to Trow or that Trow failed to appreciate its significance, it is equally possible that Pain did not mention it because he was not on the roof and did not know about it. Equally, of course, Pain may not have mentioned it because it never happened.

The latest offering on the Craig and Bentley case is *Scapegoat* by Craig's defence counsel John Parris. It is

226

a blistering and rather conceited attack on the judiciary and the police and alleges that the trial judge in the Craig and Bentley case, Lord Goddard, derived sexual satisfaction from passing the death sentence and ejaculated when doing so. Apart from this apparently unsubstantiated allegation and numerous factual inaccuracies which considerably diminish the book, it prompted a letter to the *Observer* from Lord Shawcross in which he said:

> . . . I believe the trial of Craig and Bentley was unfair, that Goddard did prejudice the issue because of his hatred of and determination to put down crimes of violence. Bentley, although clearly guilty, as a matter of strict law ought to have been reprieved by the Home Secretary. The case represents a rigid enforcement of the law which was of no credit to British justice.

There are those who would disagree that Bentley was 'clearly guilty', but would support the view that the judiciary was at fault and that Bentley should not have been hanged.

In 1948, Timothy Evans and his wife Beryl moved into the top floor flat at 10 Rillington Place. In October their daughter Geraldine was born and in the summer of 1949 Beryl became pregnant again. Beryl was desperate for an abortion and the occupant of the ground-floor flat, John Christie, convinced her that he could perform the operation for her. In early November Timothy Evans returned to 10 Rillington Place from work. Christie greeted him with the news that the operation had gone wrong. Beryl was dead. Evans did not go to the police because he understood that Christie could be charged with murder for performing an illegal abortion. Instead he helped Christie to dispose of Beryl's body and the bloodstained bedding on which she

227

had died. He also allowed Christie to (supposedly) take baby Geraldine to be looked after by a couple in East Acton, and sold the household furniture for £40, out of which he bought himself a £19 camel coat.

Evans then left 10 Rillington Place to live with relatives in Merthyr Tydfil in Wales. Here Evans 'confessed', he told various stories, one admitting his own guilt and another implicating Christie, but Christie convinced the police of his innocence. 10 Rillington Place was searched. The body of Beryl Evans was found behind a stack of wood in the wash-house and, nearby, that of baby Geraldine was discovered, a tie around her neck. Both had been strangled. Evans was charged with both murders but was tried only for that of the baby. He was found guilty and hanged on 9 March 1950. In March 1953 the new tenant of Christie's flat discovered that what he had taken to be a wall was in fact a papered-over door leading to a kitchen alcove. In the alcove he discovered what turned out to be three bodies. The police were called and a search was made. Three more bodies were found, two buried in the garden and one, Christie's wife, beneath the floorboards.

Christie had, by this time, disappeared but the police search for him was widely publicised and on 31 March 1953 he was arrested by PC Thomas Ledger. When tried for the murder of his wife, the defence, attempting to obtain a verdict of 'Guilty but insane', showed that Christie was a multiple murderer. Some believe that to aid his case Christie admitted to murders he had not committed – 'the more the merrier', as he put it – among them that of Beryl Evans. He admitted to seven murders and implied that he might have committed others which he was unable to recall but he denied having killed the baby. He was found guilty and executed.

On 18 October 1966, following the Brabin report, Timothy John Evans was given a free posthumous pardon. The report did not absolve Evans of guilt but concluded that he had been executed for the wrong crime and that he had murdered his wife but not baby Geraldine (for which crime he had been hanged). There had been a growing campaign for an inquiry and highly influential in bringing one about was the book *Ten Rillington Place* by Ludovic Kennedy. A film of the same name was released in 1970 with John Hurt as Evans and Richard Attenborough as Christie.

Chapter Sixteen

ROCK AND ROLL

Scott resigned as commissioner in 1953. During his last two years the crime figures began to drop but in the second quarter of the 1950s they began to rise again, and rapidly. In 1955 *The Times* reported that the British people were 'fast becoming ungovernable'. Perhaps it was another reflection of the instability generated by a changing world during this period: Eisenhower succeeded as thirty-fourth president of the United States, Stalin died, the Korean War came to an end. Some people even argued, as ever they will, that television had an unsettling influence.

Television, in fact, had found its way into many homes for the televising of Queen Elizabeth II's coronation. Living rooms around Britain were illuminated solely by the light of a flickering black and white screen on which were played out *The Quatermass Experiment*, *The Life and Legend of Wyatt Earp*, *77 Sunset Strip*, *Hancock's Half Hour*, *Saber of London*, *The Grove Family* and *Gunsmoke*. In 1953, television was used for the first time in England in a murder hunt when photographs of William Pettit were broadcast in connection with the investigation into the murder of René Brown in Chislehurst, Kent.

The rise in crime put considerable pressures on the police, especially the undermanned CID which managed to maintain the clear-up rate of roughly 50% (the same as twenty years earlier) despite a three-fold increase in crime. Yet, criticism of the police was also once more on the increase. The romantic aura of Scotland Yard buffered the Metropolitan Police to some degree and the image of the police was in general immeasurably helped by BBC television's *Dixon of Dock Green*. This was a series of mainly domestic dramas about friendly East End policeman George Dixon – the character who originally appeared in and was killed at the end of the 1950 movie *The Blue Lamp*. It starred Jack Warner as the likeable and solid Dixon and ran for twenty-one years (about 250 episodes) from 1955 to 1976. However, nationally, the police were rapidly losing public support and confidence.

Harold Scott was succeeded as Commissioner by Sir John Nott-Bower, the son of the City of London Police Commissioner at the time of the Siege of Sidney Street. His experience included over twenty years in the Indian Police Service and twenty years with the Metropolitan Police, which he had joined as Chief Constable in 1933. Despite these paper qualifications, David Ascoli, a voice of authority on such matters, described him as: '. . . excessively idle . . . of the nineteen holders of the office of Commissioner, Nott-Bower is the least memorable.' The choice of Scott and, to a greater extent Nott-Bower, were serious mistakes. True, it was probably advisable after the war to let the Metropolitan Police settle down and consolidate, and neither Scott nor Nott-Bower were going to turn into diehard reformers in the Trenchard mould. On the other hand, there were major problems within the Metropolitan Police at this time, and within the CID in particular, and a firmer hand on the tiller during the 1950s might have prevented the disasters of subsequent decades from which the Yard, and the CID especially, has yet to fully recover, if ever it does.

Public concern over the execution of Derek Bentley and

Timothy Evans had added weight to the growing movement to abolish capital punishment and a spurned lover named Ruth Ellis was about to enter the history books as the last woman to be hanged in Britain. The Ellis case had been handled by the Hampstead police and did not directly involve Scotland Yard until the eve of her execution when Yard detectives were asked to search for an alleged accomplice.

Born Ruth Neilson on 9 October 1926 at Rhyl in North Wales, Ruth Ellis went to London in 1940 and there met a French-Canadian soldier by whom she had a son, Clare Andria [sic] Ellis, born in 1945. Unknown to Ruth the soldier was married. She later claimed that Clare was the son of an American airman killed in action. When the war was over, Ruth managed to get a job with the local camera club as a model, sometimes posing nude. This led to her introduction to a drinking club where she found a job as a hostess, essentially a prostitute. Here she met George Johnson Ellis, an alcoholic dentist who was violent when drunk. She married him on 8 November 1950 and a daughter, Georgina, was born on 2nd November 1951. The marriage failed and the couple ceased to live together from November 1951 until their divorce in 1955.

Shortly after leaving her husband, Ruth met David Blakely, a motor engineer with something of a reputation as a racing car driver. He came from a well-respected family which was upset by his relationship with Ruth Ellis. There were several quarrels and pressure was put on him to end his friendship with her. Their relationship was stormy but Ruth was besotted. From February 1955 they lived together in a flat at 44 Egerton Gardens, Kensington. On 8th April they quarrelled and Blakely left the flat and did not return. All day on Saturday 9th April and Sunday 10th April she attempted to find him. She had managed to acquire a revolver, a .38 Smith and Wesson, and six cartridges. At

9 p.m. on the Sunday she learned that Blakely and a friend Clive Gunnell had gone to the Magdala public house. She saw Blakely's car parked outside and the two men inside.

Ruth waited outside the pub and when Blakely came out to the street she shot at him. He ran a few steps. Ruth fired again. Blakely fell face down on the pavement. She fired several more shots into his back. It was a cold, premeditated murder. The nearsighted Ruth Ellis was even wearing her glasses, rarely worn in public, so that she did not miss. She made no attempt to leave the murder scene but waited until the police arrived, handed them the gun, and asked to be arrested.

At her trial, Mrs Ellis made no attempt to defend herself. She admitted that she had been drinking heavily and had taken the gun with the intention of killing Blakely. The jury found her guilty but the defence counsel pleaded for mercy, saying that Ruth Ellis was drunk at the time of the shooting and emotionally stressed to the point of hysteria. Despite a national outcry for her reprieve, it was denied, allegedly because a passer-by had been wounded.

Expecting to be reprieved, and remaining stoic until learning this had been denied, at this point Ruth Ellis broke down. She made a statement to a solicitor, Victor Mishcon, and Scotland Yard officers undertook a last-minute investigation. There had always been a mystery about the origin of the gun she had used to kill Blakely. She said that she had taken it three years earlier as security for a debt from a customer at the club where she worked. This claim was discredited in court. Now Ruth reluctantly told Victor Mishcon that her lover Desmond Cussen had given her the gun, had earlier that day driven her to Epping Forest for firing practice and had driven her to the murder scene in Hampstead. Victor Mishcon took this statement to the Home Office and Scotland Yard was in turn contacted.

In fact, the police had already questioned Desmond Cussen.

A Mrs Harris had said that Ruth's son had shown her two guns kept in a drawer in Cussen's flat. Cussen produced an air gun and a starting pistol. Mrs Harris was unable to say whether either was the gun she had been shown by the boy. On the eve of Ruth's execution two Scotland Yard CID officers were assigned to question Cussen again but he had left his office early, apparently as a result of a telephone call apprising him of the latest developments. The police contacted Cussen's known friends and associates and looked for him in the places he was known to frequent. He could not be found. Nothing further could be done.

Ruth Ellis was highly distressed and drunk when she killed Blakely, who it was later learned had assaulted her many times and only thirteen days before the murder had caused Ruth to suffer a miscarriage. Ruth's legal advisors had withheld this information from the jury and also the part allegedly played by Desmond Cussen because they believed it would be used by the prosecution to show premeditation and thus lose Ruth any chance of escaping execution. Had Cussen been found and had he admitted the allegations then the Home Secretary might have been inclined to commute Ruth's sentence. As it was, the execution went ahead as planned on 13 July 1955 at Holloway Prison.

There was a brief renewal of police interest in the Ellis case in 1972 when John Bickford, Ruth's solicitor, went to the police and explained that he had known at the time of the trial that Cussen had given Ruth the gun, taught her how to fire it and driven her to the scene of the crime. Mr Bickford also said that Cussen had admitted the truth of these claims to him. Bickford's statement was passed to the Director of Public Prosecutions and thoroughly reviewed but it was felt that in light of the absence of corroborative evidence no proceedings could be taken against Mr Cussen. Desmond Cussen had consistently denied the allegations

235

and maintained that he left Ruth Ellis at 7.30 p.m. on the night of the murder. Although the case of Ruth Ellis did not directly involve the CID at Scotland Yard until their last-minute efforts to question Cussen, it remains important in the history of the police and society in general in that it was instrumental in bringing about the abolition of the death penalty.

In September 1958, Nott-Bower made his departure from Scotland Yard and his deputy, Joseph Simpson, accepted the commissionership. Simpson was the first Commissioner to have come through the ranks, though he had admittedly been promoted through them at great speed and had hardly spent much time slogging it on a beat. He joined the Metropolitan Police in 1931 and by 1937 was already Assistant Chief Constable of Lincolnshire, then Northumberland, and Surrey, returning to the Metropolitan Police in 1956 as Assistant Commissioner of traffic, and Deputy Commissioner in 1957.

In December 1958, the popular farceur Brian Rix was stopped by a PC Eastmond for alleged speeding. A man named Garrett became involved in the incident. There was an argument, both Garrett and Eastmond alleging assault against each other. PC Eastmond took Garrett to the police station where the station inspector refused to accept the charges. Garrett was released and then brought charges against Eastmond for assault and the police for false imprisonment. The case was settled by a payment, without admission of liability, of £300. A year later, politicians very reasonably asked why £300 of public money had been paid to Garrett if Eastmond was innocent and why, if Eastmond was guilty, he had not been subjected to disciplinary action. The upshot was a Royal Commission (the fifth in the history of the police) but on this occasion it undertook its duties with care and patience, dexterously wielding the scalpel as it dissected the police service and made some significant recommendations which resulted in the Police Act (1964).

The 1960s was a dramatic decade: John Kennedy, Martin Luther King, the Beatles, Mary Quant. It was a time of rebellion, of satire, of a refusal by the majority to accept the firmly held beliefs of a wealthy and powerful minority. Several memorable names such as Lonsdale, the Krogers, Gee, Houghton, Stephen Ward and Profumo were all *causes célèbres* in their day. All involved the CID through the Special Branch which was called in when MI5 needed things done 'nice and legal'.

In 1960 Evan Jones, the head of the Special Branch, was summoned to Leconfield House (the headquarters of MI5) in Curzon Street to talk about 'Sniper', an American Security Service informer. 'Sniper' had provided information about a Soviet spy in Britain and given enough information for suspicion to fall on Harry Houghton, a clerk in the Port Auxiliary Repair Unit in Portland, Dorset. Surveillance on Houghton had led to the identification of his mistress Ethel ('Bunty') Gee and in June 1960 to a man calling himself Gordon Lonsdale.

In September, Superintendent George Smith of the Special Branch served a search warrant on Lonsdale's bank manager and obtained access to a safe deposit box which proved to contain espionage equipment. Lonsdale was later followed by MI5 'watchers' (the Watcher Service, or surveillance squad, was headed by James Skardon. It was a division of Malcolm Cumming's 'A' Branch of MI5) and led them to Peter and Helen Kroger. By January 1961, Superintendent Ferguson Smith of the Special Branch had arrested Houghton, Gee, the Krogers and Lonsdale. The Krogers were later identified by the FBI as Morris and Lona Cohen, wanted since 1951 on suspicion of being involved with the atom bomb spies Julius and Ethel Rosenberg.

Lonsdale was a Soviet case officer named Conon Molody and 'Sniper', who by this time had defected, was a Polish Military Intelligence officer named Michal Goleniewski. The latter was also able to provide information to the British about an MI6 officer in Berlin who had betrayed MI6 agents operating in Poland. Enough detail was given to identify the man as George Blake who was then brought back to England, questioned and admitted being a Russian spy. Evan Jones, his deputy Ferguson Smith, and Chief Inspector Louis Gale arrested Blake on 4 April 1961.

At his trial in 1962, Blake received a prison sentence of forty-two years which was extraordinary for its severity. Yet Lonsdale, who had pleaded 'not guilty' and had been unco-operative, received a sentence of only twenty-five years while Blake who had made a complete admission and offered total cooperation received a sentence very nearly double Lonsdale's. Blake's defence counsel described the sentence as 'inordinate, unprecedented and manifestly excessive' but the judge stated that 'Blake's case was one of the worst that can be envisaged in times of peace'. The appeal judges concurred. Blake escaped from Wormwood Scrubs on 22 October 1966. The news was passed to Special Branch Commander Evan Jones but, as is now well-known, Blake defied efforts to recapture him and eventually surfaced in the Soviet Union.

Meanwhile, MI5 had been conducting an investigation into a suspect called John Vassall, but it was proving extremely difficult because their source, another defector, had been unable to provide much detail. On 12 September 1961 George Smith of the Special Branch arrested Vassall, then went to search his flat and in a secret compartment in a wooden bookcase found some rolls of film which established Vassall's guilt,

The Profumo Affair in 1963, on top of the Blake and Vassall cases (not to mention the notorious Kim Philby) delivered a crushing, indeed fatal, blow to Harold Macmillan's

Conservative government. However, it was in reality a storm in a teacup. M15 wanted to compromise and then blackmail the Soviet assistant naval attaché, Lieutenant-Commander Eugene Ivanov. Ivanov was friendly with society osteopath Stephen Ward who supplied girls for high-class parties, and Ward agreed to act for M15. The whole scheme began to fall apart, however, when one of Ward's girls, Christine Keeler, had an affair with both Ivanov and the Secretary of State for War, John Profumo. It was feared, particularly by the FBI, that the Russians were obtaining nuclear secrets from Profumo via Keeler. There were other slight concerns, like Ward and Keeler's visits to celebrated night-spots such as Esmerelda's Barn which was run by some twins called Kray. Ward and Keeler had also attracted the attention of the press following a shooting at Ward's flat when a man named John Edgecombe tried to break in to see Keeler.

Later, when Detective Sergeant Burrows of the Marylebone Lane police station visited Keeler in connection with her forthcoming attendance as a prosecution witness at Edgecombe's trial, she informed him of her affairs with Profumo and Ivanov, and also said that 'Ward had asked her to discover from him [Profumo] the date on which certain atomic secrets were to be handed to West Germany by the Americans'. Keeler's allegation that Ward was a spy, or as near to being a spy as to make only a pedant's difference, was a serious allegation. Burrows informed his immediate superior, Detective Inspector Anning, who in turn telephoned Detective Inspector Morgan of the Special Branch. Anning and Morgan arranged an interview with Keeler. When Special Branch Commander Evan Jones learned of Morgan's intention to interview Keeler he was concerned because Keeler was contracted to give her story to the *Sunday Pictorial*. Jones did not want the Press to become aware of Branch interest in what was likely to be a major political scandal. After discussion with his deputy commander, Douglas Grant, Jones instructed Morgan not to attend. The CID interpreted the Branch's action as a 'hands off' command and accordingly cancelled its own interview with Keeler.

The behaviour of the Branch seems decidedly odd. There was no reason why Morgan should have been introduced to Keeler as a Branch representative and no reason why the newspaper should ever have learned of the Branch's interest in Ward. Jones's action therefore seems extraordinary. No less extraordinary was the mild criticism of the CID and the Branch in the Denning Report, the result of Lord Denning's investigation of the security implications of the Profumo affair, which merely said that the failure to interview Keeler 'was due to an error in coordination, for which no one individual can be blamed'. The Denning Report is widely held to have been an exercise in damage limitation. Otherwise a whitewash. Ward was eventually tried for living off immoral earnings but on 3 August 1963, before judgement could be passed, he killed himself with an overdose of Nembutal. It was rumoured that his death was murder, not suicide, but there seems to be little substance to this claim.

The whole affair was damaging to Macmillan's teetering government and was followed by further disasters such as the defection of Kim Philby. Then there was the 'headless man' scandal – a photograph produced at the Duchess of Argyll's divorce hearings showed her performing fellatio with a man whose identity had been protected by the top of the photograph being cut off. A German newspaper claimed that the man was Conservative minister Duncan Sandys, who denied that this was the case although he admitted to an involvement with the duchess. Finally there was the shattering confession in 1964 by Sir Anthony Blunt that he had been a spy. (Blunt confessed to M15 in return

240

for immunity from prosecution.) There were other deeply embarrassing revelations that year too, concerning John Cairncross and others. These shenanigans among the rich and famous ultimately led to the resignation of Prime Minister Harold Macmillan and did considerable damage to the credibility of the Conservative Party.

Evan Jones, the head of the Branch throughout these trying times, retired in 1966 and was replaced by Chief Superintendent Ferguson Smith. During this period, the CID itself had other things to deal with, such as the Hanratty case.

On 22 August 1961, Michael Gregsten and Valerie Storie had a few drinks together at the Old Station Inn at Taplow, then drove to a cornfield at Dorney Reach, near Maidenhead, where they made love. They were disturbed when a man knocked on the window of the car and thrust a gun inside. He claimed to have been on the run for four months, although his dress and shiny shoes (as later described by Valerie Storie) seemed not to support this claim. The man who seemed to have no purpose in mind, made them drive around the suburbs of North London. They then drove out towards the village of Ampthill where the man shot Gregsten, seemingly by accident, and raped Storie, then shot but fortunately did not kill her. He then got into the car and drove off towards Luton.

The following day, after Miss Storie and her dead lover had been found, Gregsten's car was discovered abandoned in the East End of London. Suspicion fell on a man who called himself Frederick Durrant because, for five days after the murder, he had locked himself in his room at the Alexandra Court Hotel, Finsbury Park. His real name was Peter Alphon and he was able to prove that on the night of the murder he had been in a Maida Vale hotel called the Vienna. However, two cartridge cases were found in a room at the Vienna and these were shown to have come from the gun that killed Michael Gregsten. On the night before the murder the room had been occupied by a man calling himself James Ryan. Further questioning of the hotel manager revealed that the room had not been occupied by Ryan for the whole of the day of the murder. Earlier on, it had been used by Durrant/Alphon.

Detective Inspector Robert Acott, who had charge of the case, took the unusual step of publicly naming Alphon as the killer of Gregsten. Alphon immediately surrendered himself at Scotland Yard where he took part in an identity parade and was put through a gruelling interrogation. However, he was not identified by any of the various witnesses, including Valerie Storie. Next, the Vienna hotel manager said that his story about Alphon having occupied the room was untrue and so police interest switched to James Ryan. The name was the alias of a small-time North London crook named James Hanratty. After his arrest he took part in an identity parade and was identified by Valerie Storie largely, it would seem, because of his voice.

Valerie Storie's conviction that Hanratty was 'the man' proved to be the backbone of the case brought against him but her testimony cannot now be considered as valuable as it was then. By her own admission she had not seen Gregsten's killer very well and her descriptions of him varied between interviews with the police. At the Alphon identity parade she even identified the killer as a Spanish sailor who had been at sea at the time of the crime and had only partici- pated in the parade at the request of the police. Meanwhile, Hanratty damaged his defence case by changing his alibi and claiming that he had not been in Liverpool during the afternoon of the murder, but in Rhyl, North Wales. Although evidence was produced to support both alibis, they proved unconvincing to the jury and Hanratty was hanged.

Subsequently, and in different ways, Peter Alphon admit- ted to having murdered Gregsten. He had done so, he said,

242

on the instructions of others, one of those apparently being Charlie France, who had given evidence against Hanratty and later gassed himself. Alphon said that he had not been instructed to kill Gregsten, though he had been provided with a gun, but that the weapon had gone off accidentally. Whilst Alphon's credibility was for various reasons highly questionable, his tale had certain merit in that Gregsten's killer's uncertainty and indecision would fit with someone who had essentially been hired to merely frighten, possibly even kill, somebody with a view to supplying evidence by which Hanratty could be 'fitted up'. Whether Alphon was a crank and fantasist or a murderer, many people are today convinced that Hanratty did not kill Gregsten and was wrongly hanged. His execution was one of several which contributed to the movement for the abolition of capital punishment.

On the morning of 8 August 1963, the Royal Mail train from Glasgow was robbed of £2,631,634 (multiply it by ten to get the current purchasing power). The robbery was well-organised and effectively carried out by two London-based gangs.* The one led by Bruce Reynolds came from south-west London and consisted of John Daly, Ronald 'Buster'

---

* The following is a list of the Train Robbers, the number of years imprisonment to which they were sentenced, and what they are known to have been doing since release: Ronald Biggs, 30 years (escaped from Wandsworth on 8 July 1965 and eventually settled in Rio de Janeiro, Brazil); Roger Cordrey, 20 years (reduced on appeal); moved to West Country and set up business; John Daly, acquitted; Ronald 'Buster' Edwards, 15 years (on release he went back to gaol for stealing clothes from Harrods. Now runs a flower stall and was the subject of a 1988 film *Buster* in which he was portrayed by Phil Collins); Gordon Goody, 30 years; James Hussey, 30 years (with Thomas Wisbey he was imprisoned for seven years in August 1989 for trafficking in cocaine); Roy James, 30 years (charged with Wilson in 1982 with involvement in £2.5 million

Edwards, Gordon Goody, James Hussey, Roy James, James White, Charles Wilson, and outsider Ronald Biggs; from the south-east London gang came Thomas Wisbey, Robert Welch and Roger Cordrey. There were also several others involved and three who took part in the robbery but do not appear to have been publicly named: two of these from Reynolds's gang and one from a separate south-east London firm.

The Buckinghamshire police immediately called on Scotland Yard's help and Commander George Hatherhill of the CID, who was not far from retirement, took charge of the case, liaising closely with Superintendent Fewtrell of the Buckinghamshire police. It was a major police inquiry which, within days, was involving almost half the CID officers in London. Information was received suggesting that the criminals' hideout was Leatherslade Farm but by the time the police arrived the thieves had gone, leaving behind evidence that they had been there. On the same day that the farm was discovered a Mrs Clarke advertised a garage for rent in Bournemouth. A man replied to the advertisement and his behaviour and the large sum of money in his possession aroused her suspicions. She contacted the police, who were interviewing her when two men

VAT fraud. Case was abandoned when jury failed to agree. Thought now to be living in Spain); Bruce Reynolds, 25 years (convicted in 1984 for supplying drugs and imprisoned for three years); James White, 18 years (after release he returned to his former business as painter/decorator); Robert Welch, 30 years (helped with prisoner support group following release); Charles Wilson, 30 years (escaped from Winson Green Prison in 1964; subsequently found in Quebec, Canada, and returned to prison; charged with James in 1982 for tax fraud, case abandoned; shot and killed in Marbella on 24 April 1990, and was suspected of cocaine smuggling); Thomas Wisbey, 30 years (with James Hussey, imprisoned for ten years in August 1989 for trafficking cocaine).

arrived. One was William Boal, the other Roger Cordrey. Their car was found to be stuffed with bank notes and they were arrested. Gradually, evidence came in which named others involved in the robbery.

There is also the legend that the robbery was planned by a mastermind. John Gosling, in his book *The Great Train Robbery*, wrote that the mastermind was a distinguished Scottish former soldier known to the robbers as 'Johnny Rainbow'. Some of the thieves also alleged, in Piers Paul Read's *The Train Robbers*, that an Ulsterman was the brains behind the robbery.

Although the train driver was badly assaulted during the robbery, the incident generated considerable public interest and a degree of admiration for the criminals. There was widespread consternation, not least among the robbers themselves, at the severity of their sentences – up to thirty years in prison, which equated with a sentence for murder and did seem disproportionate to the crime. However, the Great Train Robbery in many respects marked a new era which had its tentative beginnings with the armed gangs of the post-war years. By the Sixties, London had become dominated by gangs like those of Chicago in the Twenties. There were the Kray Twins in east London and the Richardsons in the south, not to mention various 'firms' who committed daring armed robberies.

Chapter Seventeen

CORRUPTION AND GANGBUSTING

Very little is known about the life of Decimus Juvenal, who died c. AD 130, but his sixteen satires reveal him to have been deeply concerned with the immorality and social injustice of his age. He questioned the honesty of those who were appointed to positions of trust, such as guardians of law and order, with the query: *quis custodiet ipsos custodes?* – 'who will guard the guards themselves?' Who, indeed, polices the police?

In the late 1950s and early 1960s the drug problem was fairly minor. The Drug Squad occupied a single office on the second floor of the Yard and had access to a temperamental Hillman car but during this period use of the 'pep pill' and dope (cannabis) smoking increased. Indeed, 'smoking' became socially acceptable in certain circles and even expected in others. Harder drugs like cocaine and heroin, fashionable in the 1920s, also saw an unparalleled increase in usage. Suddenly narcotics was a big and very serious business. Likewise, pornography saw a boom in the 1960s and resulted in the creation of 'the dirty squad', less commonly but officially known as the Obscene Publications Squad.

Drugs and pornography offered rich rewards which resulted in the growth of criminal organisations hitherto largely unknown in Britain. With large amounts of money at stake, the criminals not only became predisposed to use violence, but there were also underpaid policemen who felt inclined to have a slice of the action for themselves. One such officer was Harold Challenor who had distinguished himself during the war and been awarded the Military Medal. He joined the Metropolitan Police in 1947 and displayed considerable ability, his 'zeal and industry' being praised by his superiors. However, some fellow officers entertained rather more candid opinions of their colleague, one of whom later observed:

> He was ruthless. He would plant objects on suspects, abuse prisoners as routine matters. He could be violent. We would then have to sort it out, placating people and take the heat out of the situation. Meanwhile he would carry on regardless. A crude, ignorant man.

In July 1963, a state visit to London by the King and Queen of Greece caused a number of demonstrations against the Greek regime. Among the arrested demonstrators was a man charged by Challenor and three constables with possessing an offensive weapon, viz. half a brick. The man claimed the brick was planted on him by Challenor and, after an investigation, Challenor was found to be guilty. He was also found to be insane, something hitherto unnoticed by his superiors. The sanity of the three constables who were with Challenor was unimpaired and they were imprisoned. The man with the brick or, rather, without it, was acquitted of all charges against him and the inquiry resulted in a pardon for twenty-four people imprisoned on evidence provided by Challenor. It was later learned that for two years Harold Challenor had been running a protection racket in Soho clubland, taking money from club owners in return for not raiding their establishments.

The Challenor case was the first in a series of inquiries which lifted the lid off Scotland Yard to reveal the endemic corruption within the CID. Commissioner Joseph Simpson wrote in 1965: 'An accused officer is entitled to the same benefit of the burden of proof in disciplinary inquiries as he or any member of the public is in the case of a criminal prosecution.' Few people would disagree with this statement but policemen command extraordinary powers and occupy an exceptional position of trust in society. While policemen must be afforded the same protection against unjust charges as a member of the public, any accusations against them must if anything be treated more seriously and be seen to be treated more seriously.

The problem at the Yard was that, back in 1878, in the idealistic days of Howard Vincent, the separation of the detective branch from the uniform branch did not merely separate crime detection from crime prevention but more seriously gave the CID an autonomy which included absolute authority for dealing with allegations of criminal misconduct against the police, uniformed or not. This meant that in cases of allegations against the CID, the CID investigated itself, which was a bit like having a villain's guilt assessed by villains – a parallel rather closer to the truth than the general public realised. Sir Charles Warren, it may be recalled, clashed with James Monro over the very question of CID autonomy. Monro's 'victory' on the point may therefore be seen as creating the situation which explosively emerged less than a century later. This situation had lasted too long. As Ascoli comments, corruption within the CID was a time-bomb ticking away in a cupboard. It was known to exist but complacently ignored in the hope that it would not go off. Eventually, of course, it did.

The Metropolitan Police was and is a hierarchical organisation with rank supposedly reflecting ability and implying superiority. It is not necessarily the case, of course, that rank reflects ability. For example, for years Frederick Wensley was denied promotion because this would have necessitated his transfer from H Division, which covered Whitechapel, where his abilities were particularly valued. In this hierarchical environment, transfer to the CID always seems to have been regarded as a further rung on the elitist ladder. The police training college at Hendon created an additional Oxbridge-like clique – Commissioner Simpson surrounded himself with fellow Hendonites; the four assistant commissioners were ex-Hendon and Peter Brodie, as Assistant Commissioner, Crime, was probably the most powerful man in the Met.

Brodie was widely expected to succeed Simpson. Had he done so then the history of the CID and the Metropolitan Police would have been very different indeed. However, Home Secretary James Callaghan offered the commissionership to Robert Mark, who was not an innocent as far as police politics was concerned. He was not of Hendon and thought his appointment would cause trouble. He refused the appointment. When Callaghan asked Mark's advice, Mark suggested that Deputy Commissioner John Waldron be appointed Simpson's successor. Callaghan took Mark's advice, but appointed Robert Mark Deputy Commissioner. Mark described the next four years as 'the most unpleasant years of my life'.

In 1968, a 'retired' burglar named Eddie Brennan was used by The Times newspaper as a 'consultant' for a planned series of articles about house-breaking. In the autumn of 1969 Brennan introduced a friend, Michael Perry, to Times journalists Gary Lloyd and Julian Mounter. Perry claimed that he was paying out money to his local detective sergeant, John Symonds of Camberwell, and to two Yard detectives, Detective Inspector Bernard Robson (C9 Division) and Detective Sergeant Gordon Harris, a Metropolitan CID officer seconded to No. 6 Regional Crime Squad in Brighton.

Moreover, Perry alleged extensive police corruption. Robson and Harris, he said, had planted 'evidence' on him and proceeded to blackmail him. The less predatory Symonds (who was aware of his Yard colleagues but unconnected with them) merely took money in the time-dishonoured fashion for tip-offs, turning a blind eye, and so on.

The two journalists investigated and managed to gather considerable evidence which included photographs and audio tape recordings. It was on one of these tape recordings that Symonds provided grounds for the belief that there was wholesale corruption in the Force. He described himself as 'a little firm in a firm' and observed, 'We've got more villains in our game than you've got in yours, you know.' On the evening of Friday, 28 November 1969 *The Times* handed their evidence to Scotland Yard. The next morning's edition carried the story with an explanation that the story had been published within hours of the information being given to the police because *The Times* had no confidence in the Yard's willingness or ability to conduct a full and impartial investigation into the behaviour of its own detective officers. Commissioner Waldron and the Establishment at the Yard immediately closed ranks and attempted to dismiss the article as merely another piece of irresponsible journalism. The Yard, with good reason, is concerned with its public image and the knee-jerk reaction of the Establishment on this and other occasions unquestionably did far more serious long-term damage to that image than would have been the case if it had immediately purged itself in public. It certainly did itself more damage than the corrupt officers. It gave the impression of reacting only when its back was to the wall. Ascoli succinctly remarked: 'Waldron played his cards with an ineptitude and a degree of obstructionism which would have fully justified the Home Secretary in removing him from his office.'

The Times's evidence could not be brushed aside. After a preliminary report by Chief Superintendent Lambert, Waldron ordered an internal investigation – directed first at Lloyd, Mounter and Parry. Fortunately, Home Secretary James Callaghan instituted an independent inquiry headed by Frank Williamson and a team of provincial policemen. By the spring of 1970, cooperation had developed between Williamson and Lambert, the Yard's own internal inquirer. On 26 May 1970, Lambert was suddenly replaced by Detective Chief Superintendent William Moody. On 3 March 1972 Robson and Harris were sent to prison for seven and six years respectively. Symonds disappeared and Scotland Yard could not find him. Cynics have wondered if Scotland Yard ever seriously looked. He gave himself up some years later and was sent to prison.

It is widely accepted in certain quarters that the investigation was a cover-up. Two other officers described – but not named – in *The Times* were not prosecuted, though one was demoted and the other later resigned. Robson and Harris were the only ones out of dozens of officers investigated to go to prison. The other deeply disturbing fact is that the man appointed to conduct the inquiry, Chief Superintendent William Moody, was at the time himself involved in corruption at a level which made those he was investigating rank amateurs in comparison.

There next took place an incident which gave Robert Mark the chance he had been waiting for to pounce on corruption within the CID. CID officers arrested two men for a burglary committed outside London. The men were charged and the provincial force involved were notified. Two provincial officers arrived in London to discover that charges had been withdrawn and the accused men set free. The Met CID's action had been a breach of conduct. The Director of Public Prosecutions, whose consent was required before a charge for an indictable offence could be withdrawn, had not been consulted. The provisional chief constable made a formal complaint to the Commissioner and the Metropolitan Police CID began an inquiry into its own actions. Robert Mark claims that the Metropolitan Police solicitor described the resulting report as 'so partisan as to be virtually worthless'.

The chief inspector responsible for the inquiry and the report was later promoted to chief superintendent. A cynic, and there were plenty at the time, might have thought the promotion a reward for a cover-up well done. For disputed reasons which need not concern us, Robert Mark obtained the commissioner's authority to undertake a clean-up of the Force, the CID especially. With Jim Starritt, Assistant Commissioner A, and two of his senior officers, Henry Hunt and Ray Anning, A10 was born. A10 consisted of a hand-picked team of officers drawn from the uniformed and detective branches and under the direct control of Deputy Commissioner Robert Mark. It was responsible for investigating *all* allegations of crime against members of the Force.

The second half of the 1960s had seen a boom in the distribution and sale of pornography. The owners of the Soho shops which purveyed the material protected their anonymity by operating behind front-men and the *Sunday People* and *News of the World* set out to identify and expose the faceless, nameless people running the trade. The *Sunday People* in November 1971 named Jeff Phillips, Gerry Citron, John Mason, Jimmy Humphreys, Frank Misfud, Barry Anderson, Thomas Hawksford, Rex Swift and Charles Julian as the main pornographers in London. It also levelled accusations of corrupt practices by the police in connection with these men. The chief superintendent of the Fraud Squad who was appointed to investigate the allegations received denials from those named (except Humphreys who was not questioned) and the officers of the Obscene

Publications Branch reported that they knew of none of those named being involved in the dirty books business.

In February 1972, the *Sunday People* splashed a story alleging that the head of the Flying Squad, Commander Kenneth Drury, had holidayed in Cyprus with Soho pornographer James Humphreys. Drury should have been suspended and the allegations investigated but, according to Robert Mark: 'The CID argument was that suspension would undermine CID morale, encourage criminals to do irreparable damage to the reputation of the force. Tell me the old, old story in fact.' Mark apparently had to virtually force Assistant Commissioner, CID, Brodie to take action. Drury was suspended on 6 March but resigned on 1 May before any disciplinary proceedings could be held. Nine days later, Brodie entered hospital suffering from 'excessive strain'. He never returned to duty and was replaced by Colin Woods, formerly Assistant Commissioner, Traffic.

Brodie had joined the Metropolitan Police in 1934 and was the first Assistant Commissioner, Crime, to have risen from the ranks. At earlier stages in his career he was regarded by colleagues as having used excessive zeal to rout out corruption. His personal integrity has never been questioned but his weakness was immense loyalty to his team. He apparently could not believe that colleagues and friends were rotten. Responsibility for the corruption within the Metropolitan Police must ultimately rest with the senior men like Brodie and former Commissioner Joseph Simpson. Indeed, with most of the former commissioners and assistant commissioners. Back in Trenchard's day the senior ranks knew about corruption. These men knew about the corruption but did nothing about it.

Sir Robert Mark succeeded Waldron on 17 April 1972. One of his first moves was to give the responsibility for enforcing the porn laws in Soho to the local uniformed officers. The new Assistant Commissioner, Crime, Colin Woods, directed the Serious Crimes Squad under Bert Wickstead to begin an operation directed against the Soho porn merchants. Mark then summoned the representatives of the CID into his office. With a lack of subtlety he 'told them simply that they represented the most routinely corrupt organisation in London' and threatened to put the whole lot back into uniform and start afresh if necessary. Many resignations followed. By 1973 two officers a week were prematurely leaving the Force because of Mark's purge. The CID was thrust into a state of turmoil. The next step was the creation of a special Anti-Corruption Squad, separate even from the A10 Branch. It was placed under the command of Gilbert Kelland.

Porn dealers kept the 'hard stuff' under the counter or in a back room. They wanted to display it but to do this they needed the Porn Squad officers to turn a blind eye. 'Ocular failure' was purchased. Various pornographers later told how they paid as much as £14,000 to open a shop and about £500 or more a week to keep them open. By the time of *The Times* inquiry this corruption had been going on for at least twenty years. A fragile relationship existed between the two Soho porn barons, 'godfather' Bernie Silver and Jimmy Humphreys. Both dealt with Chief Superintendent Moody and Humphreys also dealt with Commander Kenneth Drury of the Flying Squad, which the *Sunday People* exposed. Drury resigned before disciplinary proceedings could be brought against him and a short time later wrote an article for the *News of the World* in which he described Humphreys as a paid informant. It seems that Humphreys was chagrined by this slur on his otherwise tarnished character. He told the *News of the World* that far from being paid he had done the paying – and had been paying lavishly.

The next development was an allegation by a man named Peter Garfath that he had been 'injured' by Humphreys

255

and some other men following an affair with Humphreys' wife. Humphreys had fled to Holland when Mark put police operations in Soho into the hands of the local uniformed officers. He contacted Jim Starritt, the Deputy Commissioner, to say that he had not attacked Garfath and was being fitted up. Humphreys alleged that Detective Chief Inspector John Bland and certain criminal friends were framing him as payment for what he had said about Drury. Neither Starritt nor Gilbert Kelland believed the accusations. However, Starritt and Kelland now discovered that the Serious Crimes Squad had taken some personal diaries from Humphreys' home. These contained explicit details of Humphreys' dealings with senior detectives. The existence of these diaries had not been made known to Starritt. Kelland was told that this was because of pressure of work. He took charge of them from Chief Inspector John Bland. The diaries were genuine and very revealing but in themselves they did not constitute evidence. Kelland needed corroboration before he could move against the named officers.

There followed many months of arduous and detailed investigations. Late on Friday, 27 February 1976, a team of senior detectives gathered in Kelland's office. Amid great secrecy – which was breached by someone who informed the press – the following morning these officers went to arrest twelve serving or former policemen: two ex-commanders, one ex-detective chief superintendent, one ex-detective chief inspector, four detective inspectors, two ex-detective inspectors and two ex-detective constables. As a result of the investigations, fifteen officers – including the two retired commanders – were eventually tried at the Old Bailey on corruption charges and thirteen went to prison. More than forty officers were the subject of investigation and more than half left the Force. The operation was later described by Mark as 'probably the greatest ever single piece of detective work'.

It is informative to learn how an honest cop like Detective Inspector Anthony Kilkerr, who later testified against his corrupt colleagues, had been subverted. On Friday evenings the Obscene Publications Squad regularly gathered for drinks in the Squad's general office. At one of these sessions Detective Chief Inspector George Fenwick summoned Kilkerr to his office and pressed some money into Kilkerr's jacket pocket. It was that simple. Kilkerr threw the money away at St James's underground station, but he was now compromised. He knew of no one to whom he could turn because did not know how far upwards the corruption extended.

The effects of the corruption scandals are still felt. Although most people sensibly realise that the number of corrupt policemen was small in relation to the size of the Metropolitan Police and that the majority of policemen were and are honest men doing a difficult and dangerous job for less than adequate remuneration, the existence of corruption creates distrust bred of uncertainty. This is especially true when the Force itself initially attempted a cover-up and, indeed, tried to smear the accusers. Nevertheless, Sir Robert Mark did much to restore public confidence by washing the Yard's dirty laundry in public.

At the time of the internal purging – and some cynics have argued that it was an exercise in 'damage limitation' – the Yard was involved in trying to break up the cancerous growth of London's gangs. One of the most firmly entrenched of these gangs was the Messina family, Giuseppe Messina and his sons Salvatore, Alfredo, Eugenio, Attilio and Carmelo, who had claimed Soho as their turf since the 1930s. The Messinas maintained a low profile, which may explain their longevity, and made a lot of money. Yet they were toppled from power in the late 1950s and early 1960s. However, as dusk fell over the Messinas in the West, the dawn was rising on the careers of the Krays in the East and the Richardsons in the South.

Neither gang was particularly noted for keeping a Messina-like low profile. Instead, they employed singular but effective managerial methods on their various business enterprises and deflected police attention with the usual financial inducements to members of the Met's bent brigade. The Krays and the Richardsons had a healthy respect for each other, the Tibbs family in Romford and one or two other groups, but on their respective manors they generated considerable fear. The Richardsons had a worse reputation than the Krays, largely because they were believed to be particularly brutal, and it was this which ultimately proved to be the cause of their downfall. There were many people whose love for the Richardsons had been somewhat tarnished by, among other things, being suspended trouser-less from rafters and having delicate parts of their anatomy subjected to electric shocks. Although these people were understandably afraid of the Richardson brothers, once protected by the police and persuaded to recite relevant reminiscences to a judge and jury, the Richardsons became long-term clients of Her Majesty's prison service.

The end of the Kray twins came about because they did not devote themselves to executive responsibilities and from time to time undertook shopfloor activities. One little job best left to the workers was the murder of George Cornell in 1966. Cornell, a talkative ex-employee of the Richardsons, had been a thorn in the side of the twins for some time, but the main reason for his murder was his choice of words when expressing his opinion of Ronald Kray's weight and sexual preferences. He called Ronald a 'big, fat poof'. On 9 March 1966 Ronnie went to the Blind Beggar pub in Whitechapel Road and shot George Cornell dead.

The murder investigation was headed by Detective Super-intendent Jim Axon and Ronald Kray was arrested by

Detective Superintendent Tommy Butler of the Flying Squad. There was an identification parade at Commercial Street police station but the witnesses, already interviewed by a representative of the 'firm', pretended they had seen nothing, heard nothing and said nothing. The following year Reggie Kray murdered a fellow villain named Jack McVitie since the latter had threatened to kill him. It was two years before the Serious Crime Squad, headed by Detective Chief Inspector Leonard Read (nicknamed 'Nipper') and Detective Inspector Frank Cater, both working under the direction of Deputy Assistant Commissioner, CID, John Du Rose, launched a major investigation into the Krays' activities.

'Nipper' Read had worked on bringing the Great Train robbers to justice but he apparently embarked on the investigation of the Twins with little hope of success. The problem lay in acquiring evidence, persuading witnesses to talk and minimising the potential damage which could be done to the investigation by a rumoured Kray spy at the Yard. Read gathered a hand-picked team, set up his headquarters away from the Yard in a nondescript office block called Tintagel House and hid the true nature of the investigation behind a rumour that they were engaged on another police corruption investigation. Despite the security, the Krays learned of Read's team and their purpose. As with the Richardson's, the Kray's weak spots lay in their past with people they had forgotten about. Once persuaded that the police really were the half-hoped-for giant killer, these people talked. Leslie Payne talked for three weeks. The Krays had tried to kill him and he knew that eventually they would succeed, so he told the police all he knew. Other people talked too, including the barmaid at the Blind Beggar.

One night in May 1968 policemen secretly gathered at Tintagel House. That night the Twins and members of the 'firm' were arrested. The police had done their work well and the case against the Twins was solid. They were sent to prison for thirty years. At the time of writing they are still there. Ronald Kray is a diagnosed chronic paranoid schizophrenic and held in Broadmoor. It is doubtful he will ever be released. As John Pearson noted in his book, *The Profession of Violence*, the most disturbing thing about the Krays and Richardsons is that they became so big and were allowed to survive for so long.

The special teams created to investigate the London gangs survived the fall of the Krays and Richardsons. Thoroughly reorganised and placed under the command of Bert Wickstead, they became the Serious Crimes Squad, otherwise known as the 'Funny Firm'. Wickstead first turned his attention to 'Little Caesar', otherwise Phillip Jacobs, an East End pub landlord who led the Dixon Gang and threatened to replace the Krays. Jacobs had resisted intimidation by the Krays by enlisting the help of brothers George and Alan Dixon. The twins had then gone inside, leaving Jacobs with a gang, a clear field, and a philosophy of do unto others what one did not want done unto oneself, but Wickstead moved against Jacobs and the Dixons before they had a chance to move into the limelight. Next on the list was James Tibbs, a greengrocer with a sunny smile who, according to Wickstead, was looked upon by locals as a modern day Robin Hood. With his brother, George, James Tibbs ruled from Romford to Canning Town and even the Richardsons and Krays took the view that if Tibbs wanted that area then he could have it. The Funny Firm moved against the Tibbs gang in April 1972 and they received stiff prison sentences – James Tibbs fifteen years.

Gangland has not been crushed. A degree of stability among the rival gangs was apparently imposed on them by an underworld baron named Freddie Foreman but, following Foreman's murder in 1990, gangland disputes have deteriorated to a state of war. In 1991, for example, there was a shooting in a South London pub, The Bell, in Walworth, in which two people were killed, one of whom was just a visitor to the pub out for a quiet drink. The killings were believed to be in retaliation for the murder in March 1991 of a certain Ahmet Abdullah.

The Krays and the Richardsons were 'hard men' enacting serious and dangerous versions of children's gang games. They tried to forge links with the American mafia, but failed to do so. Today, gangs operate internationally, not just south or east of the river, and drugs have made gangsterism a very, very lucrative profession. The playground of the Krays and Richardsons is a far harder place these days.

Chapter Eighteen

INCREASINGLY BIZARRE
CRIMES

On 10 August 1972 an armed robbery was made on a branch of Barclays Bank in Wembley and over £130,000 in bank notes stolen. In December of the same year, Flying Squad officers in Northampton arrested Bertie Smalls for the offence. Smalls realised that information, like anything else, has a commercial value and soon after his arrest he indicated that in return for certain benefits to himself he was willing to tell all about his fellow criminals and the crimes they had committed. The police did not immediately respond to Bertie Smalls's offer. To catch criminals like the Krays and Richardsons the police had been forced to do deals with villainous sprats to catch the evil mackerels. It was not something the police liked doing because the sprats hurt people just like mackerels and both should be sent down, but sometimes it was necessary. Bertie Smalls, was different. He was a mackerel. In the argot of the street he was a rated villain banged to rights. Nobody really wanted to see him swim free, even if other rated villains were netted in consequence. In other words, he was an important criminal against whom the police had conclusive evidence of guilt. The police were unwilling to do a deal whereby charges against Smalls would be dropped in return for information which would result in the arrests of other criminals; he was too important to let go. But it was not a police decision. Any deal with Smalls was up to the Director of Public Prosecutions and, following a repetition of the offer at the time of Smalls's committal proceedings, discussions with the Director of Public Prosecutions, the police and Smalls's solicitor led to his offer being accepted. Smalls turned Queen's Evidence and named thirty-two bank robbers, the majority of whom were later prosecuted and convicted. No criminal had ever informed on such a scale and the Smalls case led to the coining of the term 'supergrass', which was apparently first employed by John E. Swain, former head of the Flying Squad. It was the start of a new trend.

A few years later, attention moved away from the sewers to the penthouses. To be more precise, 46 Lower Belgrave Street, the home of Lord and Lady Lucan. Richard John Bingham, seventh Lord Lucan, was born in 1934. He was the great-great-grandson of the third Earl Lucan who, in 1854, ordered the infamous Charge of the Light Brigade. Richard Bingham was a professional gambler whose luck had deserted him.

The Lucans had been living apart since January 1973, Lord Lucan having moved into a flat in nearby Elizabeth Street. There was considerable ill-feeling between them. On the night of 7 November 1974 Lady Lucan, her three children and the nanny, Sandra Rivett, watched television. The two youngest children were put to bed sometime around 8.30 p.m. and Sandra Rivett went to the basement kitchen to make tea. She did not come back upstairs. After about twenty minutes, according to Lady Lucan, she went to investigate the nanny's delay. She was attacked and later claimed that her assailant was her husband. When the police were summoned to investigate his wife's allegations Lord Lucan could not be found. The Lucan children were unharmed but, in the basement breakfast room, they found

264

splashes and pools of blood. In a large United States mailbag from which blood was seeping they found the body of Sandra Rivett and also a nine-inch long piece of lead piping wrapped at one end with sticking plaster. This was the weapon with which Miss Rivett had been bludgeoned to death.

Chief Superintendent Roy Ranson and Chief Inspector David Gerring took charge of the investigation and were able to establish that, some time after 8.30 p.m., Sandra Rivett had gone to the basement breakfast room to make tea. She did not return and Lady Lucan went to investigate. Lady Lucan said that she herself did not enter the basement but had been attacked by her husband at the top of the stairs. She managed to grab his genitals and the assault ceased. Lord Lucan then took her upstairs and, when he was in the bathroom fetching a cloth with which to clean her face, she fled the house, running in her nightdress to a nearby pub, the Plumbers Arms, where customers maintained that she staggered into the bar at about 9.45 p.m.

According to the doorman of the Clermont Club, an exclusive casino at 44 Berkley Square, Lord Lucan left about 8.45 p.m. and drove away in his Mercedes. Lucan appears to have gone to his flat in Elizabeth Street – where his Mercedes was found – and walked from there to Lower Belgrave Street. In a few letters and telephone calls to family and friends, Lord Lucan stated that he had been passing his house when he saw in the basement a man attacking his wife. He let himself into the house and the attacker ran off. He explained that his wife, who, he said, had a history of mental instability, had begun to hysterically accuse him of having hired the man to kill her, this accusation being one he said she had often levelled against him. He managed to calm her down, then took her upstairs and tried to clean her up. 'She lay doggo for a bit and when I was in the bathroom left the house,' he wrote. Lucan then left the house himself. He collected a car which had earlier been lent to him by a friend, wrote a few letters and made some telephone calls. He then drove to Newhaven where his car was discovered. In the boot the police found a length of lead piping wrapped in sticking plaster. It matched the one found at the murder scene. A warrant was issued for the arrest of Lord Lucan on suspicion of murder.

The case against Lord Lucan is almost overwhelming. Many people are convinced that he murdered Sandra Rivett in mistake for his wife. But did he? The reason given by Lord Lucan for entering the house could not be substantiated by the police. On being summoned to the murder scene they were unable to see into the basement because of closed venetian blinds. When the venetian blinds were open, parts of the basement could be seen from the street, but those parts showed no sign of a struggle having taken place. The venetian blinds could have been open when Lord Lucan passed by, or the struggle could have left no tell-tale signs.

Lady Lucan, of course, maintained that she did not enter the basement but was attacked at the top of the stairs. Yet under the arch of her shoe there was Sandra Rivett's blood. Lady Lucan must have stepped in a pool of the blood, all of which was in the basement. Grey-blue wool fibres believed to come from Lord Lucan's flannel trousers were found in his borrowed car, on the murder weapon, in the basement, on a bath towel and in a wash-basin. Yet no fibres were found on the mailbag into which Sandra Rivett's body had been stuffed. If Lord Lucan shed wool fibres wherever he went, why not on the mailbag into which he must have manhandled Sandra Rivett's body?

Most damning is the piece of lead pipe found in the boot of the Corsair he had borrowed. It is difficult to imagine a reason why anyone would wrap sticking plaster around a strip of lead pipe, but one cannot discount the admittedly remote possibility that Lord Lucan or someone in his household had such a reason and that the strip of pipe used to kill Sandra Rivett just happened to be found in the basement by her killer. Yet the piece of pipe does not in any event prove that Lord Lucan killed Sandra Rivett. It only proves that he was acquainted with her killer, that perhaps Lady Lucan was right and her husband did hire her attacker (and the murderer of Sandra Rivett; the same person who stuffed her body in the mailbag).

Much weight has been attached to a set of timings provided by the Lucan's ten-year-old daughter Frances. She punctuated her testimony to the police with references to television programmes. She said that she had watched *The Six Million Dollar Man* with the family and Sandra. The programme finished about 8.30 p.m. Miss Rivett then took the younger children to bed and Frances had played for a short while in the nursery before rejoining Lady Lucan. By this time, Sandra Rivett had gone to the basement to make tea. Lady Lucan expressed her concern about what had delayed the nanny and went to investigate. A little later, Frances heard a distant scream which she attributed to the cat having scratched her mother. All this happened *before* the news began on television at 9 p.m. The news had been on for about five minutes when Lord Lucan appeared in the doorway, with Lady Lucan whom he was assisting upstairs. Frances also said that some time later, after she had gone to bed, she heard Lord Lucan call for her mother. This would almost certainly have been about 9.45 p.m. when Lady Lucan had made her escape to the local pub.

According to Lady Lucan, about twenty minutes elapsed between Sandra Rivett going to make tea and her going to investigate. Miss Rivett appears to have been murdered on entering the basement but, if Lady Lucan's timings are reasonably accurate, Miss Rivett must have been murdered between 8.40 and 8.45 p.m. According to the doorman at the Clermont, Lord Lucan was at the club at 8.45 p.m. Therefore, he could not reasonably have reached Lower Belgrave Street much before 8.53 p.m. If these timings are even remotely correct then Lord Lucan could not have murdered Sandra Rivett.

The timings are also consistent with when Lady Lucan would have gone in search of Sandra Rivett and with Lord Lucan's story that he had seen Lady Lucan being attacked in the basement (though there remains the question of whether or not he could have seen into the basement at all). If Lord Lucan did hire someone to kill his wife, why was he anywhere in the vicinity of Lower Belgrave Street at the time of the murder? Was he there to make sure that he and not one of the children found Lady Lucan's body? Was the story of seeing his wife being attacked the one he would have told the police on reporting his discovery of the body? Or was he there to collect and dispose of the body? Was that why he borrowed a friend's battered Corsair when his own Mercedes was available? The murder of Sandra Rivett will probably never be solved. Neither will the fate of Lord Lucan. Most people believe he is dead. Others are equally convinced that the gambler would never have taken his own life.

The Lucan case, which will probably remain an enduring mystery, had been played out against a background of growing concern about international terrorism. Following the arrest in 1971 of members of the Angry Brigade, Scotland Yard had set up the Bomb Squad. It was soon renamed the Anti-Terrorist Squad. By 1973 the IRA had extended its terror campaign to mainland Britain. Commissioner David McNee records in his autobiography that in London between 1973 and 1982 there were 252 bomb incidents, 19 terrorist shootings, 56 deaths, and 805 people injured as a result of terrorist activities. 138 arrests were made in connection with these incidents. Apart from bombs, a new threat came from hijacks and sieges. The British police had up to now had little experience of sieges since that of Sidney Street. The first serious one to come their way was non-political and has proved to be something of an oddity.

Lillio Termine was an Italian hairdresser who shared Lord Lucan's passion for gambling, at which he was also a loser. It was later alleged that Termine owed money to a club owner named Norbert Rondel and cleared his debt by supplying information for a robbery which Rondel set up. This allegation against Rondel was never substantiated. However it came to pass, Termine learned that on Saturday nights the managers of the Spaghetti House chain of restaurants met at the one in Knightsbridge and usually had large sums of money with them. Termine realised that there would be enough money to clear his debts. Somehow his information was conveyed to a man named Franklyn Davies, who was employed by Norbert Rondel as a croupier. Davies had done a little armed robbery on the side, though this had been curtailed by a prison sentence only recently completed. Davies thought that Termine's information ought to be put to some practical use and enlisted the assistance of Wesley Dick, Anthony Munroe and Samuel Addison.

On Saturday, 27th September 1975, Addison drove the team to the Knightsbridge restaurant and Davies, Dick and Monroe entered just as the managers were leaving. At gunpoint, the managers were ordered down to the self-service basement area and went down the stairs in single file, the criminals at the rear. This enabled one of the managers to slip away unnoticed and reach a neighbouring restaurant, from where he raised the alarm. By a remarkable coincidence, as the call for cars to go to the scene was made from the Information Room, two police cars were actually passing the Knightsbridge restaurant. Both stopped and went to investigate.

The gunmen pushed their captives into a store-room and

there began a five-day siege which they made out to be of a political nature. Although the gunmen eventually released the hostages and surrendered, it was a tense and nerve-racking time for the police and distinguished by the array of devices employed by the Forensic Equipment Unit, who bugged the whole basement store-room with microphones and fish-eye cameras inserted through ventilator shafts and walls.

The police had at this time been making a careful re-examination of IRA activity in London and had uncovered what appeared to be a pattern. It was decided to mount heavy surveillance of probable IRA targets. This expensive operation involving seven hundred police volunteers was almost made redundant by an irresponsible policeman who told the *Evening News* about it. Fortunately the front page coverage of the story did not deter the terrorists, who perhaps thought the surveillance would have been called off because of the coverage. On 6 December they attacked Scott's Restaurant in Mayfair, which happened to be in the middle of the surveillance area and a large number of policemen were almost immediately on the scene. The panicked terrorists fled, but the chase effectively ended when they gained access to a flat in Balcombe Street. The police were certain that the cornered terrorists were responsible for several bombing outrages in London and the terrorists would later claim responsibility for the crimes attributed to the Guildford Four.

Although the British police had limited experience of sieges, the policy for handling them was firmly in place: the police do not give in under any circumstances. Robert Mark observed in his autobiography that at the Yard it had been decided that if any senior policeman was ever taken hostage he was to 'be written off'. Asked what the police would do in the event that the hostage was a politician, Mark replied that he would ask the hostage-takers 'if they would like a few more'. Ultimately, the policy always works. For the police, the siege becomes a waiting game while the terrorists have no way out and eventually have to give in. The Balcombe Street siege lasted almost six days.

Sir Robert Mark oversaw some significant changes within the Metropolitan Police and in the nature of crime, but monolithic structures like Scotland Yard do not adapt to change as rapidly as they should. The police is not subject to market forces in the same way as trade and industry. It does not have to change with the times and be aggressively competitive to retain a market share. After a period of change they can – and generally do – take time to sit back, rest, think and consolidate. As we have observed, commissioners like Warren, Trenchard and Mark are usually followed by a less aggressive figure. On 13 March 1977, Sir Robert Mark was succeeded as commissioner by David McNee. Three months later, McNee appointed Gilbert Kelland Assistant Commissioner, Crime, and later Geoffrey Dear and John Dellow as assistant commissioners.

Just over a year after McNee occupied that office there occured in London one of the most extraordinary acts of terrorism ever committed. It happened at a bus stop in September 1978. Forty-nine-year-old Bulgarian writer and defector Georgi Markov was on his way to Bush House in the Aldwych, where he worked as a broadcaster in the Overseas Service of the BBC. A man jabbed him in the thigh with an umbrella, mumbled an apology and left in a taxi. Markov later became ill and died. It was found that he had been injected with a tiny metal sphere believed to contain a poison called ricin.

The inquiry was taken over by Commander Jim Nevill of the Anti-Terrorist Squad and received a lot of publicity, but very little information was forthcoming. A man later interviewed by Scotland Yard detectives had apparently warned Markov several times about a plot to assassinate him and it is widely accepted that Markov was murdered by the Bulgarian security services on the orders of Todor Zhivkov, the Bulgarian communist leader. According to KGB defector Oleg Gordievsky, the umbrella and tiny poisoned pellet were provided by the KGB and the assassin by Bulgaria. According to a Bulgarian book written by two journalists, the assassin was a now-retired diplomat. However, the book's veracity has been questioned. At the time of writing, Bulgarian detectives are reinvestigating the case following the toppling of Zhivkov from power.

Amid all this crime on an international level, internal problems did not go away. In July 1978, the Met. identified what appeared to be a corrupt association between City of London policemen and armed robbers. The Commissioner of the City Force asked the Met. to undertake an investigation, but further inquiry revealed the possible involvement of Met. policemen. Therefore, the Home Office handed the investigation over to Leonard Burt, Assistant Chief Constable of the Dorset Police. Burt spread his net wide – too wide to accommodate the catch, in McNee's opinion.

Operation Countryman seems to have been an unhappy affair. The City of London and Metropolitan commissioners complained of being kept underinformed (or rather uninformed), whilst Burt's team were variously credited with complaining about being obstructed. One such accusation was levelled against Don Neesham, Commander of the Flying Squad. No firm evidence was produced to support the allegation, but it was decided to move him to other duties. He instead took early retirement.

The 1970s came to an end with a major operation by the Metropolitan Police against the IRA, followed by a number of important arrests and the discovery of arms and bomb-making materials in Greenwich. One of those arrested was Gerard Tuite, who escaped from Brixton prison whilst awaiting trial. The 1980s opened with the Iranian Embassy siege. It lasted from 30 April to 5 May and was played out before the nation on television. McNee described it as 'a unique situation, never previously encountered in the history of British policing and not least remarkable because from beginning to end a police officer in uniform – and armed – was in the heart of the building in the hands of determined terrorists'.

Whereas the sieges of 1975 came about by chance, the Iranian Embassy siege was planned. Six well-trained terrorists calling themselves 'The Group of the Martyr' held twenty-six people hostage in a building consisting of over fifty rooms. The terrorists' purpose was to attract worldwide attention to their cause, the independence of Khuzestan, an oil-rich province in south-west Iran. In London, they had obtained weapons which one theory suggests were provided by the Iraqis and had been brought to Britain under the privilege of the diplomatic bag. Inside the building was PC Trevor Lock, a member of the Diplomatic Protection Group, who was armed with a .38 Smith and Wesson. There was a massive police operation which concluded with a Special Air Services (SAS) assault on the embassy. This was televised, was dramatic and successful. Constable Lock was duly and justly rewarded for his bravery.

On 2 October 1982 Kenneth Newman, variously nicknamed 'Mighty Mouse' or 'ET', took over behind the desk in the walnut-clad Commissioner's office. For the next five years, generally swathed in a halo of Mellow Virginia, he oversaw a revolution in the organisation of the Metropolitan Police. Born in Sussex in 1926, Newman served with the RAF from 1944 to 1947, then joined the Palestine Police Force, where he served in the CID. He joined the Metropolitan Police in 1948 and was transferred to the Yard in 1972. It was a short appointment, more of a visit, because in November 1973 he was appointed Deputy Chief Constable of the Royal Ulster Constabulary. By 1976 he had become Chief Constable and, two years later, he received a knighthood.

Newman had an unenviable task. He had to overcome the corruption scandals of the Mark years and the Countryman debacle of McNee's. He also faced serious problems ranging beyond the operations of the CID, chiefly personnel short-ages and decaying law-and-order. London's crime figures had trebled since 1962 and clear-up rates had plummeted. There was a predominance of street crime and the methods of the Metropolitan Police had come under fire. There were allegations of racial discrimination, violations of suspects' rights, and offences against civil liberties.

There is little doubt that Newman, more strategist than policeman, was the right man for the job at the time, though he was not always popular and was regarded as something of reactionary. He alienated the black commu-nity by referring to them as 'coloured' and there were also charges that the changes he initiated reduced the Met's morale. It is also probably true to say that Newman's objectives failed. Figures show that there was no significant reduction in crime figures, that levels of public disorder remained high, and that public confidence in the police dropped by 6% during Newman's term of office. On the other hand, people expected change to be dramatic, whereas the effects of Newman's reorganisation needed time to percolate through.

Another bizarre, or at least highly unusual crime for Britain, was discovered at 6.15 p.m. on 8 February 1983 by a Dyno-rod employee named Michael Cattran, who was sent to investigate the cause of a blockage in the drains at 23a Cranley Gardens, Muswell Hill. In the sewer, he found a substance which he later told his boss he thought was human flesh. It had come from a pipe leading from No. 23. Since it was too dark to do anything that evening, Cattran returned with his boss the next day. The substance had disappeared. One of the occupants of the flat told them that they thought the man who lived in the attic had been to the manhole during the night. The police were called.

Although the substance had gone, Cattran had found some pieces of meat and four small bones in the wastepipe from No. 23. These were handed over to Detective Chief Inspector Peter Jay, who immediately had them examined by experts. The meat and bones were human. The occupant of the attic flat had gone to work. Detective Chief Inspector Jay, with Detective Inspector McCusker and Detective Constable Butler, decided to wait for him to come home. The attic flat belonged to an executive officer at the Job Centre in Kentish Town. His name was Dennis Andrew Nilsen. He was told about the discovery of human remains in the drains and expressed suitable horror. Jay told him to stop wasting time and tell them where the rest of the body was. 'In two plastic bags in the wardrobe next door,' said Nilsen. 'I'll show you.'

Nilsen was taken to the police station. During the ride Inspector McCusker asked Nilsen, 'Are we talking about one body or two?'

'Fifteen or sixteen,' said Nilsen.

Dennis Nilsen had murdered a dozen or more young men at his previous address and three at Cranley Gardens. Few of his victims had been missed. They had been drawn from London's underbelly of the homeless, unloved and unemployed. When asked by his solicitor why he had killed these people Nilsen replied, 'I am hoping you will tell me that.' The nearest anyone could come to an explanation was that Nilsen was lonely and felt isolated. He killed his victims to prevent them from leaving him. Brian Masters took this extraordinary explanation as the title of his award-winning exploration of the Nilsen crimes, the book *Killing for Company*.

There was never any doubt about Nilsen's guilt. He

had admitted his crimes and talked freely about them but as often is the case there was difficulty in establishing whether Nilsen was evil or insane. As had happened at the trial of Peter Sutcliffe, the Yorkshire Ripper, Nilsen's trial in effect became a trial of psychiatry, experts for both the prosecution and defence in conflict and faring badly under cross-examination. The Nilsen case again raised the question of whether or not psychiatric evidence should be used during a trial. Many experts believe that psychiatric opinion should only be raised when deciding the fate of the person charged, once his guilt has been established. Other people argue that this should be strongly resisted. The purpose of an open trial is that justice should be *seen* to be done. If psychiatric evidence is used to determine the type and length of a sentence then it must be presented in open court and opportunity given for it to be contested. In the event, Dennis Nilsen was convicted and sentenced to life imprisonment. He apparently accepted his punishment and does not expect to be released.

On Saturday, 17 December 1983, a man with an Irish accent telephoned the central office of the London Samaritans. He gave a password which identified him to the police as belonging to the IRA and said that bombs had been placed in the Harrods and Littlewoods department stores and that a further bomb had been left in a car outside Harrods. Forty minutes later, an Austin car in Hans Crescent outside Harrods exploded. Nearly one hundred people suffered injuries, some serious. PC Gordon lost both legs and part of one hand. His dog, also terribly injured, had to be destroyed. Sergeant Noel Lane and WPC Jane Arbuthnot, as well as a journalist and two women were killed. Inspector Stephen Dodd died later from injuries. Word from Dublin was that the attack was unauthorised and the IRA apologised.

On 17 April 1984, there was a public demonstration

276

outside the Libyan People's Bureau in Westminster. Most of the demonstrators were opposed to the Gadaffi régime, but there was small pro-Gadaffi group. From the first-floor window of the Bureau came a five-second burst of automatic fire. Eleven people were hit, including WPC Yvonne Fletcher who later died. There was considerable confusion. It is possible that two or three Libyans took the opportunity to leave the Bureau via the unwatched rear entrance. The Diplomatic Protection Group of the CID sealed off the Bureau. In Tripoli, Libyan troops surrounded the British Embassy and detained three Britons. In the end, nobody was brought to trial for what happened. The thirty people inside the fortress of the Bureau were protected by diplomatic immunity. Amidst British outrage, all returned to Libya.

The late 1970s saw an increase in armed robberies. One reason for this was that people were more affluent and spent more money, therefore there was more cash in banks, building societies, shops, and being transported in security vans. Despite considerable success, the police were now having to admit that crime was a problem which they were only just able to contain and Scotland Yard responded with the creation of the Robbery Squad as a section of the Flying Squad. During this period, one particular robbery stands out for the high value of the theft.

On 26 November 1983, an armed gang robbed the Brinks-Mat security warehouse in the Heathrow International industrial estate. The haul, mostly gold, was estimated to be worth about £20 million. Six Brinks-Mat employees had been deputed to see to the transfer of the valuables to an armoured van which was to take them to Gatwick Airport. Only two of those men possessed the necessary information to gain access to the vault. Somehow, three armed men had managed to breach the extensive security system. They were violent to the security men, pistol-whipping one and stabbing another. The two men who knew how to get into the vault had petrol poured over their legs and were told that it would be set alight if they did not operate the mechanisms necessary. The thieves loaded the contents of the vault into a van and made their escape.

The immediate problem was that the police could not discover any way the villains could have got into the warehouse without one of the six security guards letting them in. Suspicion therefore fell on one of the guards who, under questioning, broke down and confessed: the thieves were his sister's boyfriend and some of the boyfriend's friends.

On 1 August 1987 Sir Kenneth Newman was succeeded by his deputy, Peter Imbert, who became the twenty-first Commissioner of the Metropolitan Police. Imbert's rise through the ranks from a humble bobby at Bow Street in 1953 had been outwardly smooth and untroubled. He spent fifteen years with the Special Branch and became a terrorist expert. He was also chief negotiator with the IRA during the Balcombe Street siege in 1975 and then closely involved with the questioning of the Guildford Four who were convicted of being responsible for the bombings in Guildford, but subsequently released from prison as innocent. As Chief Constable of Thames Valley, to which post he was appointed in March 1979, he allowed BBC cameras to film a fly-on-the-wall documentary, *Police*, which police insiders thought to be a classic example of shooting oneself in the foot. Although the series provoked criticism of the police, he responded by making changes, particularly in the way police questioned rape victims. It is too early to properly assess the sort of impact which Peter Imbert's tenure behind the commissioner's desk will have made on the Metropolitan Police and Britain's policing in general. Yet his successor will face serious problems as he guides the Force towards the year 2000.

278

Chapter Nineteen

WHERE DO WE GO FROM HERE?

We have come a long way since Robert Peel's 'new' police marched on to the streets of London for the first time, but from this rapid review of 150 years of the Criminal Investigation Department one cannot escape the feeling that things have not changed. In the 1870s and 1880s the CID dealt with anarchist and Fenian terrorists. We still have terrorists today. In 1911, the CID dealt with a siege in Sidney Street. In the 1970s and 1980s, we had sieges in Balcombe Street and the Iranian Embassy.

In the post-war years of rationing, the public wanted scarce goods and were prepared to pay black-market prices to get them. This resulted in an increase in certain types of crime and an appropriate police response. Responsibility for this lay with the people who bought or otherwise turned a blind eye to the buying of black-market goods. The bottom fell out of black marketeering when rationing stopped, but there was a long-term effect. Just as bootlegging in the Prohibition years of the United States created the boom in organised crime which still plagues that country today, so the days of black marketeering created the environment for gangs like the Krays and Richardsons.

Drug abuse in particular has transformed the character of urban crime. Drug dealing is big business and it leads to crime on several levels. Crimes are committed to raise the cash to get into dealing, while lesser crimes are committed to enable addicts to raise the cash to finance their habit. Moreover, it pervades all levels of society. Money and drugs buy and corrupt respectable professionals, even the police and the judiciary. This, in turn, corrupts society in general. The widespread corrupting influence of drug money is a threat to ordered society which should not be underestimated. The Krays and the Richardsons have passed on. They were the bridge between old-style gangsterism which had operated for generations and the new-style criminals who, Mafia-like, invest (otherwise launder) large sums of drug money in property and legitimate businesses. Yet the drug business is not the only threat to our society. Lower down the scale are the growing number of street gangs, loosely knit groups who 'control' areas in most British cities and act like mini-gangsters, dealing drugs, running protection rackets and so on. Politicians and some police say that there are no 'no-go areas' in Britain. This may be true, but there are certainly some 'go warily' areas where in recent years we have seen some truly appalling outbursts of social unrest. Gang development is already showing an alarming increase in immigrant communities where criminal groups are exercising Mafia-like intimidation reinforced by extreme violence. Chinese Triads like the Wo Sing Wo, Sui Fong and 14K are moving into London and other major British cities from Hong Kong in preparation for its return to the People's Republic in 1997. A Chinese Intelligence Unit exists in West End Central and Interpol has a Triad Intelligence Desk for the coordination of police operations against these groups throughout Europe.

So far, Britain has been lucky. In spite of these very alarming trends, in fact we enjoy a lower crime rate than many other countries, including Holland, Germany, Australia and Canada, and in 1988 and 1989 the recorded crime rate actually fell. It began to rise again in 1990 and in

1991 showed a quarterly increase of about 14% over the previous year.

However, statistics are difficult to interpret. Comparison of the present murder rate with that of the nineteenth century suggests that Britain is a much safer place to live – there were 12.5 homicides per million population in 1989, almost exactly the same figure as that for 1857, the year that records began, but 1989 was close to a murder peak while 1957 was the bottom of a trough. Britain therefore *looks* like a safer place, but many victims of crime today receive medical treatment and survive, whereas they would have died from their injuries in Victorian times.

Whatever the statistics tell us, what really matters is what society *perceives* as being the reality: when we fear what we perceive as the burgeoning crime rate, we demand stiffer penalties and even the reintroduction of capital punishment. But whatever the future of crime has in store for us, one thing must be realised: whilst the threat of punishment deters most of us from crime, it does not deter the dedicated criminal. The criminal weighs the risks and gambles his freedom against the odds of being caught. In 1931 Frederick Porter Wensley concluded his autobiography with these words:

> . . . vindictive punishments are not, as a rule, effective deterrents. Not quite so well appreciated is the fact that the only way to stamp out crime is to impress the criminal with the certainty that he will be caught and punished – within limits the amount of punishment does not matter. The only way to that end is by the use of an adequate number of efficient detectives, efficiently organised and adequately equipped.

With some police forces saying that under-funding means that they may not be able to respond to 999 calls, Wensley's

281

insights into preventing crime should perhaps be listened to. Whether they will or not is something the Scotland Yard files 150 years from now will reveal.

Bibliography

ABBERLINE, Frederick George
Annotated Press Cutting Book
Unpublished.

ADAM, H.L.
C.I.D.: Behind the Scenes At Scotland Yard
London: Sampson Low, Marston, n/d

ANDERSON, Robert
The Lighter Side of My Official Life
London: Hodder, 1910

ASCOLI, David
The Queen's Peace: The Origins and Development of the Metropolitan Police 1829–1979.
London: Hamish Hamilton, 1979

BEGG, Paul
Jack the Ripper: The Uncensored Facts
London: Robson Books, 1988

BEGG, Paul, FIDO, Martin, and SKINNER, Keith
The Jack The Ripper A to Z

Introduction by Donald Rumbelow
London: Headline, 1991

BENTLEY, William George
My Son's Execution
London: W.H. Allen, 1957

BOROWITZ, Albert
The Bermondsey Horror: The Murder That Shocked Victorian England
London: Robson Books, 1989.
(Published in the United States in 1988 as *The Woman Who Murdered Black Satin*)

BROWNE, Douglas G.
The Rise of Scotland Yard: A History of the Metropolitan Police.
London: Harrap, 1956.

BUNKER, John
From Rattle to Radio
Studley, Warwickshire: K.A.F. Brewin Books, 1988

BUNYAN, Tony
The History and Practice of the Political Police in Britain.
London: Julian Friedmann, 1976.

CARLIN, Francis
Reminiscences of an Ex-Detective
London: Hutchinson, n/d

CATER, Frank, and TULLETT, Tom
The Sharp End: The Fight Against Organised Crime
London: The Bodley Head, 1988

CHESTER, Lewis, LEITCH, David, and SIMPSON, Colin
The Cleveland Street Affair
London: Weidenfeld and Nicolson, 1977

CLARKSON, Charles Tempest, and RICHARDSON, J. Hall
Police!
London: Field and Tuer, The Leadenhall Press, 1889

COBB, Belton
Murdered on Duty: A Chronicle of the Killing of Policemen.
London: Brown Watson, 1966 (1961).
First published by W.H. Allen. The Brown Watson edition
is abridged and contains additions of post-1961 cases.

COBB, Belton
*Critical Years at the Yard: The Career of Frederick William-
son of the Detective Department and the C.I.D.*
London: Faber and Faber, n/d

COBB, Belton
*The First Detectives and the Early Career of Richard Mayne,
Commissioner of Police.*
London: Faber and Faber, n/d

COX, Barry, SHIRLEY, John, and SHORT, Martin
The Fall of Scotland Yard
London: Penguin, 1977

CRITCHLEY, T.A.
A History of Police in England and Wales 1900–1966
London: Constable, 1967

DEW, Walter
I Caught Crippen

London: Blackie and Co., 1938

DICKENS, Charles
'A Detective Police Party'
London: *Household Words* 27 July and 10 August 1850

DILNOT, George
Scotland Yard: Its History and Organisation
London; Geoffrey Bles, 1929

DIVALL, Tom
Scoundrels and Scallywags and Some Honest Men
London: Ernest Benn, 1929

DU ROSE, John
Murder Was My Business
London: W.H. Allen, 1971

FELSTEAD, S. Theodore
Shades of Scotland Yard: Stories Grave and Gay of the World's Greatest Detective Force
London: John Long, 1950

FIDO, Martin
Murder Guide to London
London: Weidenfeld and Nicolson, 1986

FIDO, Martin
The Crimes, Detection and Death of Jack the Ripper
London: Weidenfeld and Nicolson, 1987
London: Weidenfeld and Nicolson, 1989 (Revised paperback)

FOOT, Paul
Who Killed Hanratty?

London: Jonathan Cape, 1971
London: Granada, 1973 (paperback with additional post-script)
London: Penguin Books, 1988 (paperback with further post-script)

FRIEDLAND, Martin L.
The Trials of Israel Lipski
New York: Beaufort Books, 1984

GODDARD, Henry
Memoirs of a Bow Street Runner
Introduction and notes by Patrick Pringle
London: Museum Press, 1956.

GOSLING, John
The Ghost Squad
London: W.H. Allen, 1959

GOULD, Robert W., and WALDREN, Michael J.
London's Armed Police: 1829 to the Present
London: Arms and Armour Press, 1986

GREENO, Ex-Det. Chief Supt. Edward
War on the Underworld
London: John Long, 1960

GRIBBLE, Leonard
Great Manhunters of the Yard
Foreword by John Capstick
London: John Long, 1966

HAMBROOK, Walter
Hambrook of the Yard

London: Robert Hale, 1937

HANCOCK, Robert
Ruth Ellis: The Last Woman to be Hanged
London: Weidenfeld and Nicolson, 1985, paperback (first published 1963)

HATHERILL, George
A Detective's Story
Introduction by Nicolas Bentley
London: André Deutsch, 1971

HOBBS, Dick
Doing the Business: Entrepreneurship, The Working Class, and Detectives in the East End of London
Oxford: Oxford University Press, 1988

HOWE, Sir Ronald
The Pursuit of Crime
London: Arthur Barker, 1961

HOWE, Sir Ronald
The Story of Scotland Yard
London: Arthur Barker, 1965

HOWELLS, Martin, and SKINNER, Keith
The Ripper Legacy
London: Sidgwick and Jackson, 1987

HOWGRAVE-GRAHAM, H.M.
Light and Shade At Scotland Yard
London: John Murray, 1947

HOWSON, Gerald:
It Takes a Thief: The Life and Times of Jonathan Wild

London: Hutchinson, 1970.
Previously published in hardback as *Thief-Taker General*

HYDE, H. Montgomery
The Cleveland Street Scandal
London: W.H. Allen, 1976

JAMES, P.D., and CRITCHLEY T.A.
The Maul and the Pear Tree: The Ratcliffe Highway Murders 1811
London: Constable, 1971

KEE, Robert
The Green Flag
London: Weidenfeld and Nicolson, 1972

KELLAND, Gilbert
Crime In London
London: The Bodley Head, 1986

KENNEDY, Ludovic
Ten Rillington Place
London: Victor Gollancz, n/d

KRAY, Reg and Ron with Fred Dinenage
Our Story
London: Sidgwick and Jackson, 1989

LITTLECHILD, Chief Inspector John
'Great Crimes and their Detection. A Talk With Ex-Chief Inspector Littlechild'
London: *Police Review and Parade Gossip*, 29 May 1893

LITTLECHILD, Chief Inspector John
'Inspector Littlechild's Recollections'

London: *Daily Graphic*, April 1893

LITTLECHILD, John
The Reminiscences of Chief Inspector Littlechild
London: The Leadenhall Press, 1894

LOCK, Joan
*Dreadful Deeds and Awful Murders: Scotland Yard's First
Detectives 1829–1878*
Taunton: Barn Owl Books, 1990

MARK, Sir Robert
In the Office of Constable
London: Collins, 1978

MARNHAM, Patrick
Trail of Havoc: In The Steps of Lord Lucan
London: Viking, 1987

McINTYRE, Patrick
'Scotland Yard. Its Mysteries and Methods'
London: *Reynolds' Newspaper*, February – May 1895

McNEE, Sir David
McNee's Law
London: Collins, 1983

MONRO, James
Memoirs
Unpublished.

MOORE-ANDERSON, A.P.
Sir Robert Anderson and Lady Agnes Anderson
Foreword by Lord Caldecote
London: Marshall, Morgan and Scott, 1947

MOYLAN, J.F.
Scotland Yard and the Metropolitan Police.
London: G.P. Putnam, 1929

OLIVER, Hermia
The International Anarchist Movement in Late Victorian England
London: Croom Helm, 1983

ORWELL, George
Decline of the English Murder and Other Essays
London: Penguin Books, 1965
('Decline of the English Murder' first appeared in *Tribune* in 1946)

PAGET, (Q.C., M.P.) R.T., and SILVERMAN, (M.P.) S.S.
Epilogue by Christopher Hollis, M.P.
Hanged and Innocent
London: Victor Gollancz, 1953

PARRIS, John
Scapegoat
London: Duckworth, 1991

PAUL, Philip
Murder Under the Microscope: The Story of Scotland Yard's Forensic Science Laboratory
Foreword by Lord Walton
London: Macdonald, 1990

PEARSON, John
The Profession of Violence: The Rise and Fall of the Kray Twins' Vicious Criminal Empire
London: Weidenfeld and Nicolson, 1972

London: Granada, 1973 (revised edition)

PIKE, Alan R.
Man From the Yard: A History of the Metropolitan Police C.I.D.
Unpublished manuscript

PORTER, Bernard
The Origins of the Vigilant State: The London Metropolitan Police Special Branch Before the First World War.
London: Weidenfeld and Nicolson, 1987

PROTHERO, Margaret
The History of the Criminal Investigation Department at Scotland Yard from the Earliest Times Until To-Day
London: Herbert Jenkins, 1931

READ, Piers Paul
The Train Robbers
London: W.H. Allen, 1978

ROSE, Andrew
Stinie: The Murder on the Common
London: The Bodley Head, 1985

RUMBELOW, Donald
The Complete Jack the Ripper
London: Penguin, 1988
(many revised editions since original publication in 1975)

RUMBELOW, Donald
I Spy Blue: The Police and Crime in the City of London from Elizabeth to Victoria.
Foreword by Sir Arthur Young
London: Macmillan, 1971

RUMBELOW, Donald
The Houndsditch Murders and Siege of Sidney Street
London: Macmillan, 1973
London: W.H. Allen, 1988 (revised edition)

Lord RUSSELL of Liverpool
Deadman's Hill: Was Hanratty Guilty?
London: Secker and Warburg, 1965

SAVAGE, Percy
Savage of the Yard
London: Hutchinson, n/d

SCOTT, Sir Harold
Scotland Yard
London: André Deutsch, 1954

SLIPPER, Jack
Slipper of the Yard
London: Sidgwick and Jackson, 1981

SWEENEY, John
At Scotland Yard: Being the Experience During Twenty-seven Years' Service of John Sweeney, Late Detective Inspector, Criminal Investigation Department, New Scotland Yard
Edited by Francis Richards
London: Grant Richards, 1904

TAYLOR, Bernard
Cruelly Murdered: Constance Kent and the Killing at Road Hill House
London: Souvenir Press, 1979

THOMSON, Sir Basil
The Story of Scotland Yard

London: Grayson and Grayson, 1935

TROW, M.J.
Introduction by Ludovic Kennedy
'Let Him Have It, Chris': The Murder of Derek Bentley
London: Constable, 1990

WARD, David
Foreword by Richard Whittington-Egan
King of the Lags
London: Elek Books, 1963

WARREN, Sir Charles
'The Police of the Metropolis'
London: *Murray's Magazine*, November 1888

WOODCOCK, George
Anarchism: A History of Libertarian Ideas and Movements
London: Pelican Books, 1963

WENSLEY, Frederick Porter
Detective Days: The Record of Forty-Two Years' Service in the Criminal Investigation Department
Introduction by George Dilnot
London: Cassell, 1931

YALLOP, David
To Encourage The Others
London: W.H. Allen, 1971
London: Corgi, 1990 (revised and updated paperback)

Index

A10 253
Abberline, Insp. Frederick
95–7, 126, 138, 189
Abdullah, Ahmet 261
Addington, Henry, 1st
Viscount Sidmouth 14–15
Agar, Ted 45–6
Agnew art gallery 157, 158–9
Albert Victor, Duke of
Clarence, Prince 130–31,
138–9
Alphon, Peter 241–3
anarchists 102, 142–3, 163
Anderson, Dr (*later* Sir)
Robert: in Fenian Office
86, 90–91; Asst. Com., CID
108, 120, 123–4, 125, 126,
127–9, 133–6, 154, 155, 160;
memoirs 117–18
Angel, Miriam 112, 114–16
Anti-Corruption Squad 255
Anti-Terrorist Squad 268
Antiquis, Alec de 218, 219
Area Superintendents 190
Argyll, Duchess of 240
arsenic 137, 178–9
Ascoli, David 3, 11, 215,
232, 249

Baker, Supt. 28, 31

Balcombe Street siege 270–71
Baldwin, Charles 20
Balfour, A. J. 109, 110
Balfour, Jabez 147–8
Barrett, Michael 62
Barrow, Eliza 179
Batt, Charles 57–8
Bean, John William 34
Beard, John 198
Beck, Adolf 152–5
Benedix, Clara 184–5
Benson, Harry 71–8
Bentley, Derek, 219–27
Bentley, Sgt. Robert 171
Beron, Leon 173–8
Biggs, Ronald 243–4
Billington, James 152
black marketeering 279
Blake, George 238
Blakely, David 233–5
Bland, Chief Insp. John 256
Bloody Sunday, *1887* 112, 121
Blunt, Sir Anthony 240
Bodle, George 178
bombs 86, 93–9, 103, 104,
107–8, 142–3, 268, 276
Bourdin, Martial 143
Bow Street 6–14
Bow Street Foot Patrol
10

Bow Street Horse Patrol 8, 9, 10, 13

Bow Street Runners 7–8, 10, 23–4, 46; Dickens writes of 42

Bradford, Col. Sir Edward Riley 145, 162

Brennan, Eddie 250

Brett, Sgt. 60–61

Briggs, Thomas 53–4

Brinks-Mat security warehouse 277–8

Brodie, Peter 250, 254

Brown, Hannah 24–5

Browne, Douglas G. 110

Browne, Frederick Guy 201–202

Bullard, Charles (Charles Wells) 158

Burke, Capt. Richard O'Sullivan 59–60, 61

Burnham, Alice 183–4

Burrows, Albert 202

Burt, Leonard 272

Burton, Harry 95, 98

Busalin, Insp. John 20–21

Buswell, Harriet 68–9

Byng of Vimy, 1st Viscount 209–10

Bywaters, Frederick 195–7

Calcraft, William 41, 51, 55

Callan, Thomas 107–8

Capstick, John 216

Carlin, Chief Insp. Francis 190

Carlton, Billie 205

cars 141, 192; police 192–3

Carson, Edward 149–50

Cass, Elizabeth 112–14, 120

Cater, PC John 166

Cavanagh, Tim 18–19, 44–5

Cavendish, Lord Frederick 89

Challenor, Harold 248–9

Chang, Brilliant (Chan Nan) 205

Chapman, Annie 126, 128

Charles, Fred 143

Chartists 47, 87

Childers, Hugh 103–4, 111

Childs, Sir Wyndham 203

Chinese Triads 280

Choate, PC Walter 171–2

Christie, John 227–9

CID see Criminal Investigation Dept.

City of London 1–2, 3, 9, 11, 12, 16, 272

Civil War 3

Clarke, Insp. George 74, 75, 76

Clerkenwell prison 61–2

Cleveland Street scandal 137–9

Cobb, Belton 20, 25, 76

Cobb, Sgt. 84–5

Cole, PC George 84, 85

Colquhoun, Patrick 12–13

Communists 163

Condon, Edward 60–61

constables, early 2, 8

Cornell, George 258

Cornish, George 193, 194

Courvoisier, François 31, 32–3

Covent Garden Journal 7
Craig, Christopher 219–27
Cream, Thomas Neill 147
Criminal Investigation
   Dept. (CID), origin 79,
   81–8, 89–90
Criminal Record Office 161
Crippen, Hawley Harvey and
   Cora 167–70
Cummins, Frederick Gordon
   212–13
Cunningham, James Gilbert
   95, 96–8
Cussen, Desmond 234–6
Cutbush, Thomas 131
Cuthbert, Insp. 103

Daily Mirror 164
Daily News 33
Daily Telegraph 69, 72, 77, 88
Daly, John 93
Dance, Alf and 'Squibs' 216
Davies, Franklyn 269
de Goncourt, Mme la
   Comtesse 72–3
de Lava, Thelma 200, 202
de Veil, Thomas 6
Deasy, Capt. 60
Denning Report 240
Detective Branch 34–51,
   53–69, 71–9
Dew, Insp. Walter 163,
   167–70
Dickens, Charles 32–3,
   41, 42; *Household Words*
   article 42–4
Die Freiheit 87

Divisional Detectives
   64–7, 189
Dixon, Alan and George 260
Dixon, PC Charles 166
Drug Squad 247
drug trafficking 205, 247,
   279–80
Druitt, Montague John 110,
   131, 132
Drummond, Edward 39
Drury, Com. Kenneth 254, 255
Druscovitch, Insp. Nathanial
   74–5, 76
Dubof, Yorka 171, 172
Dunnaway, Sgt. 57
Dyer, Amelia 152

Eagles, PC Charles 166
Eastmond, PC 236–7
Eddowes, Catharine 127, 130
Edwards, Major James 164
Ellis, Ruth 233–6
Emsley, Mary 50, 51
Endacott, PC Bowden 113–14
espionage 3, 163–4, 181;
   German 164, 181–3
Euston, Lord 138–9
Evans, Beryl and Timothy
   227–9
Evening News 270
Evening Standard 209
extradition 54–5, 62

Fabian, Robert 218–19
Fairfax, Det. Cons. Frederick
   220–22, 225

Farrow, Edward and Ann 162
Fascists, British Union of 211
Faulds, Dr Henry 160
Felstead, S. Theodore 182–3
Fenian Office 63, 86
Fenians (Irish Republican
  Brotherhood) 59–63, 86,
  89–110, 111
Fenwick, George 257
Ferguson, Michael 49
Fido, Martin 133, 136
Field, Insp. Charles Frederick
  25, 26–7, 43
Fielding, Col. 63
Fielding, Henry 6–9
Fielding, John 9–10
fingerprints 155, 160–62
Fitch, Det. Cons. Herbert T.
  163
Fletcher, WPC Yvonne 277
Flying Squad 192–207
Ford, Richard 13
Foreman, Freddie 260
Forensic Equipment Unit 270
forensic science 141, 160–3,
  178–9, 207
Fowler, Henry 150–51,
  152
France, Charlie 243
Francis, John 34
fraud 147–8
Fraud Squad 215, 253
Freemasons 179
Froest, Insp. Frank 148,
  152–3, 163
Froggatt, Edward 74
Fulton, PC 191

Gainsborough, Thomas,
  painting of Duchess of
  Devonshire 157, 158–9
Gale, Sarah 24–5
Galton, Sir Francis 160–61
Game, Sir Philip 211
gangs 257–61, 280
Gardner, Margery 216–17
Gardner, PC William 35
Gardstein, George 171–2
George III, King 8, 9, 10
Geraghty, Christopher 218–19
Gerard, Emilienne 186
Ghost Squad 216
Glasgow 12
Goddard, Baron 227
Goddard, Henry 23
Goddard, Sgt. 204, 206
Goff, Sgt. Charles Burgess
  25, 26, 38
Gold, Isaac Frederick 87–8
Goleniewski, Michal ('Sniper')
  237–8
Good, Daniel 33, 34–6
Gordon Riots, 1780 7, 10, 11
Gosling, Sgt. John 216
Gosselin, Major Nicholas 91
Gould, Richard 30
Grantham, PC Joseph 19
Great Bullion Robbery,
  1855 45–6
Great Scotland Yard Scandal,
  1876 71–9
Great Train Robbery,
  1963 243–5
Greaves, PC 176
Greenacre, James 24–5

Greeno, Chief Insp. Edward 212–13

Gregsten, Michael 241–3

Greig, PC 191

Grimwood, Eliza 26

Guildford Four 278

Gull, Sir William 131

Gutteridge, PC 200–201

H Division 27, 96, 106, 250

Hall, Edward Marshall 169–70, 178, 184, 207

Hambrook, Walter 192

Hamilton, William 34

Hammond, Charles 137–8

hanging 152; public 32–3, 41, 55, 62

Hanratty, James 242–3

Harcourt, Sir William 87, 97–8, 99–100

Hari, Mata 184–6

Harkins, Michael 106–8, 110

Harriott, Capt. John 12–13

Harris, Det. Sgt. Gordon 250–51, 252

Harris, H.S. 179

Harrods bomb 276

Hart, Sarah 39

Hassel, Dr 68–9

Hay, Capt. William 42

Haynes, Insp. John 37–8, 44, 47

Heath, Neville George 216–18

Hefeld, Paul 165–6

Henderson, Lt.-Col. Edmund 63–7

Henderson, Sir Edward 103–4, 111

Hendon training college 250

Henry, Sir Edward 160, 161–2, 182

Hitchen, Charles 4–5

Hogg, Phoebe 146–7

Home Office 98, 102, 123–4, 136; special branch for Irish affairs 63, 90–93

homosexuality 5, 137–9, 149

Horwood, Gen. Sir William 209

House of Commons: bomb 95–7; Select Committees 9, 14, 15–16, 22

Household Words article 42–4

Hubbard, William 26

Humphreys, Hames 253, 254, 255–6

identification 141, 152–5

Imbert, Peter 278

Interpol 197–8, 216, 280

IRA 211, 268, 270, 272–3, 276

Iranian Embassy siege 272–3

Ireland: Royal Irish Constabulary 11; Home Office Dept. for 63, 90–3; *see also* Fenians; IRA

Irish Bureau (Section B) 89–110, 146

Ivanov, Lt.-Com. Eugene 239

Jack the Ripper 110, 121, 123–36, 147

Jackson, Harry 161
Jacobs, Phillip 260
Jacoby, Henry Julius 193–4
James, Henry 87
Jenkins, Supt. 165, 166
Jenkins, Harry 218–19
Jenkinson, Edward G. 90–93, 97–102, 108–9
Jones, Evan 237, 238, 239–40, 241
Joscelyne, Ralph 165, 166
Jubilee Plot 104–10
Justices of the Peace 2, 11–12

Kee, Robert 60
Keeler, Christine 239–40
Kelland, Gilbert 255, 256, 271
Kelly, Mary 128, 131
Kelly, Capt. T. J. 59
Kendall, Sgt. Edward 44
Kendall, Norman 211
Kennedy, William 201–202
Kent, Constance 47–50
Kilkerr, Det. Insp. Anthony 257
King's Police Medal for Gallantry 166
Kosminski, Aaron 131, 133–6
Kray, Reginald and Ronald 239, 258–60, 261
Kroger, Peter and Helen 237
Kurr, William 72–7

Labour Party 183
Langley, Sgt. Edward 40–41, 44

Larkin, Philip, hanged 60–61
Lawende, Joseph 130
Le Caron, Henri 91
Le Neve, Ethel 168–70
Le Queux, William 163–4, 181, 182
Leeson, Det. Sgt. 172
LeFroy, Percy 88, 126
Lepidus, Jacob 165–6
libel, seditious 87
Libyan People's Bureau 277
Liddell, Guy 212
Lipski, Israel 112, 114–16, 120, 129
Littlechild, Insp. John 71, 102, 149, 150
Lock, PC Trevor 273
Lody, Carl Hans 182
London United Workingmen's Committee 103
Long, PC John 19–21
Lonsdale, George 237–8
Lucan, Richard Bingham, 7th Lord 264–8
Lushington, Godfrey 101, 116, 117

Macdonald, Sir Archibald 11
Mackenna, Roger 109–10
Macmillan, Harold 238, 240, 241
Macnaghten, Sir Melville 101n, 110, 118–19, 131–3; Chief Cons., CID 141, 146, 160; Asst. Com. 173, 181
Macready, Nevil 190
magistrates 11–12

Mahon, Patrick 198–9
Mainwaring, William 11
Manchester stamp robbery
    55–9
Manning, Frederick 40–41
Manning, Marie 40, 41–2
Marching Watch 1–2
Marine Police Office 11–12
Mark, Sir Robert 210, 250,
    252–7, 270–71
Markov, Georgi 271–2
Marr family, murdered 13
Marsh, James 178
Marshall, Doreen 217
Matthews, Henry 111–12, 113,
    116, 121, 123, 124, 128, 136,
    141, 144–5
Maybrick, Florence and
    James 136–7
Mayne, Com. Richard 25, 27,
    31, 37, 42, 57, 62–3
McLean, Roderick 34
McNaghten, Daniel 38–9
McNee, David 268, 271,
    272, 273
Meiklejohn, Insp. John 67,
    74–5, 76
Melville, Joseph 105–6, 107
Messina family 257–8
Messiter, Vivian 203–4
Metropolitan Police:
    development 2, 10, 15,
    16, 17–36; districts 67;
    Divisions 189–90
Metropolitan Police
    Improvement Bill,
    1829 11, 16

Meyrick, Kate 204–5, 206
MI5 181, 182, 237–40
Middlesex Justices Act,
    1792 11
Miles, PC Sidney 220–25
Millen, Gen. 104–6, 107–9
Miller, Insp. 29–30
Milsom, Albert 150–51, 152
Money, Sir Leo Chiozza 202–3
Monro, James: Head of
    Detective Dept. 76, 91–3,
    95, 97–101; Asst. Com., CID
    111, 116, 118–20; Head of
    Secret Dept. 101–9, 118–20,
    123; resigns from CID
    123–4; at Home Office 123;
    Com. 18, 97–9, 136, 138,
    142; resigns 143–5
Moody, Chief Supt. William
    252, 255
Morony, John J. 106
Morrison, Stinie 173–8
Most, Johann 87
Müller, Franz 54–5
Mullins, James 50–51, 53
'Murder Squad' 163
Murdoch, Charles 155
Murray, Edwin 75, 76–7
Muswell Hill murders 150

National Political Union of the
    Working Classes 22
Neesham, Don 272
Neil, Chief. Supt. Arthur 190,
    193, 195
New Police, nineteenth
    century 18–36

New Scotland Yard 18, 142
New York Times 125, 158
Newlove, Henry 138
Newman, Sir Kenneth
 273–4, 278
News of the World 253, 255
Nichols, Mary Ann 126
Nicholson, Margaret 8
Nilsen, Dennis 275–6
Nolen, Joseph 105–6, 107
Nott-Bower, Sir John 232, 236
Nutkins, Insp. 150

O'Brien, Michael 60–61
Obscene Publications Squad
 247, 253–7
O'Connor, Patrick 40
Operation Countryman 272
Orrock, Thomas Henry 84–5
Ostrog, Michael 131, 132–3
Otway, Sgt. Charles 28–9,
 30–31
Oxford, Edward 33–4

Pain, PC Claude 220, 225, 226
Pall Mall Gazette 112,
 113, 116
Palmer, Insp. William 74, 76
Pankhurst, Emmeline 167
Parris, John 227
Pate, Robert 34
Payne, Leslie 259
Peace, Charles 82–4
Pearce, Insp. Nicholas 27,
 28–9, 30, 31–2, 36, 37, 38
Pearcy, Mrs Eleanor 146–7

Peel, Sir Robert 11, 15–16, 39
pensions, police 143–5, 187
Perry, Michael 250–51, 252
Peters, Jacob 171, 172
Pettit, William 231
Petty, Maria 28
Philby, Kim 240
Phillips, Charles 32
Pierce, William 45–6
Pierrepoint, Albert and
 Thomas 202
Pinkerton, Robert 159
Piper, PC Walter 170–71
Pitt's Bill, *1785* 11
Pizer, John 134
plain-clothes men 21–3,
 64–5, 67, 90
Podmore, William Henry
 203–4
Police Act, *1964* 237
Police documentary
 programme 278
Police Gazette 11
Police Orders 21–2, 23, 37, 64,
 89, 90, 193
Police Review 7
Polti, Francis 143
Popay, William 22
pornography 247, 253–5
Potter, Insp. 57–8
Profumo, John 238–40
Prothero, Chief Insp. J. 203–4
psychiatric evidence 276
Puritans 3

Quarterly Pursuit of Criminals
 10

Queen's Evidence 264

racism 274
railways 45–6, 53, 88;
  robberies 45–6, 243–5;
  telegraph 39
Randall, Joseph 23–4
Ranger, PC G. 57–8
Ratcliffe Highway murders 13
Read, Det. Chief Insp.
  Leonard 259
Reilly Joseph ('Little Joe')
  158, 159
rewards 13, 32, 51
Reynolds, Bruce 243–4
Rice, Peter 60
Richardson brothers 258, 260
Rising Sun pub 94–5
River Police 12
Rivett, Sandra 264–8
Robbery Squad 277
Robinson, PC Edward 83–4
Robson, Det. Insp. Bernard
  250–51, 252
Roche, Bertha 186
Rojas, Francesca 161
Rolston, Charles 166
Rolt, Terence 218–19
Rose, Thomas 36
Rowan, Com. Charles
  18, 25, 37, 42
Ruggles-Brise, Evelyn 116–17
Rumbelow, Donald 171
Russell, Lord William 31, 32

Salnish, Christian (Jacob
  Fogel) 170, 173

Sapwell, William 20–21
Savage, Chief Insp. Percy
  198–200
Savidge, Irene 202–3
Sayer, John 8
Schonfeld, Peter 148
Schwartz, Israel 129–30
Scot, Walter 18
Scotland Yard, name 17–18
Scott, Sir Harold 215, 219
Scott's Restaurant, Mayfair
  270
Seaman, William 151–2
Secret Dept.: Home Office
  63; (Section D) 100–109,
  118–20, 123, 146
Seddon, Frederick Henry 179
Serious Crimes Squad 255,
  256, 260
Shackell, Insp. Joseph 38
Shaw, Sgt. Frederick 37, 44
Shaw, Norman 142
Shaw, Richard 58
Shore, Supt. 159
Sidney Street, siege 172–3
Silver, Bernie 255
Simpson, Com. Joseph 236,
  249, 250, 254
Smalls, Bertie 263–4
Smith, Ferguson 237, 238, 241
Smith, Super. George 237, 238
Smith, George Joseph 183
Smith, Henry 150
Smith, Sgt. Henry 44, 46
Smith, John ('Lord
  Willoughby'; William
  Thomas) 152–5

Somerset, Lord Arthur 138–9
Spaghetti House, Knights-
   bridge 269–70
Special Branch 89, 94, 102,
   141, 146, 163, 167, 187
Spicer, Sidney Edward 190–91
Spilsbury, Bernard 184, 186,
   207, 212, 218
Stamp Office Robbery,
   Manchester 55–9
Starritt, Jim 253, 256
Statute of Westminster,
   1285 1, 2
Stephen, Sir James Fitzjames
   2, 115, 137
Stephens, Revd Joseph 38
Stephenson, William and
   Caroline 27–8
Storie, Valerie 241–2
Stow, John: *Survey of
   London* 17
Stratton, Albert and Alfred
   162
Stride, Elizabeth 127, 129–30
strikes 120, 187; General 206;
   police 145, 187–8
suffragettes 166, 183
Summers, Lawrence 20
Sunday People 253–4, 255
Sunday Pictorial 239
Sutcliffe, Peter 276
Svaars, Fritz 171, 172–3
Swanson, Insp. Donald 87, 88,
   126–7, 129, 131, 139, 159,
   160; marginalia 134–5
Sweeney, Sgt. John
   94–5

Swinscow, Charles Thomas
   137–8
Syme, Insp. John 188
Symonds, John 250–51, 252

Tabram, Martha 125–6
Tanner, Sgt. Richard 46,
   50–51, 53–5
Tawell, John 39, 41
television 231, 232, 278
Templeman, John 29–30
Termine, Lillio 269
terrorism 59, 142–3, 268; *see
   also* bombs
Thackeray, William
   Makepeace 32
thief-takers 4
Thompson, Edith and
   Percy 195–7
Thomson, Basil Home 176,
   181, 183, 185, 187, 189;
   arrested 200, 202
Thomson, Insp. James J.
   55–9, 68
Thornton, Sgt. Stephen 36,
   37, 40, 46, 47, 51; Dickens
   writes of 43
Tibbs, George and James
   258, 260
Times, The 19, 31–2, 41,
   55, 77, 111–12, 231,
   250–51, 252
tipstaves 8, 63
Titley, Thomas 85–6
Toplis, Francis Percy 190–92
Tottenham outrage, *1909*
   164–6, 170–73

Tower of London, bomb,
 1885 95–7
Townsend, John 8
Trafalgar Square, riots
 103, 121
training 161, 250
Trenchard, 1st Viscount
 210–11
Trow, M.J. 225, 226
True, Ronald 194
Tucker, Sgt. 171
Tuite, Gerard 272
Tyler, PC William 165, 166

unemployment 120
uniform 18–19, 67

Vassall, John 238
Vassileva, Nina 172, 173
Victoria, Queen 31, 160;
 assassination attempts
 on 33, 34
Vincent, Sir Howard 66–7,
 78–9, 81, 85–6, 89–90, 91,
 111, 249
Voison, Louis 186–7
Vucetich, Juan 161

Waldron, Dep. Com. John
 250, 251–2
Walker, Supt. Robert 43,
 103, 111
Walsh, J.S. 109–10
Ward, Stephen 239–40
Warren, Sir Charles 91, 102,
 104, 111–12, 116–21, 123,
 136, 249

watchmen, *seventeenth
 century* 3–4
Welch, Saunders 7, 8–9
Wensley, Frederick Porter
 250; Det. Sgt. 151–2; Det.
 Insp. 172, 174, 175–8; Chief
 Insp. 186–7, 189–90, 195–6;
 Chief Cons., CID 204, 206;
 autobiography 281
Westwood, Robert 27–9
Whicher, Sgt. Jonathan 41,
 43, 46, 47–50
Whitechapel: H Division 27,
 96, 106, 174, 250; Murders
 124–36
Wickstead, Bert 255,
 260
Wild, Jonathan 4–5
Wilde, Oscar 148–50
Wilkes, John 9
William, John 13
Williamson, Adolphus
 Frederick: Det. Sgt.
 44–7; Det. Chief
 Insp. 53, 63, 67,
 69, 75, 78; Chief
 Supt. 81; at Irish
 Bureau 89–90, 92,
 93–4, 95, 100; Chief
 Cons., CID 111, 118,
 140, 159
Williamson, Frank 252
Williamson, John 13
Wilson, Charles 244
Winter (Dawson) 99
Women's Social and Political
 Union 166–7

Woods, Colin 254–5
World War I 181–6
World War II 211–13
Worth, Adam (Harry
  Raymond) 157–9
Worth, Percy 216
Wright, Sampson 10–11

Yallopp, David 220, 223–4,
  226
Yates, Gertrude (Olive
  Young) 194

Zelle, Margerette (Mata
  Hari) 184–6